Project Math

Tools and Techniques
for
Project Managers,
Agile Coaches and Scrum Masters,
Project Sponsors,
Project Management Offices,
Aspiring Team Members,
Business Analysts,
and
Engaged Stakeholders

Dr. James A Robison, PMP, PMI-ACP, CFPIM

ISBN: 978-1-71800-999-8

May all your projects finish on time, on budget, and on scope.

This book is dedicated to my late wife Kathie,

who supported, or at least tolerated,

my many projects over our 40 years of marriage.

Preface

I wrote this book for you. You are probably not a "math person." No; you are probably more of a "people person." Successful project managers are skilled leaders, team builders, motivators, conflict resolvers, negotiators, and coaches. They have great "people skills" but they rarely have great math skills. If that is you, then you have the right book.

Successful project managers are also good decision makers and communicators. They know how to use quantitative analysis to make good decisions, and they know how to summarize data and make meaningful presentations to team members, sponsors, and other stakeholders. Successful project managers have overcome whatever initial resistance to mathematics they may have had, and have become comfortable and confident crunching numbers. If that is your objective, then you have the right book.

It might be useful to think of it as a left brain, right brain thing. In our brain, the left hemisphere deals with analytics, logic, and reasoning; the skills of math. The right hemisphere deals with creativity, imagination, and intuition; the skills of leadership. You can be a successful project manager with good people skills and mediocre math skills, but you cannot be a successful project manager with good math skills but only mediocre people skills. You are, or believe you can be, a successful project manager, and that is why I think you are a right-brained "people person" and not a left-brained "numbers person."

Most of us appear to favor one hemisphere over the other, but "ambidextrous thinkers" can develop their weaker hemisphere, just as a right-handed athlete may train to develop their left hand to become more competitive.

I was an operations manager in industry for thirty years. Since retirement, I have spent the last twenty years teaching strategy, statistics, management information systems, operations management, and project management at Sonoma State University in Northern California. My project management students are working adults, either currently project managers, project team members, or transitioning into the profession.

They quickly grasp the people topics like communications and stakeholder engagement, but they struggle with the math. I tried various texts, but none seemed to approach the topic at the right level. Like Goldilocks and the three bears, some were too hard and some were too soft. But, unlike Goldilocks, I could not find one that was just right.

I decided to write a book to fill the gap. My intent was that it could be used as the math text for a traditional project management class or it may be enjoyed a la carte by individuals focusing on either overcoming a weakness in their project management skill set or preparing for a project management certification exam.

I wrote this book to help you become an ambidextrous thinker. My assumption, as stated above, is that you are comfortable leading others but that you are less comfortable crunching numbers. I have tried to present the various topics in a simple, conversational tone. Each topic begins with a short scenario so you understand *why* you are doing the math. In most cases, I present a formula, but I have tried to use words rather than algebraic symbols or Greek letters whenever possible. I then replace the words with numbers and show the resulting value. But the value is frequently not the answer. The value leads us to a decision, which I present in words. In some cases, a larger value may lead us to the correct decision, in other cases, a smaller value may be better. For example, if we are talking about net present value, bigger is better, but if we are talking about payback period, then smaller is better. (Don't worry, we'll cover both net present value and payback periods later on.)

This is a desk reference, but I first recommend you read the book from cover to cover. It's a bunch of very short stories (in the traditional sense, not the agile sense). It's easy to stop, take a break, and then pick up where you left off. There is a practice problem at the end of most topics, with the answer following. I recommend you do the practice problems to ensure you understand the topics. If you don't understand why the right answer is the right answer; stop, go back, and review the topic; before you continue to the next topic. In operations management, that's called quality at the source.

A simple pocket calculator will be adequate for most of the topics. Some of the more complicated formulas, however, are better handled using Microsoft® Excel®. I am going to assume you have access to Excel, but that you are not an Excel guru or power user. All of the Excel formulas and functions we use will be fully explained. They have all been around for a while, so you don't need the latest version of Excel; and either a Windows® PC or an Apple® Mac will meet our needs.

After you have finished the book, keep it nearby as a desk reference. Rather than starting at the front of the book, start with the index at the back. Find your topic of interest and go right to it. Some of the topics build on a story from prior topics, but from a pure math perspective, each is a standalone problem with all of the required data and formulas.

Which of the topics presented in this book are the most important?

A master carpenter knows how to use a hammer, saw and screwdriver, but his or her skill is in knowing which tool to use for the task at hand. Consider this book your toolbox. You should know how to use all of the tools, but your mastery of project math will be demonstrated in selecting the most appropriate tool for each problem.

Each tool is presented as a discrete topic, but many can be used in conjunction with each other. This might be considered as tailoring your resources to meet the specific needs of the project or problem. An example of this will be found early in the book where we combine analogous estimating with parametric estimating to calculate a total cost estimate for a new cleanroom.

Many topics include footnotes. These could justifiably be classified as scope creep, so feel free to skip them if you are behind schedule, if your schedule performance index, SPI, is less than one. On the other hand, if you have some slack or float time, you will find them educational and possibly even entertaining.

I like to start new topics on a new page, and that means some topics ended with a few lines at the top of an otherwise blank page. I don't feel comfortable charging you money for blank pages, so I added some stories, which I call filler, to the most offending pages.

Fillers are true stories from my 30 years in operations management, with one exception, a joke I tell my statistics students.

I started this conversation with references to "successful project managers," but what are they?

A common definition of a successful project manager is someone who finishes their projects on time, in budget, and in scope, so I used Time, Budget and Scope as categories to hold the various topics.

These are often called the three legs of the Project Constraint Triangle. This grouping is not perfect, but it works as well as any other arbitrary grouping, such as initiating, planning, executing, monitoring and controlling, and closing, which, in my opinion, are well overused in project manager literature.

There is some overlap in the groupings. For instance, you will find three-point estimating in both the Time and the Budget sections. Also, I used the Scope section for all topics that didn't fit neatly into Time or Budget.

Risk, which is sometimes considered the forth leg of the project triangle is included in both Time and Budget. Quality, a significant topic in this book, is included in Scope where it rightfully belongs. The quality of our deliverable could be defined as to how well it conforms to the scope.

May all your projects finish on time, in budget, and in scope.

Jim Robison
August, 2018

Thank You

A special thank you to Alana Kelly and Victoria Saltariche for proof reading and finding numerous errors and typos in the draft version of this publication. Given that, I remain solely responsible for any and all remaining errors and typos.

Legal Stuff

Project Math is an independent publication and is not affiliated with, nor has it been authorized, sponsored, reviewed, or otherwise approved by Microsoft Corporation®. All screenshots of Excel® spreadsheets are copyrighted by Microsoft Corporation.

This book assumes a basic understanding of project management as presented in *A Guide to the Project Management Body of Knowledge (PMBOK Guide) Sixth Edition*® published by the Project Management Institute®. However, *Project Math* is an independent publication and is not affiliated with, nor has it been authorized, sponsored, reviewed, or otherwise approved by the Project Management Institute.

Table of Contents

In Budget

It's clearly a budget. It's got a lot of numbers in it.

George W. Bush

The budget is not just a collection of numbers, but an expression
of our values and aspirations.

Jacob Lew

To reduce deficit spending and our enormous debt, you reign in spending.
You cut the budget. You don't take more from the private sector and grow
government with it. And that's exactly what Obama has in mind with this
expiration of Bush tax cuts proposal of his.

Sarah Palin

Money is only a tool. It will take you wherever you wish, but it will
not replace you as the driver.

Ayn Rand

Money it talks, but it don't sing and dance.

Neil Diamond

Money, money, money. Must be funny in the rich man's world

ABBA

Money makes the world go 'round.

Liza Minnelli and Joel Grey, Cabaret

A penny saved is a penny earned.

Benjamin Franklin

The love of money is the root of all evil.

1 Timothy 6:10

The lack of money is the root of all evil.

Mark Twain

Analogous Cost Estimation

An analogous cost estimate is a relatively quick, and therefore relatively inexpensive, method of estimating total costs for major activities or entire projects. It is considered a "top-down" estimate because you are estimating the total cost of the project or activity. Later you can divide this total into components such as labor, materials, and rent.[1]

Scenario

You are at the company cafeteria getting your morning cappuccino. The plant manager joins you and orders a latte.[2] You exchange greetings and she says she has been meaning to talk to you. She is considering building a new cleanroom and asks you approximately what it will cost.

You recall that the last cleanroom the company built cost $1,000,000.[3] This is known as analogous estimating and the million bucks is known as a point estimate. The new cleanroom is analogous to the old cleanroom. Maybe add ten percent for inflation, and another hundred thousand as CYA[4] padding. That would put your point estimate, your guesstimate, at $1,200,000. (1,000,000 X 1.1) + 100,000 = 1,200,000.

Process

But, if you answer that a new cleanroom will cost $1,200,000, the plant manager is liable to think that is an exact number, down to the penny. How do you communicate an approximate number without getting into standard deviations, statistically significant variances, and all that stuff?

You decide to respond with a rough order of magnitude estimate.

A rough order of magnitude, also known as a "ballpark estimate," is a range from 25% below your point estimate to 75% above.[5]

Optimistic estimate (lower cost) = point estimate X 0.75
    Your optimistic estimate is $1,200,000 X 0.75 = $900,000

Pessimistic estimate (higher cost) = point estimate X 1.75
    Your pessimistic estimate is $1,200,000 X 1.75 = $2,100,000

Results

You tell her your ballpark estimate for a new cleanroom is between $900,000 and $2,100,000, with a most likely estimate of $1,200,000.[6]

She asks if you are available to lead the project for the new cleanroom.

Footnotes

(1) In contrast, a "bottom-up" estimate would first estimate the individual costs for labor, materials, rent, etc. and then add them together to get the total cost.

(2) A cappuccino is one third espresso, one third steamed milk, and one third foamed milk, whereas a latte has more milk and less foam. The difference between a latte and a cappuccino therefore is the milk to foam ratio. The cappuccino has a stronger coffee taste and the latte, with more milk, has a softer taste. Yum!

(3) Don't guess. An estimate is not the same as a guess. If you don't remember the cost of the previous cleanroom, tell her you will look it up when you get back to your office.

(4) CYA stands for Cover Your Assumptions or something like that.

(5) To subtract 25% from a value, we multiply it by 0.75. to add 75%, multiply the value by 1.75.

(6) Later on, we will see a couple of way we can use these three estimates; optimistic, pessimistic, and most likely; to calculate both costs and durations for individual activities and for the entire projects.

Filler:

The concept of a contamination controlled environment originated in the mid-19th century in hospital operating rooms. Modern cleanrooms, however, were born out of the need for precision manufacturing in clean environments during World War II and the subsequent race to space.

Parametric Estimating

Parametric estimation uses the value of a common parameter, such as size or capacity, of a previous activity or project to estimate the cost or duration of a future activity or project. The assumption[1] is a linear relationship between the chosen parameter and the cost (or duration) and that all things other than the chosen parameter are relatively similar.

Scenario

The plant manager says that your analogous estimate seems low. You ask how large the proposed cleanroom will be. She replies that it will have six work stations. Well, that changes things! The prior cleanroom only had four workstations. You need to refine your original estimate in light of this new information.

Process

Given your knowledge of cleanrooms, you assume that a six-station cleanroom will cost about 150% that of a four-station cleanroom (6/4 = 1.50). You are assuming a linear relationship between workstations and cost. This is known as parametric estimating. You are using a parameter, in this case the number of workstations, to improve your analogous estimate and come up with a new rough order of magnitude estimate.

Analogous estimate X parametric factor = parametric estimate

$$\$1,200,000 \times 1.50 = \$1,800,000$$

Results

You then convert your new point estimate to a rough order of magnitude, ROM, with a range of -25% to +75%. Your estimate for a six-station cleanroom is between $1,350,000 and $3,150,000.

$$1,800,000 \times 0.75 = 1,350,000 \text{ and } 1,800,000 \times 1.75 = 3,150,000$$

She says that is about what she expected and she invites you to conduct a more detailed cost analysis.

Scenario

Assume the prior cleanroom consisted of two major components; the room itself, which cost $800,000, and a heating, ventilation, and air conditioning (HVAC) unit, which cost $200,000. Further, you discover that this model HVAC unit can support up to eight workstations. What are your revised rough order of magnitude optimistic, most likely, and pessimistic estimates?

Process

You use analogous estimating for the HVAC because the new unit will be the same as the old unit, adjusted only for inflation of 10%.

$$\$200,000 \times 1.10 = \$220,000$$

You use parametric estimating for the rest of the cleanroom, adjusting for both inflation of 10% and the increased capacity of $6 / 4 = 1.50$.

$$\$800,000 \times 1.10 = \$880,000$$
$$\$880,000 \times 1.50 = \$1,320,000$$

Results

Your new most likely estimate is $220,000 + $1,320,000 = $1,540,000.[2]
Your optimistic estimate is $1,540,000 X 0.75 = $1,155,000 and your pessimistic estimate is $1,540,000 X 1.75 = $2,695,000.

Footnotes

(1) Be sure to document all of your assumptions in the project assumption log or the project management plan. I'll just mention this once, but we will frequently be making assumptions, and we should be sure to document all of them.

(2) Accountants in the audience will note the similarity of this to fixed costs and variable costs. We'll talk more about fixed costs and variable costs when we get into breakeven analysis.

Definitive Estimate

A definitive estimate has less deviation around the mean, or the point estimate, than a rough order of magnitude (ballpark) estimate. You have taken the time to eliminate many of the unknowns or assumptions. You are more confident of the range within which the final number will fall.

Scenario

The plant manager gives you a folder containing the specifications for the new cleanroom and asks you to provide a "definitive estimate" as soon as possible for inclusion in the formal project proposal.

A definitive estimate is a bottom-up estimate. It takes more time to complete than a parametric estimate, and it costs more if your time is charged to it, but it is a lot more accurate. Each of the individual costs are estimated and then totaled. The total is then expressed as a lower and upper range, such as plus or minus some percentage. Frequently –5% and +10% are used, but symmetrical deviations, such as ± 5% or ± 10% are not uncommon. Check with your project management office, PMO, to see what the organization prefers.

Process

Back in your office you calculate the various costs to procure all of the components, assemble, and test the six-station cleanroom. You then add the costs together and come up with the most likely total cost point estimate of $1,350,000.

Optimistic definitive estimate (lower cost) = point estimate times 0.95. Your optimistic definitive estimate is $1,350,000 X 0.95 = $1,282,500.

Pessimistic definitive estimate (higher cost) = point estimate times 1.10. Your pessimistic definitive estimate is $1,350,000 X 1.10 = $1,485,000.

Results

You document your definitive estimate for the six-station cleanroom as between $1,282,500 and $1,485,000 and give it to plant manager.

Discussion

What does this mean? Why did the plant manager ask you to invest your time (and therefore company money) in this activity? The goal was not to calculate some numbers; the goal was to help make the right decisions.

The plant manager is obviously considering building a new cleanroom. Why? Probably to increase production, sell more product, and increase organizational profits.

But will the additional profits justify the cost of the cleanroom? How long will it take to recover the cost of the cleanroom? Should she build the new cleanroom or outsource the additional production? If she builds the cleanroom, how much should she budget for it?

All of her decisions have a greater likelihood of being correct because you have provided her with the best possible estimates for the project cost.

Practice

Your project is to improve the energy efficiency of your company buildings. In particular, you are interested in the cost to install solar panels on the roofs of each of your buildings. A pilot project was conducted on a 50,000 square foot, one story building. The cost to install the solar panels was $35,000.

What is the analogous cost to install solar panels on a two-story building?

What is your rough order of magnitude estimate for this job?

What is your parametric point estimate for a 100,000 square foot building? What is your rough order of magnitude (ballpark) estimate for this building?

You have calculated a bottom up estimate for the 100,000 square foot building to be $64,000. What is your definitive (0.95/1.10) estimate?

Answers

The analogous cost to install solar panels on the two-story building is the same as on the one-story building: $35,000. Remember, in analogous estimating, we are assuming the two projects are exactly analogous, despite the obvious difference in roof height and, possibly, roof size and shape, tall trees or buildings nearby that would block the sun, and the expected electrical needs of the building.

The rough order of magnitude estimate is:

$$\text{Optimistic} = \$35,000 \times 0.75 = \$26,250$$
$$\text{Pessimistic} = \$35,000 \times 1.75 = \$61,250$$

The parametric point estimate for the 100,000 square foot building is:

$$\$35,000 \times \left(\frac{100,000}{50,000}\right) = \$35,000 \times 2 = \$70,000$$

The rough order of magnitude (ballpark) estimate is:

$$\text{Optimistic} = \$70,000 \times 0.75 = \$52,500$$
$$\text{Pessimistic} = \$70,000 \times 1.75 = \$122,500$$

The definitive, bottom up, estimate is:

$$\text{Optimistic definitive estimate} = \$64,000 \times 0.95 = \$60,800$$
$$\text{Pessimistic definitive estimate} = \$64,000 \times 1.10 = \$70,400$$

Discussion

If someone says they have spent a lot of time calculating the project cost, they are probably saying they were doing a bottom-up definitive estimate rather than a top-down analogous or parametric estimate.

But, on the other hand, you might want to confirm that before putting too much faith in their data. It might be that they are just slow and not very productive, or they don't really know what they are doing. If that is the case, give them a copy of this book.

Three-Point Cost Estimation

In project management, a three-point estimate is the average (or the weighted average) of a pessimistic estimate, an optimistic estimate, and an estimate of the most likely outcome. The simple average is known as a triangular distribution and the weighted average is a beta distribution.[1]

Scenario

You need to estimate the cost of several activities. Some activities are well known and you can establish cost estimates based on historical data, but other activities are less understood, even by experts.

Triangular Distribution

Process

Rather than asking your expert for a single point estimate, you ask for a most likely, an optimistic, and a pessimistic estimate.[2] A typical response from an expert might be: "I think it will cost about $30,000, but it could cost as little as $20,000 or as much as $52,000." Note that the most likely does not have to be midway between the optimistic and the pessimistic. Your expert should be able to explain how they determined each of their three estimates, or they forfeit their expert badge.[3]

Given the estimates, there are three techniques you can use to get an expected cost for the activity. The simplest is to simply use the most likely, but that does not take into consideration the optimistic and pessimistic estimates. Two techniques that do consider all three estimate are triangular distribution and beta distribution.[4]

Triangular distribution is simply the average of the three estimates.

$$Duration = (Optimistic + Most\ Likely + Pessimistic)/3$$

In the above example:

$$Duration = \frac{20,000 + 30,000 + 52,000}{3} = \frac{102,000}{3} = 34,000$$

The expected cost for the activity is $34,000.

Triangular distribution assumes our three estimates are equally likely.

The probability plot for a triangular distribution would look like this:

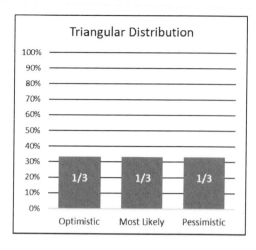

Beta Distribution

Beta distribution places more emphasis on the most likely value than it does on the optimistic or pessimistic values. The formula is:

$$Duration = \frac{Optimistic + 4(Most\ Likely) + Pessimistic}{6}$$

Using the estimates of $30,000 for the most likely, $20,000 for the optimistic, and $52,000 for the pessimistic, we get:

$$Duration = \frac{20,000 + 4(30,000) + 52,000}{6} = 32,000$$

With the beta distribution, we get $32,000 for the expected cost of the activity. With triangular distribution, we had an expected cost of $34,000. Notice that the beta distribution "pulled" the expected value closer to the most likely estimate of $30,000.

Beta distribution assumes the "most likely" estimate is, in fact, more likely than either of the other two, which is probably not a bad assumption to make.

The probability plot for a beta distribution would look like this:

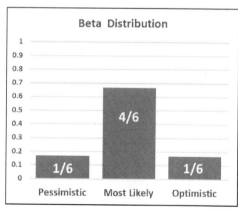

Discussion

We have three choices for our estimated activity cost. The most likely is easy to get, but it ignores the valuable information contained in the optimistic and pessimistic estimates. Triangular distribution considers the range between the optimistic and the pessimistic and beta distribution recognizes the significance of the most likely. Our choice of estimating methods really comes down to the relative importance we place on the most likely estimate. If we have a lot of confidence in the most likely estimate, use it as the expected value. If we have very little confidence in it, use triangular distribution. For a compromise between the two, use beta distribution. Whichever we choose, we will document the rationale for our selection in our project management plan.[5]

An important byproduct of three-point estimating is it gets us to think early on about what could go right (optimistic) and what could go wrong (pessimistic). We will document these as opportunities and threats and include them in our risk management plan. We can even include the optimistic and pessimistic values when evaluating risks and contingencies reserves.[6] More on them later.

Practice

Your project is to restore the company parking lot. The project consists of three activities: repair, resurface and restripe. You have consulted with vendors and with team members and have compiled the following costs:

Repair: optimistic $41,000, pessimistic $80,000, most likely $50,000.

Resurface: optimistic $30,000, pessimistic $72,000, most likely $60,000.

Restripe: optimistic $8,000, pessimistic $22,000, most likely $12,000.

Using only the most likely estimate, what is the cost for each activity and what is the expected total cost for the project?

Using triangular distribution, what is the cost for each activity and what is the expected total cost for the project?

Using beta distribution, what is the cost for each activity and what is the expected total cost for the project?

Answers

Single point (most likely):

Repair = $50,000

Resurface = $60,000

Restripe = $12,000

Total = $50,000 + $60,000 + $12,000 = $122,000

Triangular distribution:

$$\text{Repair} = \frac{41,000 + 50,000 + 80,000}{3} = \frac{171,000}{3} = 57,000$$

$$\text{Resurface} = \frac{30,000 + 60,000 + 72,000}{3} = \frac{162,000}{3} = 54,000$$

$$\text{Restripe} = \frac{8,000 + 12,000 + 22,000}{3} = \frac{42,000}{3} = 14,000$$

Total = $57,000 + $54,000 + $14,000 = $125,000

Beta distribution:

$$\text{Repair} = \frac{41,000 + 4(50,000) + 80,000}{6} = \frac{321,000}{6} = 53,500$$

$$\text{Resurface} = \frac{30,000 + 4(60,000) + 72,000}{6} = \frac{342,000}{6} = 57,000$$

$$\text{Restripe} = \frac{8,000 + 4(12,000) + 22,000}{6} = \frac{78,000}{6} = 13,000$$

Total = $53,500 + $57,000 + $13,000 = $123,500

Footnotes

(1) In the 1950's project managers realized they needed a way to incorporate an expected range of activity estimates. Three-point estimating was developed to help project managers estimate activity costs and durations while recognizing the importance of the range or spread in the various estimates. Three-point estimating is nearly the same for project cost or duration. The only difference is that we add all of the expected activity costs together to get the expected total cost for the project whereas we only add the activity durations for activities on the critical path. We will see the same formulas when we discuss activity and project duration and the critical path, and also when we discuss risk probability and impact, but for now, let's talk money.

(2) The pessimistic estimate includes everything that could go wrong with the activity. We can use it to establish our contingency reserve for the activity. The optimistic estimate assumes everything will go right. Both pessimistic and optimistic activity estimates should generate entries in our risk register.

(3) Your organization should have an established definition for optimistic and pessimistic estimates. For example, the person responsible for the estimate should be 95% confident that the actual cost will not be greater than their pessimistic estimate, and 95% confident that the actual cost will not be less than their optimistic estimate. A 95% confidence interval is fairly common in business statistics.

(4) Which technique we use depends on organizational policy and guidance from the project management office. Whichever we use, we should be consistent and use the same one throughout the project.

(5) Could we create our own three-point distribution formula such as 25%, 50% and 25%? Of course we could! But the only two formulas recognized in popular project management literature are triangular distribution and beta distribution. We would need a good justification for a new formula, such as a historical analysis of project cost estimating accuracy within the organization.

(6) A contingency reserve may be associated with an activity having significant risk. It is included in the project budget and usually is available to the project manager without the need for an approved change request.

Filler

I once visited the west coast distribution center of a major retailer. They were taking a "wall-to-wall" physical inventory every month end, and I was hoping to sell my consulting services to implement a daily cycle counting program. As I toured the facility with the distribution center manager, I noticed a lot of empty, or near-empty shelves. I asked if this was normal. My host replied it was not, but that they were getting ready for the physical over the coming weekend. I joked that they were minimizing the stock to make it easier to count. He chuckled and said that was not the reason. When he told me the real reason for the empty shelves, I knew I had no chance of selling my cycle counting services.

Corporate management back east was concerned about high inventory levels. They wanted to increase the inventory turnover rate, which is average cost of goods sold divided by average inventory at cost. To motivate managers to make prudent inventory decision, they gave a monthly incentive bonus to all managers based on their turnover rate.

Remember the formula, sales divided by inventory. To improve the ratio, you can sell more or you can stock less; and the corporate accountants back east used the month-end physical inventory as the value in the inventory turnover computations, and the bonus.

So what did the distribution manager do? He shipped everything he could to the stores the week before the scheduled count. What else did he do? You guessed it. He stopped receiving goods the week before the count. As I walked back to my car, I saw about a dozen padlocked semi-trailers in the parking lot, full of goods that would be "delivered" after the weekend. Daily cycle counting would expose this little game to senior management.

Be careful when designing your incentive systems. They should be simple to understand, but difficult to artificially manipulate.

Total Project Cost

In the last topic we began by saying three points are better than one, but then we conclude with a single point estimate, the expected value, with no indication of our confidence in that number. Wouldn't it be better if we could provide three estimates for the total project cost? In addition to the expected total cost, we can provide an optimistic total cost estimate and a pessimistic total cost estimate. In addition to indicating our confidence in the expected value, we will find some other uses for this valuable information.

Discussion

You will need a calculator with a square root key for this. Later, when we are working with activity durations and total project duration, rather than activity costs and total project cost, we will use Microsoft Excel. Either method, of course, will give us the exact same answers.[1]

Scenario

You have a simple project with three sequential activities. For each activity, you have an optimistic cost, a most likely cost, and a pessimistic cost. What is the total optimistic, most likely, and pessimistic cost for the project?

Activity	Optimistic	Most Likely	Pessimistic
A	22	40	82
B	48	60	90
C	42	63	120
Total:	112	163	292

Discussion

In the old days, we would have only asked our experts for their most likely estimate and then declared that the total project cost would be 163. But, we know better than that now. We know to ask our experts for their optimistic and pessimistic estimates in addition to their most likely guess.

Next, we will calculate the expected cost for each activity. Given a choice between triangular distribution and beta distribution, we will use beta distribution.

Process

We calculate the following expected values using beta distribution:

Activity A = (22 + 4(40) +82) / 6 = 44
Activity B = (48 + 4(60) + 90) / 6 = 63
Activity C = (42 + 4(63) + 120) / 6 = 69

Results

Using beta distribution, we get a total project cost of (44 + 63 + 69) = 176 rather than the 163 we got by only using the most likely estimates.

Scenario

What is the optimistic, expected, and pessimistic costs for the project?

Discussion

We might be tempted to use the sum of the optimistic estimates, 112, and the sum of the pessimistic estimates, 292, but that would be incorrect. Activity risks are assumed to be independent. It is unlikely that a series of independent events would always be positive or always be negative.

Further, optimistic and pessimistic estimates that are further away from the expected value are of more concern to us than nearby estimates, so we need to weight them accordingly.

The way we do that is to square the difference between the optimistic or pessimistic estimate and the expected value (not the most likely value) for each activity.

Next, we add the squares for each activity, and then calculate the square root of the sum of the squares.

Finally, we subtract the square root of the optimistic difference from the expected value of the project total for our optimistic total, and we add the square root of the pessimistic difference to the expected project total to get the pessimistic total.

Process

The difference between the estimate values:

Optimistic A = 44 – 22 = 22   Pessimistic A = 82 – 44 = 38
Optimistic B = 63 – 48 = 15   Pessimistic B = 90 – 63 = 27
Optimistic C = 69 – 42 = 27   Pessimistic C = 120 – 69 = 51

Squares and totals:

Optimistic A = 22 X 22 = 484   Pessimistic A = 38 X 38 = 1444
Optimistic B = 15 X 15 = 225   Pessimistic B = 27 X 27 = 729
Optimistic C = 27 X 27 = 729   Pessimistic C = 51 X 51 = 2601
Total = 484 + 225 + 729 = 1438   Total = 1444 + 729 + 2601 = 4774

Square roots and total cost estimates:

Optimistic = $\sqrt{1438}$ = 37.92   Pessimistic = $\sqrt{4774}$ = 69.09

Optimistic cost estimate = 176 – 37.92 = 138.08 = 138
Pessimistic cost estimate = 176 + 69.09 = 245.09 = 245

Results

The expected cost of our project is 176, with an optimistic estimate of 138 and a pessimistic estimate of 245.

Discussion

We have replaced the single point project estimate with a three-point estimate that includes our optimistic/pessimistic range. The pessimistic estimate could be used to set a management reserves and the optimistic estimate could be used to set a project bonus incentive.

Footnote

(1) Starting with paper, pencil and a calculator helps us understand the theory behind the process. Once we know what's going on, we can use Excel to simplify and speed up the process.

Break-Even Analysis

Costs are willingly incurred in order to produce revenue, and when revenue exceeds cost, we have a profit. The break-even point is where revenue exactly equals cost. Less than that, and we are losing money, more than that, we are making a profit. Some projects we do because we have to, such as complying with governmental regulations; but many projects are undertaken to generate a profit for the organization. Before these projects are approved, a break-even analysis will be conducted and the break-even point will be determined. The first step is to identify the fixed costs, the variable costs per unit, and the revenue per unit sold.

Scenario

You are writing the project charter to develop the Genesis digital camera. The marketing manager plans to position the Genesis directly against our major rival, with a retail price of $80. The manufacturing manager believes the total fixed costs to launch the Genesis will be $7,000,000 and the variable cost will be $45 per unit.

How many Genesis units must be sold before the product breaks even, recovers the initial investment of $7,000,000, and starts to generate a profit for the company?

Process

We will assume there is no inflation. Future profit dollars have the same value to you as current investment dollars. Of course, this is not true, but it's okay as long as we acknowledge our results are contingent upon this assumption. We'll talk more about the time value of money later on.

We will subtract the variable cost from the retail price. That will give us the profit contribution of each unit sold. (We are going to assume we can sell everything we produce.) We then divide the profit margin into the fixed costs to see how many units we need to sell to repay the fixed cost and break even. Any additional units sold will generate a profit equal to their profit margin.

Results

Break even units = Fixed costs / (Price – Variable cost)

$$7,000,000 / (80 - 45) = 7,000,000 / 35 = 200,000$$

We must sell 200,000 Genesis units to break even and start generating a profit.

Discussion

Senior management rarely gets involved in units; they aggregate units into dollars so they can compare different products, different product lines, and even different divisions of the company. So how much sales, in retail dollars, does the Genesis have to generate to break even?

Process

Since we already know the break-even point in units, we can simply multiply the units by the retail price. The break-even point does not change; we are only changing the unit of measure we use to define the break-even point.

Breakeven Units X Retail Price = Breakeven Dollars

$$200,000 \text{ X } \$80 = \$16,000,000$$

Results

We must sell $16,000,000 worth of Genesis units to break even and start earning a profit.

Discussion

As we have seen, calculating the break-even point is not difficult; but explaining it to others might be. For that, a break-even chart is frequently used. The horizontal (x) axis displays units and the vertical (y) axis displays cost and revenue. When units are zero, revenue is also zero, and total costs equal the fixed cost. Below 200,000 units, total costs are greater than revenue; we are losing money. At 200,000 units we break even. Above 200,000 units our total revenue is greater than our total cost and we are making a profit. Whoopee!

Scenario

Earlier we assumed there was no inflation and those future dollars are the same as current dollars. That may not be a problem if the future is next week or next month, but suppose we won't hit the break-even point for several years! We will discuss the future value of money later, but for now, let's at least determine when we will hit the break-even point.

After the launch of the Genesis, approximately how long will it take us to reach the break-even point?

Based on our analysis of the competitors' sales, our sales manager believes we can sell 130,000 Genesis units a year at a retail price of $80.00 each.

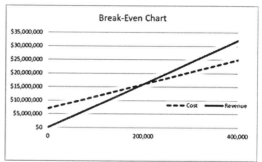

Process

This is easy. We simply divide our break-even quantity by the annual sales rate.

Breakeven units / Annual sales in units = Years to break even

200,000 / 130,000 = 1.54 years

Of course there are 52 weeks in a year, so we multiply by 52

1.54 years X 52 = 80 weeks

Results

If our assumptions are correct, we will break even in about 80 weeks after launch. We will have sold 200,000 units and produced $16,000,000 in revenue, equaling our total cost of $16,000,000.

Discussion

The minimum amount of time required to recover the fixed cost is sometimes called the payback period. As we saw above, it can be expressed in years, months or weeks. Very small projects might even have a payback period best expressed in days. For example, we rent a booth at the county fair to sell candy apples. The fair lasts 5 days and we expect to recover the rental fee and break even on day 3.

Practice

The manufacturing manager has suggested we build a smaller factory for the Genesis and run two shifts a day. That would reduce the fixed costs in half, to $3,500,000 but would increase the variable costs to an average of $60 per unit due to the overtime we would have to pay the swing-shift crew.

If we used the small-factory, swing-shift model for Genesis production, what would be the break-even point, in units and in dollars, and how long would it take, in weeks, to reach the break-even point? Should we stay with the original model, or change to the small-factory, swing-shift model?

Assume the Genesis will still retail for $80 and the expected demand will remain at 130,000 units per year.

Answers

Fixed cost = $3,500,000
Variable cost = $60 per unit
Retail price = $80
Expected demand = 130,000 units per year

Break-even units:

$$\frac{3,500,000}{(80-60)} = \frac{3,500,000}{20} = 175,000 \text{ units}$$

Break-even dollars:
$$175,000 \text{ X } \$80 = \$14,000,000$$

Break-even time:

$$\frac{175,000}{130,000} = 1.35 \text{ Years}$$

$$1.35 \text{ years } X \text{ } 52 = 70 \text{ weeks}$$

We should use the small-factory, swing-shift model because the break-even point is less (175,000 units compared to 200,000 units; or $14,000,000 compared to $16,000,000) and because we will reach the break-even point sooner (70 weeks compared to 80 weeks).

Discussion

Suppose actual demand is a lot less than 130,000 units a year. With the large-factory model we would be stuck with an under-utilized $7,000,000 plant, but with the small-factory model, we can lay off some or all of the swing shift.

On the other hand, suppose demand is much greater than 130,000 units a year. With the large-factory model we can add a swing shift, and even a graveyard shift. With the smaller factory, our maximum output will be limited by our maximum three-shift capacity.

How can we resolve the dilemma of the unknown demand?

Expected Monetary Value

Expected monetary value, EMV,[1] is used to estimate the value of future income, or loss, given conditions of uncertainty. It does not consider the time value of money, but it can be used to compare similar alternatives.

Scenario

We need to build a new factory to produce the new Genesis digital camera. Should we build a large factory or a small factory? We saw with break-even analysis that we can calculate profit relatively accurately if we know what demand will be. The problem is, we <u>never</u> really know what future demand will be. We have estimates, but no guarantees. Future demand, like risk, is uncertain. (Maybe risk and demand are the same thing?) How can we make good decisions in an uncertain environment?

Process

The first step is to estimate the probability of uncertain events; in this case, demand. For simplicity, let's say there are three possible levels of demand: low, average, and high. [2]

We estimate the probability of low demand as 20%, the probability of average demand as 50%, and the probability of high demand as 30%.

Based on an analysis of fixed and variable production costs, and expected sales in the three different demand environments, we have estimated the following annual profit and loss amounts:[3]

- A large factory with low demand will have a $1,000,000 loss.
- A large factory with average demand will have a $2,000,000 profit.
- A large factory with high demand will have a $5,000,000 profit.
- A small factory with low demand will have a $500,000 loss.
- A small factory with average demand will have a $2,500,000 profit.
- A small factory with high demand is high will have a $3,500,000 profit.

The expected monetary value, EMV, for either option, large factory or small factory, is the sum of the profit and loss resulting from each of the three demand probabilities, low, average, and high.

Large factory	Demand	Probability	Profit (Loss)	Value
	Low	20%	-$1,000,000	-$200,000
	Average	50%	$2,000,000	$1,000,000
	High	30%	$5,000,000	$1,500,000
EMV (Large factory)				$2,300,000

Small factory	Demand	Probability	Profit (Loss)	Value
	Low	20%	-$500,000	-$100,000
	Average	50%	$2,500,000	$1,250,000
	High	30%	$3,500,000	$1,050,000
EMV (Small factory)				$2,200,000

The values are simply the profit or loss multiplied by the demand probability percent. For example, -$1,000,000 X 0.20 = -$200,000.

Results

The expected monetary value for the large factory is $2,300,000 and the expected monetary value for the small factory is $2,200,000. Given the greater expected monetary value, we should build the large factory.

Filler:

Toyota Motor Corporation is spending a billion dollars to build a new factory in central Mexico. The plant will employ 2,000 workers and have the capacity to produce 200,000 vehicles annually. Corolla production will begin there in 2019 starting with the 2020 model.

"Our next-generation production facility in Mexico will be a model for the future of global manufacturing and set a new standard for innovation and excellence," said Jim Lentz, chief executive of Toyota North America. "Transforming our Canadian vehicle assembly plants is an equally important part of our strategic plan to position the North America region for sustainable long-term growth."

40

Decision Tree

Expected monetary value tables are sometimes displayed as a decision tree. This can be especially useful when explaining complex problems involving lots of "branches." Compare the decision tree below to the EMV table above. Both contain the same data. Which is more intuitive?

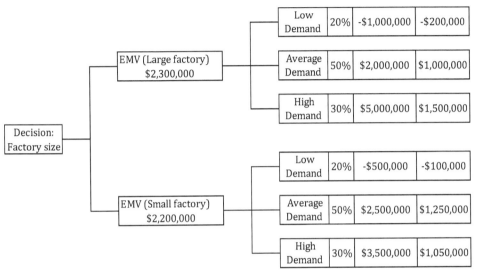

Practice

Rather than building a new factory, we could acquire and renovate an existing factory. This would get us into the market faster but with a less efficient operation. Use the large factory and demand date above, but replace the small factory option with an "acquire and renovate" option:

- If we acquire and renovate a factory and demand is low, we will lose $250,000.

- If we acquire and renovate a factory and demand is average, we will make $3,000,000.

- If we acquire and renovate a factory and demand is high, we will make $4,000,000.

Should we build the new large factory, or should we acquire and renovate an existing factory?

Answer

We should acquire and renovate a factory because the EMV is higher ($2,650,000 > $2,300,000):

Build factory	Demand	Probability	Profit (Loss)	Value
	Low	20%	-$1,000,000	-$200,000
	Average	50%	$2,000,000	$1,000,000
	High	30%	$5,000,000	$1,500,000
EMV (Build large factory)				$2,300,000

Acquire factory	Demand	Probability	Profit (Loss)	Value
	Low	20%	-$250,000	-$50,000
	Average	50%	$3,000,000	$1,500,000
	High	30%	$4,000,000	$1,200,000
EMV (Acquire and renovate factory)				$2,650,000

Here's the same data in decision tree format:

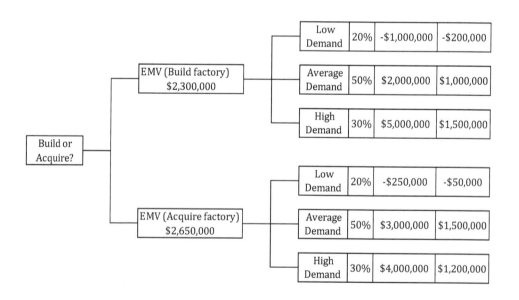

Discussion

This did not need to be a two-step operation. We could have constructed a single EMV table with all three options: large factory, small factory, and acquire and renovate. Most EMV tables will also include a "do nothing" option. Sometimes the downside (negative risk) is so significant that the rewards (positive risk) do not justify the project; in which case "do nothing" might be our best option.

Maximizing profit is nice, but money may not be our only concern. How can we include non-monetary factors in our decision-making process? For example, our factory decision could include political, economic, social, technological, environmental and legal considerations.[4] We will see how we can include subjective data in the decision making process when we get to factor weighted tables.

Footnotes

(1) Don't get confused between Expected Monetary Value, EMV, and Earned Value Management, EVM. Another example of why I dislike acronyms.

(2) I used three demand estimates, but there is nothing special about three. You should use whatever is most appropriate for the situation.

(3) The profit and loss estimates include fixed costs, variable costs, and revenue from sales. To simplify this example, we will bypass these calculations and use net profit (or loss) to make our decision. For a discussion of fixed costs, variable costs, and revenue, see break-even analysis.

(4) Political, economic, social, technological, environmental and legal considerations make up a PESTEL analysis, which is a common strategic management tool. Of course, building a new factory or acquiring and renovation an existing factory, would certainly be considered a strategic decision.

Project Cost Estimation

We used triangular distribution and beta distribution to improve the quality of our activity cost estimates. We took the resulting expected value for each activity and added them together to get the expected project cost. We concluded with the question; wouldn't it be better if we could provide the expected, optimistic and pessimistic costs for the entire project? Well, we can.

The following technique will give the decision makers three cost estimates: expected, optimistic, and pessimistic. The expected cost is the same values they are currently getting, using the traditional method of adding the expected costs of each of the activities. The optimistic and pessimistic estimates are the result of a little statistics using the "addition rule for the variances of independent random variables."

The rule says we cannot simply add the optimistic estimates for each activity and get an optimistic estimate for the project, nor can we add the pessimistic estimates. But, we can add their variances.

Discussion

Most project management literature defines a variance as the difference between the actual value and the expected value. Looking at the data for our project, we might expect that the optimistic and pessimistic estimates are variances from the most likely estimate for each activity. They are not.

Here we need to forget the project management definition of a variance and look to statistics instead, where a variance is defined as the square of the standard deviation. Think of the difference between an optimistic estimate for an activity and the expected value as the "optimistic standard deviation" and the difference between the expected value and the pessimistic as the "pessimistic standard deviation."[1]

The statistics rule for addition is that we must convert each standard deviation into its variance by squaring it, adding the variances, and then finding the square root of the total. We do this separately for optimistic variances and pessimistic variances because it is unlikely our data are symmetrical; we probably have an optimistic or pessimistic skew.

Scenario

We are planning a relatively simple project with only four activities. For each activity, we obtained an optimistic, a most likely and a pessimistic cost estimate from subject experts.

	A	B	C	D
1	Activity	Optimistic	Most Likely	Pessimistic
2	A	$1,200	$2,000	$2,200
3	B	$4,400	$5,000	$5,300
4	C	$7,800	$8,400	$9,000
5	D	$5,800	$6,500	$6,900
6				

Don't confuse these optimistic, most likely, and pessimistic estimates we got from our experts with the rough order of magnitude estimates we calculates ourselves at the bottom of page 18, where we simply subtracted 25% and added 75%.

Process

What is the expected total project cost? We will use beta distribution to calculate the expected cost for each activity. Grab your smartphone or pocket calculator.

$$Expected\ Cost(A) = \frac{1,200 + 4(2,000) + 2,200}{6} = 1,900$$

$$Expected\ Cost(B) = \frac{4,400 + 4(5,000) + 5,300}{6} = 4,950$$

$$Expected\ Cost(C) = \frac{7,800 + 4(8,400) + 9,000}{6} = 8,400$$

$$Expected\ Cost(D) = \frac{5,800 + 4(6,500) + 6,900}{6} = 6,450$$

We then added the expected costs for the four activities to get the expected project cost of $21,700. This is as far as we went in the prior topic and, sadly, as far as most project management literature goes too.

We have access to some really valuable information: expert opinions on optimistic and pessimistic costs for each activity. Why not include them in our discussion of the total project cost? It's time to put down the calculator and boot up Excel.

Microsoft Excel

First, a brief introduction to Excel, the most popular electronic spreadsheet and a true killer application.[2]

Good spreadsheet design labels each of the variables and then uses cell references to place the variables into formulas and functions. Clearly displaying each of the variables makes it easy to read and update.

Formulas always begin with the equal sign so Excel knows the cell contains math and not text. Excel will interpret 2+2 as text and will display 2+2, but it will interpret =2+2 as a formula and will return 4.

The slash is used for division; =6/2 will result in 3. The asterisk is used in Excel to multiply; =2*4 will be 8. The caret is used to indicate an exponent: three squared is =3^2 is 9 and 3 cubed is =3^3 is 27. We use decimal or fractional exponents for square roots: =9^0.5 or =9^(1/2) is 3. We could also use the SQRT function in Excel to do this. See below. The colon is used to show a range of cells. For example, A1:A5 includes cells A1, A2, A3, A4 and A5. A1:B3 includes A1, A2, A3, B1, B2 and B3.

Formulas are things we create and are limited only by our imagination. Functions, on the other hand, are built into Excel and must follow a specific syntax. For example, =(B1 + B2 + B3)/3 is a formula, and =AVERAGE (B1:B3) is a function[3]. Functions are definitely preferred for complicated formulas. We will discuss a few of them in the following pages. Some example are =SUM(2,5) is 7, =AVERAGE(4,6) is 5, and =SQRT(9) is 3.

It is best not to "hide" values in formulas and functions (as I did above), but rather to refer to cells that are labeled and contain the values. If the correct values are in the cells indicated =SUM(A2,A3), AVERAGE(B5,C5) and SQRT(D4) would all be preferable to my examples above. There are hundreds of functions in Excel and each new Excel version adds more. To remain backward compatibility, older functions are rarely removed.

So, how do we find a function that will meet our needs? Memorize all of them? I think not!

The function wizard is a very useful tool for finding functions. Click on the *fx* (just left of the edit window) to open the wizard. Type a word into the search box and click "Go." You don't need to memorize a bunch of Excel functions if you know how to use the function wizard.

You can also select a category in the function wizard and scroll through the list. When you find something that looks like it might meet your needs, click on the "Help on this function" link which will open a dialogue box where you can fill in the required and optional cell references.

Scenario

And now, back to our story. What are the expected, optimistic, and pessimistic costs for our project?

Process

	A	B	C	D	E	F	G	H	I
1	Activity	Cost (Dollars)				Optimistic Std. Dev.	Optimistic Variance	Pessimistic Std. Dev.	Pessimistic Variance
2		Optimistic	Most Likely	Pessimistic	Expected				
3	A	$1,200	$2,000	$2,200	$1,900	$800	640,000	$200	40,000
4	B	$4,400	$5,000	$5,300	$4,950	$600	360,000	$300	90,000
5	C	$7,800	$8,400	$9,000	$8,400	$600	360,000	$600	360,000
6	D	$5,800	$6,500	$6,900	$6,450	$700	490,000	$400	160,000
7				Sum	$21,700	Sum of Var.	1,850,000	Sum of Var.	650,000
8						Square Root	$1,360	Square Root	$806
9				Expected	$21,700	Optimistic	$20,340	Pessimistic	$22,506

Our estimates have been entered in cells B3:D6. The formula in cell E3 is =(B3+(4*C3)+D3)/6. Cell F3 is =C3–B3. Cell G3 is F3 square, =F3^2. Cell H3 is =D3–C3, and cell I3 is H3 square, =H3^2. Similar formulas are used for the activities B, C and D in rows 4, 5 and 6. The expected total cost of the project is in cell E7 with =SUM(E3:E6). Cell G7 is =SUM(G3:G6) and cell I7 is =SUM(I3:I6). Cell G8 is the square root of G7 using =SQRT(G7) and cell I8 is =SQRT(I7). The optimistic project outcome in cell G9 is =E9–G8 and the pessimistic project outcome in cell I9 is =E9+I8.

Note that the optimistic square root is subtracted from the expected value (21,700 – 1,360 = 20,340) while the pessimistic square root is added to the expected value (21,700 + 806 = 22,506).

Results

Our expected project cost of $21,700 did not change, but we now can add considerable value to this point estimate by including an optimistic estimate of $20,340 and a pessimistic estimate of $22,506.
All three estimates will be reported to management. This will give the organization some insight into the degree of risk inherent in the project.

Remember analogous estimation, parametric estimation, rough order of magnitude, and definitive estimates? We used them when we were doing top-down project estimating. Now that we are using bottom-up estimating, we can still include information regarding the expected accuracy of our point estimates.

Rather than saying, "My estimate for the total cost is $21,700" we can say, "My estimates for the total cost are $20,300 to $22,500" (rounded).

Our project sponsor might consider our pessimistic estimate when deciding upon a management reserve[5] for the project. The size of the pessimistic estimate may even be cause to reconsider the wisdom of the project itself or, at least, to better understand the major risks before breaking ground. Lastly, deciding between competing projects based on all three estimates will probably yield better decisions than comparing expected values alone.

Practice

Your business is growing and you need to expand the employee parking lot. The project involves two activities: preparing the land and installing the asphalt. The most likely cost to prepare the land is $1,400, with an optimistic cost of $800 and a pessimistic cost of $2,000. The most likely cost for the asphalt is $1,800, with an optimistic of $1,000 and a pessimistic of $2,600.

Using beta distribution, what is the expected cost for each activity?

What are the optimistic, most likely, and pessimistic costs for the entire project?

Process

		Cost (Dollars)			Optimistic	Optimistic	Pessimistic	Pessimistic
Activity	Optimistic	Most Likely	Pessimistic	Expected	Std. Dev.	Variance	Std. Dev.	Variance
Prepare land	$800	$1,400	$2,000	$1,400	$600	360,000	$600.00	360,000
Install asphalt	$1,000	$1,800	$2,600	$1,800	$800	640,000	$800.00	640,000
			Sum	$3,200	Sum of Var.	1,000,000	Sum of Var.	1,000,000
					Square Root	$1,000	Square Root	$1,000
			Expected	$3,200	Optimistic	$2,200	Pessimistic	$4,200

Our estimates are entered in cells B3:D4. The formula in cell E3 is =(B3+(4*C3)+D3)/6 and cell E4 is =(B4+(4*C4)+D4)/6. Cell E5 is =SUM(E3:E4) and, to show all of our results on the bottom line, cell E7 is simply =E5. By the way, =SUM(E3:E4) could have been entered as =SUM(E3,E4) since we only have two cells in our range. Your choice.

Cell F3 is =C3–B3, cell G3 is =F3^2, cell H3 is =D3–C3, and cell I3 is H3^2. Similar formulas are in row 4 for the install asphalt activity.

Cell G5 is =SUM(G3:G4) and cell G6 is =SQRT(G5). Cell I5 is =SUM(I3:I4) and cell I6 is =SQRT(I5). Cell G7 is =E7–G6 and cell I7 is =E7+I6.

Answer

The expected cost to prepare the land is $1,400 and the expected cost to install the asphalt is $1,800. The expected cost for the entire project is $3,200, with an optimistic cost of $2,200 and a pessimistic cost of $4,200.

If you did not get these results, you should check your formulas.[6]

Discussion

These were nice round numbers, but in the real world, especially with square roots in our process, we will frequently get decimal results. I recommend rounding off these decimal results to a level equal to our input. In this case, our experts gave us estimates to the nearest $100, so our results should be rounded to the nearest $100. Otherwise, we are implying a level of accuracy that we cannot justify.

Footnotes

(1) I made up these terms; please don't try to find them in a statistics text. The differences between the optimistic and the most likely, or between the most likely and the pessimistic, are not really standard deviations and when squared, they are not really variances, but the logic behind this process is based on established statistical concepts involving the addition of independent events.

(2) What is a "killer application", or "killer app?" Applications are software that run on hardware. A killer application is a software program that is so useful that it alone justifies the entire purchase price of the hardware. The killer app for the Apple 2 was VisiCalc, the first "electronic spreadsheet." The killer app for the IBM PC was Lotus 1-2-3, another spreadsheet. Before desktop publishing for the Macintosh and the Internet for everything from smart phones to your doorbell, Microsoft Excel was the killer application for graphical user interface (GUI) machines like Windows and Macintosh. Generalizing a bit, we could argue that spreadsheets have been the driving force behind the personal computer since 1979. We could also argue that since about 1998, the Internet has been the killer app for all things digital.

(3) Excel displays function names in capital letters, so I will follow that convention in this text.

(4) Unlike a contingency reserve, a management reserve is outside the project budget and is usually controlled by the project sponsor. An approved change request will usually be required to make management reserve funds available to the project.

(5) Displaying the formulas in Excel is a convenient way to find errors of inconsistency. Depending on the version of Excel you are using, look in either the View menu or the Formulas menu for "Display Formulas." It's a simple toggle button for the entire worksheet. You may need to adjust some column widths when you toggle back to the normal view.

Payments

So far our formulas have been simple enough to do by hand, but there are many complex project management decisions that warrant the use of Microsoft Excel, and specifically the built-in functions. The payment function is a good example, and a good place to start.

Scenario

You are preparing the budget for your new project. One of the project deliverables involves purchasing a crawler excavator. Adams Equipment has one for $60,000 with no down payment, 2 year financing at 14.4% interest, with payments due at the end of each month. What would be the monthly payment? What is the total cost? (We will assume no inflation for now, but not for long.)

Process

Cell B2 is the annual percentage rate (APR) of 14.4%. We will be making monthly payments, so cell B3 converts the APR to a monthly rate with =B2/12. Cell B4 is the length of the loan in years and cell B5 converts it to months with =B4*12. Cell B6 is the amount of our loan, $60,000.

	A	B
1	Crawler excavator payment analysis	Adams Equipment
2	Interest rate (per year)	14.4%
3	Interest rate (per month)	1.2%
4	Years	2
5	Months	24
6	Loan amount	$60,000
7	Future value	$0
8	Due (0 = end of period, 1 = start)	0
9	Monthly payment	-$2,892
10	Total cost	-$69,411
11		

After the 24 months, the loan will have no value,[1] so cell B7 is zero. Cell B8 indicates if our payments are due at the start of the month (1) or at the end (0). Cell B10 is =B9*B5 to give us the total of the payments.

Finally, cell B9 contains our payment function. The syntax for the Payment function is =PMT(interest rate per period, number of periods, present value, future value, and type). Future value and type are optional, all else are required. Cell B9 is =PMT(B3, B5, B6, B7, B8)[2]. For a lease, the residual value is the future value. Type is a binomial; enter 1 if the payment is due at the start of the period and 0 if at the end of the period.

In all Excel functions, the sequence of the input variables is mandatory, and the variables must be separated by commas. If I had decided to omit the future value, because the default is zero, I would use =PMT(B2, B4, B5, , B7). If I also wanted to use the default type, which is zero, I could have used =PMT(B2, B4, B5). Excel does not expect or require commas for optional variables at the end of functions; they are only placeholders.

Results

Our payments for the crawler excavator will be $2,892 due at the end of each month, for 24 months. In total, we will have paid $69,411.

Discussion

Cell B3 converts the annual interest rate into a monthly interest rate and cell B5 converts the number of years into months. Both are necessary because the payments will be made monthly. A common error made when entering financial functions is failure to convert annual variables to periodic variables like weeks, months, or quarters.

Note that the monthly payment and the total cost are negative because we are paying money out. Since our values are well labeled, we could display them as positive if we wanted (assuming no objections from the organization or the project management office) simply by placing a negative sign at the start of the payment function in cell B8. The present value (the loan amount of $60,000) is positive because we are getting "money" in, in the form of a crawler excavator worth $60,000.

Practice

You have decided to shop around for your crawler excavator. Another dealer, Earthmovers Inc. will sell you the same model crawler excavator as Adams Equipment for only $55,000, with 3 year financing at 18.0% interest and payments due at the start of each month. What would be the monthly payments and the total cost? Based on total cost, should you buy the crawler excavator from Adams Equipment or from Earthmovers Incorporated?

Answer

	A	B	C	D
1	Crawler excavator payment analysis	Adams Equipment	Earthmovers Incorporated	
2	Interest rate (per year)	14.4%	18.0%	
3	Interest rate (per month)	1.2%	1.5%	
4	Years	2	3	
5	Months	24	36	
6	Loan amount	$60,000	$55,000	
7	Future value	$0	$0	
8	Due (0 = end of period, 1 = start)	0	1	
9	Monthly payment	-$2,892	-$1,959	
10	Total cost	-$69,411	-$70,524	
11				

The formulas for Adams Equipment, cells B2:B10, are as previously discussed. Cell C2 is the APR charged by Earthmovers, and the monthly rate is in cell C3 with = C2/12. Cell C4 is the 3 year period and C5 converts it to months with =C4*12. Cell C6 is the purchase price from Earthmovers, $55,000. The loan has no future value so cell C7 is zero. Payments will be due at the start of the month, so cell C8 is 1. The formula in cell C9 is =PMT(C3, C5, C6, C7, C8). Cell C10 is =C9*C5.

Discussion

Even though Earthmovers had a lower selling price ($55,000 < $60,000) and lower monthly payments ($1,959 < $2,892) the total cost is higher than Adams Equipment ($69,411 < $70,524), because of the higher interest rate (18% > 14.4%) and the longer finance period (36 > 24).

Based on this analysis, we should purchase the crawler excavator from Adams Equipment and not from Earthmovers because the total cost is lower by over $1000.

For Adams Equipment, we borrowed $60,000 and repaid $69,411, so we paid $9,411 in interest over the total life of the loan. How much interest did we pay each month? Dividing $9,411 by 24 does not work. In the next topic we'll see how to determine monthly principal and interest.

Save your Excel file. We will use it again when we get to what-if analysis.

Footnotes

(1) Don't confuse the future value of the loan with the future value of the crawler excavator. Loans rarely have future values. The equipment should be worth something after only two years of use. We could consider this the salvage value. Also, our accountants may want to depreciate the crawler excavator over a period longer than the length of the loan. These are all valid business considerations, but they have no bearing on the monthly loan payments.

(2) I have included spaces in function syntax to make them easier to read. Spaces should not be included in Excel formulas and functions. If you forget, Excel will remove them for you, free of charge.

Filler

SOLA Optical, a global manufacturer of lenses for eyeglasses, planned to introduce a new product on a specific launch day. As materials manager for the Petaluma plant, I was responsible for sending the packaging design to the other plants. The design, developed by the artists in our marketing department, featured an enhanced picture of vary attractive eye; fair complexion, blue iris, nice eyelashes and eyebrows. All of us who saw the artwork were impressed. I sent the digital file to the other plants.

Within hours, I started to receive very negative emails. The basic theme was: "Don't you stupid Yanks know anything! Most of the world does not have blue eyes, they have brown eyes!" The artists quickly changed the eye color from blue to a non-offensive hazel-brown color.

After I sent out the revised artwork, I paused to reflect on the problem. There was no official review committee, but everyone who had seen the original design was white. No people of color had been involved in the process. There was no one to speak up and say "Hey, that doesn't look like anybody in my family."

On that day, I learned to appreciate the value of diversity on a team or in the workforce. Give ten white guys a problem and you get a white guy solution. The broader the diversity of the participants, the more likely it is that we will arrive at the optimal solution. The power of the rainbow!

Principal and Interest

Most loan payments are comprised of two components; principal and interest. It may be important to know how much of a given payment is a repayment of the principal we borrowed, and how much of it is interest. For example, repayment of principal is not tax deductible, but payment of interest is.

Due to compounding interest practices, the ratio of principal to interest will change every period. Assuming a fixed periodic payment, we start off paying a lot of interest, and not much principal. As we gradually pay down the principal, the amount of interest on it, not the rate, is reduced, so more of our payment is applied to the principal and less to interest.

Scenario

To finance your project, you borrowed $1,000,000 at 12% interest, with equal payments made at the end of each of the next 12 months. What is the monthly interest rate? What is the monthly payment? What proportion of the payment for month 1 is interest? What proportion of the payment for month 12 is interest?

	A	B
1	Interest rate (per year)	12.0%
2	Interest rate (per month)	1.0%
3	Months	12
4	Loan amount	$1,000,000
5	Monthly payment	-$88,849
6		

Process

Our annual percentage rate, APR, of 12% is entered in cell B1. Cell B2, with the formula =B1/12, gives us the monthly interest rate. The number of periods is in cell B3 and our principal, the amount we borrowed, is in cell B4. Cell B5 contains the payment function =PMT(B2, B3, B4). So far, this has been a review of the stuff we covered in the last topic.

To get the interest amount per period and the principal amount per period, we will use the Excel IPMT and PPMT functions respectively. We will then calculate the percent of the total monthly payment that each component represents.

We constructed a simple Excel table to display interest and principal amounts and percent by month.

Month	IPMT	PPMT	Total	Interest	Principal
1	-$10,000	-$78,849	-$88,849	11.26%	88.74%
2	-$9,212	-$79,637	-$88,849	10.37%	89.63%
3	-$8,415	-$80,434	-$88,849	9.47%	90.53%
4	-$7,611	-$81,238	-$88,849	8.57%	91.43%
5	-$6,798	-$82,050	-$88,849	7.65%	92.35%
6	-$5,978	-$82,871	-$88,849	6.73%	93.27%
7	-$5,149	-$83,700	-$88,849	5.80%	94.20%
8	-$4,312	-$84,537	-$88,849	4.85%	95.15%
9	-$3,467	-$85,382	-$88,849	3.90%	96.10%
10	-$2,613	-$86,236	-$88,849	2.94%	97.06%
11	-$1,751	-$87,098	-$88,849	1.97%	98.03%
12	-$880	-$87,969	-$88,849	0.99%	99.01%

The syntax for interest payment is =IPMT(interest rate per period, period number, number of periods, present value, future value, type). As with the PMT function, future value and type are optional, with defaults of zero. The period number must be between 1 and the number of periods. In our case, the month number in column A.

The principal payment function follows the same syntax, =PPMT(interest rate per period, period number, number of periods, present value, future value, type), with future value and type optional and defaulting to zero.

The formula in cell D2 is simply =B2+C2. The formula in cell E2 is B2/D2 and the formula in cell F2 is C2/D2. Note that the total of principal and interest for each period always equal the total payment amount, but the proportion of each payment applied to interest decreases from 11.26% to 0.99%, while the proportion of each payment applied to the principal increases from 88.74% to 99.01%. Here's a chart that depicts that:

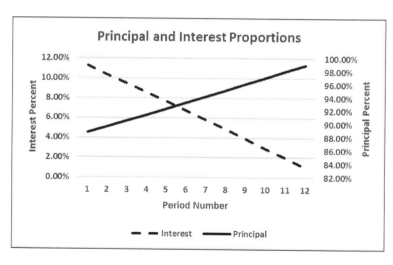

Practice

You borrowed $250,000 to finance your 4 month project at an annual percentage rate, APR, of 18%. Payments were made at the end of November, December, January, and February. The accounting department has asked you how much principal and how much interest you paid in November and December.

Answer

Cell B1 is your annual percentage rate of 18%. Cell B2 converts the APR to a monthly rate with =B1/12. Cell B3 indicates the loan covers 4 months (periods) and cell B4 is the loan amount of $250,000.

	A	B	C
1	APR	18.00%	
2	Per period	1.50%	
3	Periods	4	
4	Loan amount	$250,000	
5			
6		Interest	Principal
7	Nov (1)	-$3,750	-$61,111
8	Dec (2)	-$2,833	-$62,028
9	Totals	-$6,583	-$123,139
10			

Cell B7 is =IPMT(B2, 1, B3, B4) and cell B8 is = IPMT(B2, 2, B3, B4). Cell B9 is simply =B7 + B8.

Cell C7 is =PPMT(B2, 1, B3, B4) and cell C8 is = PPMT(B2, 2, B3, B4). Cell C9 is, of course, =C7 + C8.

In November and December, you paid a total of $6,583 in interest and $123,139 in principal, both rounded to the nearest dollar.

Discussion

Working with tables in Excel, it is frequently easiest to enter a formula in one cell and then copy it to other cells. This introduces the exciting topic of relative and absolute cell references.

B5			f_x	=PPMT(B1,A5,B2,B3)
	A		B	
1	Per period		1%	
2	Periods		6	
3	Principal		$1,000	
4				
5		1	-$163	
6		2		
7		3		

We have entered =PPMT(B1, A5, B2, B3) in cell B5, and we would now like to copy the function to cells B6:B10.

The problem is that, by default, cell references in Excel are *relative references*. In other words, the "B1" in the cell B5 formula actually tells Excel to use the value in the same column and four rows above the current cell; that is *relative* to the current cell.

If we copy the formula in cell B5 to cell B6, we get =PPMT(B2, A6, B3, B4), all our cell references moved down one

	A	B
		=PPMT(B2,A6,B3,B4)
1	Per period	1%
2	Periods	6
3	Principal	$1,000
4		
5	1	-$163
6	2	$0
7	3	

row. That's fine for A6 for period 2, but B1, B2 and B3 should have stayed where they were. For example, the function in B5 uses the principal in cell B3, the value in the same column and two rows above the current cell. But the function in cell B6 is using cell B4, which is empty, as the principal of the loan. That is not what we wanted.

We need to copy the formula in B5 to other cells without changing the references to B1, B2, and B3. We do this by changing these relative references to *absolute references*, by placing a dollar sign (which does not imply money) in front of rows or columns we don't want to change.

We edit our formula in cell B5 to be =PPMT(B$1, A5, B$2, B$3). This tells Excel not to change the row numbers for B1, B2 and B3, when we copy the formula to other cells, but it's okay to change A5 to A6, A7, A8 or whatever, because it is still a relative reference.

In the example below, cell B5 was edited to create absolute references, and then copies to cells B6:B10. The formulas in B5:B10 are displayed in cells C5:C10. Note the $ before references to rows 1, 2, and 3.

By the way, when editing formulas, you can use the function 4 (F4) key to quickly toggle cell references from relative to absolute and back again.

	A	B	C
1	Per period	1%	
2	Periods	6	
3	Principal	$1,000	
4			
5	1	-$163	=PPMT(B$1,A5,B$2,B$3)
6	2	-$164	=PPMT(B$1,A6,B$2,B$3)
7	3	-$166	=PPMT(B$1,A7,B$2,B$3)
8	4	-$167	=PPMT(B$1,A8,B$2,B$3)
9	5	-$169	=PPMT(B$1,A9,B$2,B$3)
10	6	-$171	=PPMT(B$1,A10,B$2,B$3)
11			

Present Value

Inflation causes a given amount of money to be worth less, to buy less, in the future than what it is worth in the present. Present value is what we would pay today for a future sum of money, or stream of cash flow. Important considerations are the expected interest rate, how long we have to wait for the return on our investment, and our risk appetite.

Scenario

For an initial cost of $100,000, you could renovate the first floor of your office building and lease it as retail space. You could get a 10 year lease for it with monthly payments of $2500 paid at the start of each month.

You assume a 6% interest rate over the next 10 years. The proposed renovations will have a 10 year life expectancy, so there would be no remaining value in the project at the end of the 10 year period.

What is the present value of this cash flow? Is the present value greater than the required initial investment of $100,000? Should you approve the project?

We will use the Present Value, PV[1] function in Excel to solve this annuity problem. What's an "annuity problem" you ask? An annuity is a stream of equal periodic income or expenditures at a constant interest rate, like a car loan, house payment or even rental income. The Excel PV function works for annuities.

	A	B
1	Interest rate (per year)	6.00%
2	Interest rate (per month)	0.50%
3	Years	10
4	Months	120
5	Rent received start of month	$2,500
6	Value at end of lease	$0
7	Present value	-$226,310
8		

Process

The formula in cell B2 is =B1/12 and the formula in B4 is =B3*12. The syntax for the Present Value function in Excel is =PV(interest rate per period, number of periods, payment amount, future value, type). If the payment is due at the start of the period, type = 1. If the payment is due at the end of the period, type = 0, or may be omitted as 0 is the default type value. The formula in cell B7 is =PV(B2, B4, B5, B6, 1).

The present value of $226,310 is displayed in cell B7 as a negative because that is what we would have to pay to get this cash flow in an annuity with this interest rate. Money coming in, like rental income, is displayed as a positive value; money going out, like an initial investment or periodic payments, is displayed as a negative value. This is true throughout the land of Excel.

Results

The present value of the proposed project is worth $226,310, well over the initial investment of $100,000. You should approve the project to renovate the ground floor of your office building and lease it as retail space.

Scenario

You need to purchase a truck. The project budget will cover a $5,000 down payment plus $500 monthly payment (due at the end of the month) for 60 months. The annual interest rate will be 9% on a 5 year loan.

What is the maximum you can pay for the truck and stay within budget?

Again, we use the Present Value function in Excel to solve this annuity problem.

Process

The formula in cell B2 is =B1/12. The formula in cell B4 is =B3*12. The formula in cell B7 is =PV(B2, B4, B5, B6, 0). Note that the payment in cell B5 is entered as a negative amount.

	A	B	C
1	Interest rate (per year)	9.00%	
2	Interest rate (per month)	0.75%	
3	Years	5	
4	Months	60	
5	Payment due at end of month	-$500	
6	Future value	$0	
7	Present value	$24,087	
8	Down payent	$5,000	
9	Maximum vehicle cost	$29,087	
10			

After we have determined the present value of the loan, we add the down payment, $5000 in cell B8. The formula in cell B9 is =B7+B8, and that is the maximum we can spend.

Results

We can afford to spend about $29,000 on the truck and stay within our project budget.

Discussion

Don't mistake the future value in the Present Value formula for the value of the truck in 5 years. The truck will probably have some value, but we cannot use that to justify going over budget. We could submit a change request to increase the project budget, arguing that the resale value of the truck should be taken into consideration, but that's a topic for another book.

Practice

A project will generate an income of $16,000 a month for 8 years. The interest rate is 12%.

- What is the present value if the income is received at the end of the month?

- What is the present value if the income is received at the beginning of the month instead?

- What is the total income for each option?

- What is the difference between the two present values?

Answers

Use the Present Value function in Excel to solve the first two problems. Then subtract one present value from the other to get the difference. Remember that present values for positive incomes will appear negative. For the total income, multiply the monthly income times the number of months. Both options should generate the same total income, but the differences in their present values will make one more attractive than the other.

The input data are the same. The only difference is in the Present Value functions. The formula in cell B8 is =PV(B3, B5, B6, B7, **0**) and the formula in cell C8 is =PV(C3, C5, C6, C7, **1**). That last variable indicates when the income is received; 1 for the start of each period and 0 or omitted for the end of each period.

	A	B	C
1	Income received monthly	Start	End
2	Interest rate (per year)	12.00%	12.00%
3	Interest rate (per month)	1.00%	1.00%
4	Years	8	8
5	Months	96	96
6	Income received per month	$16,000	$16,000
7	Future value	$0	$0
8	Present value	-$994,288	-$984,443
9	Difference		$9,844
10	Total income	$1,536,000	$1,536,000

While both options generate the same total income of $1,536,000, the present value is greater, by $9,844, when we receive the income at the start of each month compared to receiving it at the end. Why? If I said I would give you $100 next month, would you rather have it at the start of the month or the end of the month? Not only does getting it early allow you to use it during the month, but it also eliminates the risk of not getting it at all. Suppose I got run over by a bus? A bird in the hand is worth two under the bus.

When using present value to decide between different projects or different options, we always choose the one with the larger present value. If the negative sign makes this confusing, let's say we always choose the option with the larger absolute value as that is what we would have to pay to purchase this income stream. By the way, you can use the Absolute function in Excel (=ABS) to convert negative values to absolute positive values. Adding a minus sign to the answer is another common practice.

Footnote

(1) In most project management literature, "PV" usually means Planned Value, not Present Value. Be careful not to get the two confused. Planned value is the value of the work to be completed by some future date. It is the authorized budget to do the authorized work. So, planned value is a future value, not a present value. Also, planned value does not consider the future value of money. We'll use planned value when we get into project performance measurements later on.

Future Value

To calculate the present value, we used the future cash flow and the interest rate. Now we will reverse the process and use present value and interest rate to calculate the future value.

Scenario

You are negotiating with a contractor who is requesting $5,000 at the start of each month for 3 years. At the end of the 3 years, you expect the deliverable to be worth $250,000. The annual interest rate is 12%. If you deposited $5,000 a month in a savings account, at 12% compounded monthly for 3 years, would you have more or less than $250,000? If less, the contractor is offering you a fair deal; if more, you need to negotiate a more favorable offer, or find another contractor.

Process

The Future Value function in Excel has the syntax =FV(interest rate per period, number of periods, payment amount, present value, and type)[1]. The present value is optional in the function and is assumed to be zero if it is omitted. As with the PV function, type = 0 is used for the end of the period and type = 1 is used for the beginning of the period. Type is also optional with a default value of zero.

The formula in cell B2 is =B1/12 and the formula in cell B4 is =B3*12. The monthly payment of $5,000 is entered in cell B5 as a negative value because it represents money going out. There is no present value, so cell B6 is zero.

	A	B
1	Interest rate per year	12%
2	Interest rate per month	1%
3	Years	3
4	Number of payments	36
5	Monthly payments	-$5,000
6	Present value	$0
7	Future value	$217,538
8		

The formula in cell B7 is =FV(B2, B4, B5, B6, 1). The type is 1 because the $5,000 payment is required at the start of each month. We can use the value "1" in our function, rather than a cell reference, because the timing of payment is not likely to change during the decision making process.

We said that the present value argument is optional, with a default of zero. Since there is no present value in this situation, the formula in cell B7 could have been =FV(B2, B4, B5, , 1). Note that two commas are used to keep the "type" in its proper

	A	B
1	Interest rate per year	12%
2	Interest rate per month	1%
3	Years	3
4	Number of payments	36
5	Monthly payments	-$5,000
6	Present value	$0
7	Future value	$217,538
8		

place. If we did not use the double commas, silly old Excel would think the "1" was the present value, and that the type was zero. Two errors, just for the lack of a comma!

Results

Investing $5,000 a month for 36 months, at 12%, would yield $217,538. Paying the same amount to the contractor will result in a deliverable worth $250,000. All else being equal, we should accept the offer.

Practice

A project deliverable will cost $500 a month for 18 months, payable on the first of each month. Assuming an annual interest rate of 6%, what is the future value of the deliverable? Payments of $500 for 18 months total $9000. Why is your future value different? (Discussed on the next page.)

Answer

The formula in cell B2 is =B1/12. The formula in cell B6 is =FV(B2, B3, B4, B5, 1). The type is 1 because payment is made at the start of the month. The future value of the deliverable is $9,439.86, or about $9,440. Let's not imply a level of accuracy we cannot defend.

	A	B
1	Interest rate per year	6.00%
2	Interest rate per month	0.50%
3	Number of payments	18
4	Monthly payments	-$500.00
5	Present value	$0
6	Future value	$9,439.86
7		

Discussion

If we put $500 in a shoe box every month, at the end of 18 months we would have $9,000, so why is our future value $9,440? It's called the time value of money. In financial management, the time value of money assumes a dollar in the present is worth more than a dollar in the future because of variables such as inflation and interest rates.

In our example, the $9,000 today is worth $9,440 in 18 months.

In project management, we agree with inflation and interest, but also include risk. Having $9,000 in the bank today involves no risk, while an offer of $9,440 in the future includes the risk of non-delivery.

Footnote

(1) If the Future Value function syntax looks familiar, that's because the Future Value function has basically the same syntax as the Present Value function. The only difference is that we include present value in the Future Value function to get the future value, and we included the future value in the Present Value function to get the present value.

Filler

SOLA Optical made plastic lenses from polymer and monomer and generated a lot of scrap byproduct. As materials manager, one of my duties was to award an annual contract for the disposition of the scrap. Polymer was easy because it can be recycled and I always had several companies bidding on it. Monomer was the problem. About 75% of our scrap was monomer and nobody wanted it. We had to pay someone to dump it in landfill where it will remain forever. One year, I decided to do something about it.

That year, my request for quotation, RFQ, stated that I would only accept bids for both monomer and polymer. Most recyclers complained, but one company in China requested some monomer samples. A few weeks later, they had invented a way to recycle monomer. They got the contract and all of our polymer and monomer; and we changed the future of monomer recycling throughout the world.

Rate of Return

In the last two topics we calculated present value based on the future value and the interest rate, and we calculated the future value based on the present value and the interest rate. The obvious next step, the third side of the triangle, is to calculate the interest rate, the rate of return, based on the present value and the future value.

Scenario

Your project will cost $100,000 and be worth $200,000 in five years, with no other expenses or incomes during the 5 years. The sponsoring organization has a required rate of return, RRR or "hurdle rate," of 12% APR. Does your project clear the hurdle?

Process

We can use the Excel RRI function to determine the rate of return on your project.[1]

The syntax is =RRI(number of periods, present value, future value). The formula in cell B4 is =RRI(B1, B2, B3).

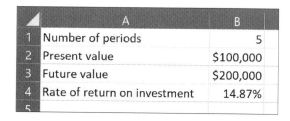

	A	B
1	Number of periods	5
2	Present value	$100,000
3	Future value	$200,000
4	Rate of return on investment	14.87%
5		

Results

Our APR of 14.87% is greater than the required rate of return, the RRR, of 12% so our project clears the hurdle.

Scenario

In the above example, interest was compounded annually. Suppose organizational policy assumes that interest is compounded monthly?

What is our revised annual percentage rate given monthly compounding?

Process

The formula in cell B2 is =B1*12 and the formula in cell B6 is =B5*12. The formula in cell B5 is =RRI(B2, B3, B4). Cell B5 tells us the monthly interest rate is 1.16% and cell B6 multiplies that by 12 to give an annual percentage rate of 13.94%.

	A	B
1	Number of years	5
2	Number of months	60
3	Present value	$100,000
4	Future value	$200,000
5	Rate of return per month	1.16%
6	Rate of return per year	13.94%

Results

We are still within the required rate of return, even if it assumes monthly compounding. Note that with monthly compounding we can achieve our objective of $200,000 with a lower APR than with annual compounding of interest, 13.94% compared to 14.87%.

Annual percentage rate, APR, is the standard way of expressing and comparing interest rates, even if the actual compounding is some other unit of time, such as quarters, months, or even days. Be sure you understand what is customary in your organization. If in doubt, ask your project management office, your PMO.

Footnote

(1) What does RRI stand for? I have been unable to find the official meaning of this function name. My guess is Rate of Return on Investment. The RRI function was introduced in Excel 2013.

Filler:

The most expensive project in history is the U.S. interstate highway system, which cost $459 billion and took 35 years to build. It was proposed by President Eisenhower as a way to quickly move troops if the U.S. was attacked. He got the idea from the Autobahn in Germany, which allowed the Nazi's to quickly reposition their forces during World War II.

Interest Rate

Okay, given present value and future value, we can find the interest rate, but suppose we don't know the future value. If we know the payment amount, we can still find the interest rate, even without a future value.

Scenario

To finance your project, you will borrow $1,000,000 for 5 years, with payments of $25,000 due at the start of each month. What interest rate will you be paying?

Process

We will use the Rate function in Excel for this. The syntax is =RATE (number of periods, payment amount, present value, future value, type, and guess). Future value, type, and guess are optional. If future value or type are omitted, the default value of zero is used. If guess is omitted, 10% is used. If RATE returns #NUM! try a different guess.

Cell B1 contains the number of years for our loan. Cell B2 converts it to months with =B1*12. Cell B3 is our monthly payment of $25,000. It is negative because we are paying money out.

	A	B
1	Number of years	5
2	Number of months	60
3	Payment	-$25,000
4	Present value	$1,000,000
5	Payment due (type)	1
6	Rate of return per month	1.497%
7	Rate of return per year	17.96%

Cell B4 is the present value of the loan, $1,000,000, which is positive because money is coming in. Cell B5 indicates that the payments are due at the start of the month. We would enter zero in cell B5 if the payments were due at the end of the month. Loans have no future value, so there is no need for a future value cell. Cell B6 is =RATE(B2, B3, B4, 0, 1). Because the default for future value is zero, we could have entered =RATE(B2, B3, B4, , 1) in cell B6. Cell B7 converts the monthly rate of 1.497 to an annual rate of 17.96 with =B6*12.

Results

Our million dollar, five year loan will cost us 17.96 percent interest. Ouch!

Practice

Eighteen percent interest is a lot. You decide to shop around. Another lender offers you $1,000,000 for four years, with payments $27,500 due at the end of the month. What would be the annual percentage rate, APR, on this loan?

Answer

	A	B
1	Number of years	4
2	Number of months	48
3	Payment	-$27,500
4	Present value	$1,000,000
5	Payment due (type)	0
6	Rate of return per month	1.195%
7	Rate of return per year	14.35%
8		

Monthly payments increased from $25,000 to $27,500, but the number of payments decreased from 60 to 48.

Additionally, payments are not due until the end of the month, which gives you free use of the payment amount for a month, effectively lowering the rate.

The formula in cell B6 is =RATE(B2, B3, B4), which could also be entered as =RATE(B2, B3, B4, 0, B5). Either way, we get 1.195% per month, or 14.35% per year. This is much better than the 17.96% APR we got from the first lender, so we decide to go with the second lender.

Filler

Supposedly the bank robber Willie Sutton was asked by a reporter why he robbed banks. His reply: "Because that's where the money is."

Sutton denied making the statement in his 1976 book *Where the Money Was:* "Why did I rob banks? Because I enjoyed it. I loved it. I was more alive when I was inside a bank, robbing it, than at any other time in my life. I enjoyed everything about it so much that one or two weeks later I'd be out looking for the next job. The money was the chips, that's all."

Internal Rate of Return

Continuing our discussion of interest rates, suppose our project includes incomes or expenses during the project? The RRI function does not allow that, but the Internal Rate of Return (IRR) function does, as long as the incomes and expenses are at regular intervals.

Scenario

A proposed project will cost $50,000 and will generate revenue of $12,000 a year for five years, giving a total revenue of $60,000. The alternative is to keep the $50,000 in the bank where it will earn 5% interest per year. We will assume the project has no greater risk than keeping the money in the bank. (See filler on the prior page.)

What is the effective interest rate for a $50,000 investment that returns $12,000 a year for five years? Should we approve the project or keep our fifty grand in the bank? We will use the Internal Rate of Return (IRR) function and compare that to the 5% interest we would get from the bank.

Process

In Excel we enter the labels as shown in cells A1:A7 and the values in cells B1:B6. Note that the investment is negative and the incomes are positive. The syntax for the IRR function is super simple, =IRR(values). The only requirement is that the values be listed in

	A	B
1	Initial investment	(50,000)
2	Income for the first year	12,000
3	Income for the second year	12,000
4	Income for the third year	12,000
5	Income for the fourth year	12,000
6	Income for the fifth year	12,000
7	Internal rate of return	6.40%

chronological sequence and that they contain at least one positive value and one negative value. The formula in cell B7 is =IRR(B1:B6). Excel calculates and displays the internal rate of return of 6.40%.

Results

We decide to approve the project because we will earn 6.40% on our investment compared to the 5% we are currently getting from the bank.

Scenario

An alternative to the project described above has been suggested. It would require the same initial investment of $50,000 and the risk is considered the same. Income would only be $6,000 in the first four years, but income in year five would be $40,000. A total income of $64,000 is better than $60,000, but having to wait until year five for most of it may be a problem.

We use the IRR function to calculate the internal rate of return for the alternative project. Based on their respective internal rates of return, should we switch to the alternative project or stay with the original project?

Process

The formula in cell B8 is =Sum(B2:B7), cell D8 is =Sum(D2:D7), cell B9 is =IRR(B2:B7), and cell D9 is =IRR(D2:D7).

	A	B	C	D
1		Original		Alternative
2	Initial investment	(50,000)		(50,000)
3	Income for the first year	12,000		6,000
4	Income for the second year	12,000		6,000
5	Income for the third year	12,000		6,000
6	Income for the fourth year	12,000		6,000
7	Income for the fifth year	12,000		40,000
8	Net income	10,000		14,000
9	Internal rate of return	6.40%		6.36%
10				

Results

Although the alternative project has a higher net income ($14,000 compared to $10,000) it is slightly less attractive because the internal rate of return is only 6.36% compared to the 6.40% offered by the original project. Our decision is not only based on how much money we will get, but when we will get it. We should stick with the original project.

Discussion

We have assumed that the risks for the two projects are the same, but that may not be a valid assumption. With the alternative project, we are putting a lot of faith in our assumption that we will reach year five with no problems. Suppose there is a fire, an earthquake, a tornado, or a law suit (the unknown unknowns) that effectively kills the project before year five. In any year prior to year five, we will have earned more income, and lost less in total, with the original project than with the alternative. So, even if the alternative project had had a slightly higher internal rate or return, we might have opted for the original project just to be on the safe side. Quantitative analysis is fine, but let's not totally ignore qualitative judgement in our decision-making process.

The internal rates of return, 6.36% and 6.40% are annual percentage rates, APRs, because we used years as our unit of time. If we had used months, the output would have been the interest rate per month, which we would then multiply by twelve to convert to annual percentage rates.

Scenario

A short and simple project will cost $9,750 in January and will return $1,000 in February, $2,000 in March, $3,000 in April, and $4,000 in May. What is the monthly internal rate of return? What is the annual rate of return? If the organizational required rate of return is 12% a year, does the project qualify?

Process

The expense of $9,750 is entered in cell B1 as a negative value and the positive monthly revenues are entered in cells B2:B5. The formula in cell B6 is =IRR(B1:B5). Because we used monthly periods, the value in cell B6 is the interest rate per month. To get the annual interest rate, we multiply the monthly rate by 12, and that is done in cell B7.

	A	B
1	Jan	$ (9,750)
2	Feb	$ 1,000
3	Mar	$ 2,000
4	Apr	$ 3,000
5	May	$ 4,000
6	IRR (Mo)	0.85%
7	IRR (Yr)	10.18%

Results

The project annual internal rate of return of 10.18 is below the organizational required annual rate of 12%. There may be other valid reasons to continue with the project, such as legal compliance or strategic initiatives, but based on return on investment (ROI) alone, we will have to pass on this one. Sorry.

Discussion

Multiplying the monthly rate by 12 to get the annual rate, or dividing the annual rate by 12 to get the monthly rate, is done all the time, but it is not exactly accurate. It ignores the compounding effect of interest. For example, if the annual rate is 12% and we divide by 12, we get a monthly rate of 1%. Compounding 1% monthly interest rate for 12 months is 1.01 to the twelfth power (1.01^{12}) which is actually 1.1268, or 12.68% APR. The error gets exponentially larger as the interest rate increases. With 20% a year, converting to 1.6667 (20/12) and compounding monthly we get an APR of 21.94%.

Again, using 12 to convert between months and years is very common. If we are comparing projects of roughly the same size and APR, we should not have a problem as long as we document our methodology. If in doubt, ask the project management office.

We will learn some techniques later on to deal with compound monthly interest. Also, consider that all years have 12 months, but not all months have 30 days, nor do all years have 365 days. We will discover ways to deal with all these timely issues very shortly.

Practice

Your project will cost $100,000 in year 1, but will return $20,000 in year 2, $30,000 in year 3, $40,000 in year 4, and $50,000 in year 5. The organizational required return rate, the hurdle rate, is 12%.

What is your project internal rate of return? Does your project meet the required return rate? We will assume all five years have the same number of days.

Process

The initial cost of $100,000 is entered in cell B1 as a negative. Incomes are entered in cells B2:B5 as positive values. Be sure to enter them in the correct sequence.

The labels in cells A1:A6 are helpful to us, but they mean nothing to Excel. The formula in cell B6 is =IRR(B1:B5). Since we are dealing in years, there is no need to convert the output of 12.83% to anything else.

	A	B
1	Year 1	$(100,000)
2	Year 2	$ 20,000
3	Year 3	$ 30,000
4	Year 4	$ 40,000
5	Year 5	$ 50,000
6	IRR	12.83%
7		

Results

The annual internal rate of return for your project is 12.83%, just slightly above the required 12%. Better slightly above than slightly below!

Filler

While installing an enterprise resource planning (ERP) system, I learned that a senior buyer in the purchasing department was very hostile to the new system, posting comments like "SAP sucks."

Rather than discipline her, I assigned her to the project team to write the user training documents for the purchasing department. When we went live, she conducted the purchasing training.

She had been the local expert on the legacy system, and she would lose her unofficial leadership position with the new system. By making her the department expert on the new system, she retained her status within the purchasing department and actively supported her coworkers as they struggled to learn the new ERP system.

Net Present Value

We used the Present Value (=PV) function to select the best option for periodic payments or incomes of equal value, but what if the amounts are not equal? In that case, we can use the Net Present Value (=NPV) function instead.

The periods must still be evenly spaced, like weeks, months or years, but the amounts can be anything; positive, negative, or even zero. That's the good news. The bad news is that NPV does not allow payments or incomes at the start of a period, only at the end of a period. That will complicate initial project investments, or down payments, that happen on day one.

Also, names can be deceiving. The Net Present Value function in Excel does not actually give us the true net present value, it only gives us the present value of the cash flow. We may still need to include initial investments to get the true net present value. That's not difficult; I'll show you how it's done. We just have to remember to do it.

Scenario

You are offered a project that will require a $36,000 investment at the start of year one. Revenue from the project will be nothing in year one, $5,000 at the end of year two, $10,000 at the end of year three, $15,000 at the end of year four, $20,000 at the end of year five, and $25,000 at the end of year six.

If you do not invest in the project, you could safely earn six percent annual interest on your $36,000 at the bank over the next six years. That's called the "opportunity cost." Investing in the project means we forfeit the opportunity of investing at the bank.

Should you risk your hard-earned cash on the project, or put it in the bank? That depends on the present value of the cash flow compared to the required investment of $36,000. It also depends on your risk appetite, the amount of risk you are willing to accept in exchange for the potential reward.

Process

We are working with annual periods, so there is no need to convert the annual interest rate in cell B1 to months. The initial investment in cell B9 is negative and the income amounts in cells B2:B7 are positive. Remember, in Excel, money going out is negative and money coming in is positive.

The syntax for the Net Present Value function is =NPV(interest rate for one period, range with expected incomes (or payments) at the end of equally spaced periods).

The formula in cell B8 is =NPV(B1,B2:B7), which is the net present value without consideration for our initial investment.

The investment of $36,000 is shown in cell B9. Note that cell B9 is not allowed in the NPV function since it takes place at the start of a period. The formula in cell B10 is simply =B8 + B9.

	A	B
1	Interest rate	6%
2	Income, end of year 1	$0
3	Income, end of year 2	$5,000
4	Income, end of year 3	$10,000
5	Income, end of year 4	$15,000
6	Income, end of year 5	$20,000
7	Income, end of year 6	$25,000
8	Present Value	$57,297
9	Initial investment	-$36,000
10	NPV adjusted for investment	$21,297

Results

The true net present value of $21,297 is displayed in cell B10, not in cell B8, which contains the misleadingly named Net Present Value, NPV function.

Filler:

The cost to start a winery range from about $560,000 for a 2,000 case per year winery to about $2,340,000 for a 20,000 case per year winery. The cost to purchase an established winery, with inventory and reputation, can be a lot more. Location also contributes to the cost and the value.

Discussion

We determined that the present value of the cash flow at the start of period one is $57,297, and we can "buy" it for only $36,000, giving us a net present value of $21,297. But all projects have risks. Does the potential reward of $21,297 justify the project risk? Should we play it safe and put our 36 grand in the bank? Unfortunately, there is no Excel function for risk appetite decisions. It's totally your call. More on risk management later.

Practice

Your project has two options. Option 1 will cost $64,000 at the start of month 1 and will return $5,000 at the end of month 1, $10,000 at the end of month 2, $20,000 at the end if month 3, and $40,000 at the end of month 4, for a total of $75,000. The annual interest rate is 6%, or 0.50% per month. What is the net present value of Option 1?

Option 2 will cost $66,000 at the start of month 1 and will return $40,000 at the end of month 1, $20,000 at the end of month 2, $10,000 at the end if month 3, and $5,000 at the end of month 4, for a total of $75,000. The annual interest rate is 6%, or 0.50% per month. What is the net present value of Option 2?

Assuming both options are equally <u>low risk</u>, which option should you choose? Why?

Assuming both options are equally <u>high risk</u>, which option should you choose? Why?

Discussion

Interesting choice. Both options offer the same payback of $75,000. Option 1 costs less, but Option 2 has a better cash flow. Let's do the quantitative analysis first, then we'll consider risk in a qualitative analysis.

Answers

The net present value of Option 1 is $9,789 (73,789 – 64,000) and the net present value of Option 2 is $8,355 (74,355 – 66,000). Option 1 has the higher net present value, it is more valuable, so that is our quantitative choice.

	A	B	C
		Option 1	Option 2
1			
2	Cost	-$64,000	-$66,000
3	Annual interest rate	6.00%	6.00%
4	Monthly interest rate	0.50%	0.50%
5	Month 1	$5,000	$40,000
6	Month 2	$10,000	$20,000
7	Month 3	$20,000	$10,000
8	Month 4	$40,000	$5,000
9	Present value (NPV)	$73,789	$74,355
10	Net Present Value	$9,789	$8,355
11			

The formula in cell B9 is =NPV(B4,B5:B8) and the formula in cell B10 is simply =B2 + B9. Similar formulas are in C9 and C10 for Option 2.

Discussion

Risk is difficult to quantify, but it is real and it should be considered.

Making good project decisions is much more than simply calculating the correct answer to a math problem

Note that both options offer the same payback of $75,000 but halfway through the project, at the end of months 2, you have only recovered $15,000 (20%) with Option 1, whereas with Option 2, you have recovered $60,000 (80%). If both options are equally high risk, it might be prudent to go with Option 2. Be sure to document the rationale for your decision.

Net Present Value with Irregular Periods

The Net Present Value function allowed us to use unequal amounts, but they still had to be at the end of evenly spaced periods. Unfortunately, events in the real world do not always occur at nice evenly spaced time periods. For that we can use the XNPV[1] function, an extension of NPV.

Unlike the NPV function, XNPV does not require payments and incomes to be at the end of a period; they can be any amount we want, positive or negative, and any time we want, or whenever Mother Nature dictates. Also, XNPV gives us the true net present value because it uses dates to calculate interest rather than fractions of a year; there is no need to convert annual percentage rates to weeks or months and back again.

Scenario

The project management office, PMO, says that organizational policy specifies using NPV to evaluate projects with unequal income and expense amounts, adjusting the NPV output with the project cost to get the true present value. You would prefer to use XNPV as it allows more flexibility and you offer to demonstrate the differences in the functions using a simple project that has recently been approved.

The project begins with an initial investment of $10,000 on January 1, 2020. The project returns $5000 on December 31 of 2020, 2021, 2022, and 2023. The interest rate is 12%.

Process

The APR of 12% in cells B2 and C2 is the same regardless of function used, and does not need to be converted for NPV because we are working with annual periods. The initial cost of $10,000 is in cells B3 and C3, at the start of year 2020.

	A	B	C
1		NPV	XNPV
2	Annual interest rate	12.00%	12.00%
3	1/1/2020	-$10,000.00	-$10,000.00
4	12/31/2020	$5,000.00	$5,000.00
5	12/31/2021	$5,000.00	$5,000.00
6	12/31/2022	$5,000.00	$5,000.00
7	12/31/2023	$5,000.00	$5,000.00
8	NPV Output	$15,186.75	
9	Net Present Value	$5,186.75	$5,186.75

Revenue of $5000 is received at the end of years 2020 thru 2023.

The formula in cell B8, =NPV(B2,B4:B7), displays $15,186.75, which is the "present value" of the income stream but it does not consider the initial expense of $10,000 because that takes place at the start of a period rather than at the end. The true present value of $5,186.75 is displayed in cell B9 using the formula =B3 + B8.

The syntax for the eXtended Net Present Value function is =XNPV(interest rate, range of values, range of dates), and the formula in cell C9 is =XNPV(C2, C3:C7, A3:A7). The net present values are the same regardless of function used; but the XNPV function allows the flexibility to change dates as needed.

For example, if the initial investment was not made until January 2nd, because January 1st is a holiday, XNPV would note the difference, while the NPV would not. XNPV is clearly the more agile function.

	A	B	C
1		NPV	XNPV
2	Annual interest rate	12.00%	12.00%
3	1/2/2020	-$10,000.00	-$10,000.00
4	12/31/2020	$5,000.00	$5,000.00
5	12/31/2021	$5,000.00	$5,000.00
6	12/31/2022	$5,000.00	$5,000.00
7	12/31/2023	$5,000.00	$5,000.00
8	NPV Output	$15,186.75	
9	Net Present Value	$5,186.75	$5,191.46

Scenario

The PMO has approved the use of XNPV for your project, which consists of five phases and will last a little over a year. Each phase is a different length, and each will require an investment early in the phase and will generate revenue later in the phase.

You have listed the dates, the expenses (negative) and the incomes (positive) in the table. The assumed annual interest rate is 9%. What is the net present value of your project?

Process

All of the data in the table are values except for the net present value formula in cell C13, which is =XNPV(C12, C2:C11, B2:B11)

	A	B	C
1	Phase	Date	Amount
2	One	3-Jan	-$30,000
3	One	9-Feb	$15,000
4	Two	8-Apr	-$60,000
5	Two	9-Jun	$40,000
6	Three	24-Jul	-$70,000
7	Three	24-Oct	$65,000
8	Four	29-Oct	-$60,000
9	Four	26-Nov	$75,000
10	Five	28-Jan	-$30,000
11	Five	26-Feb	$95,000
12	Interest rate		9.00%
13	Net present value		$30,854

Discussion

Look at that! Different amounts at different intervals, and not one at the start or the end of a period. We could never have done that with NPV.

Results

The net present value for your project is $30,854. We could use this amount to compare it to other projects, selecting the project with the highest net present value; all else, such as risk, resource availability, and strategic importance, being equal.

Practice

You are considering two competing projects. Each project includes income and expenses at different dates. The interest rate is 5% regardless of the project selected. Assuming all else is equal, which project should you choose; which project has the greater present value?

	A	B	C	D	E
1	Project A			Project B	
2	Date	Amount		Date	Amount
3	3-Mar	-$10,000		5-Mar	-$12,000
4	20-Apr	$3,000		24-Apr	$2,000
5	9-Jun	-$10,000		21-Jul	-$9,000
6	11-Jul	-$9,000		12-Sep	$5,000
7	1-Sep	$5,000		25-Sep	$20,000
8	15-Sep	$25,000			

Answers

The interest rate of 5% is entered in cells B9 and E9. The formula in cell B10 is =XNPV(B9, B3:B8, A3:A8) and the formula in E10 is = XNPV(E9, E3:E7, D3:D7). Project B offers a greater present value ($5,487 > $3,499) and should be selected over Project A.

	A	B	C	D	E
1	Project A			Project B	
2	Date	Amount		Date	Amount
3	3-Mar	-$10,000		5-Mar	-$12,000
4	20-Apr	$3,000		24-Apr	$2,000
5	9-Jun	-$10,000		21-Jul	-$9,000
6	11-Jul	-$9,000		12-Sep	$5,000
7	1-Sep	$5,000		25-Sep	$20,000
8	15-Sep	$25,000			
9	Interest	5%			5%
10	PV	$3,499			$5,487

Footnote

(1) XNPV was introduced with Excel 2013. If you are using an older version of Excel, you will not have it.

Internal Rate of Return with Irregular Periods

We enjoyed learning about the Net Present Value function in Excel, only to be disappointed that it could not accommodate irregular periods. (Sometimes the real world does not have regular periods.) We were then overjoyed to discover that the eXtended Net Present Value function worked with dates instead of fixed periods. Unlike my high school prom, we can have any date we want!

You should not be surprised, therefore, that the Internal Rate of Return (IRR) function in Excel, which has the same fixed period requirements as the Net Present Value function, was enhanced with the eXtended Internal Rate of Return function that works just fine with any dates.[1]

Scenario

Let's return to a project we introduced in "NPV with Irregular Periods." Your project consists of 5 phases and will last a little over a year. Each phase is a different length, and each will require a cash expense early in the phase and will generate revenue later in the phase. What is the internal rate of return for the project?

Process

You have listed the dates, the expenses (negative) and the incomes (positive) in the table. You have entered the data in an Excel spreadsheet as values (no formulas) except for the internal rate of return. Cell C12 is =XIRR(C2:C11, B2:B11)

The syntax for the XIRR function is =XIRR(value range, date range, guess).

Guess? What do you mean guess?

	A	B	C	D
1	Phase	Date	Amount	
2	One	3-Jan	-$30,000	
3	One	9-Feb	$15,000	
4	Two	8-Apr	-$60,000	
5	Two	9-Jun	$40,000	
6	Three	24-Jul	-$70,000	
7	Three	24-Oct	$65,000	
8	Four	29-Oct	-$60,000	
9	Four	26-Nov	$75,000	
10	Five	28-Jan	-$30,000	
11	Five	26-Feb	$95,000	
12	Internal rate of return:		60.17%	
13				

In most cases you do not need to provide a guess for your XIRR function. If omitted, as I did in cell C12, Excel assumes guess to be 10%. Excel uses an iterative technique for calculating XIRR, like it did with XNPV. Starting with guess, Excel cycles through the calculation until the result is accurate within 0.000001 percent or until it has completed 100 iterations, (then it returns an error message.) If you get an error, just change the guess and try again.

Results

The project has an internal rate of return of just over 60%. Not too shabby!

Discussion

Because XIRR uses dates rather than weeks, months, fortnights or whatever, the output will always be the annual interest rate[2].

Practice

You are considering two competing projects. Both have similar risk and strategic value and both involve multiple expenses and revenues. What is the internal rate of return for each, and which do you recommend?

Process

The data has been entered into an Excel spreadsheet. Enter the XIRR function in cells B12 and C12. You use the XIRR function, rather than the IRR function because the periods between the incomes and expenses are not evenly spaced. Also, XIRR avoids having to convert the output to an annual percentage rate as it does that for you automatically.

	A	B	C
1	Date	Project A	Project B
2	10-Jan	-$25,000	-$20,000
3	30-Jan	-$15,000	-$10,000
4	25-Feb	$5,000	$5,000
5	15-Mar	$5,000	$5,000
6	15-Apr	$5,000	$5,000
7	5-May	-$10,000	-$20,000
8	20-May	$5,000	$5,000
9	15-Jun	$5,000	$5,000
10	15-Jul	$10,000	$10,000
11	20-Aug	$20,000	$20,000
12			

Results

Project A has an internal rate of return of 30.65% and Project B has an internal rate of return of 37.52%. All else being equal, Project B would be preferred (37.52% > 30.65%).

	A	B	C
1	Date	Plan A	Plan B
2	10-Jan	-$25,000	-$20,000
3	30-Jan	-$15,000	-$10,000
4	25-Feb	$5,000	$5,000
5	15-Mar	$5,000	$5,000
6	15-Apr	$5,000	$5,000
7	5-May	-$10,000	-$20,000
8	20-May	$5,000	$5,000
9	15-Jun	$5,000	$5,000
10	15-Jul	$10,000	$10,000
11	20-Aug	$20,000	$20,000
12	XIRR	30.65%	37.52%

Discussion

Both IRR and XIRR assume that positive cash flows from a project are "reinvested" at the project internal rate of return. Is this realistic? Probably not. We spent a considerable amount of time planning our project, with an eye toward maximizing output and minimizing input. Unless some new information becomes available, our project is properly financed to reach its' objective. Throwing more money at the project will not increase the value of the deliverable; it will just increase the cost of the project.

The sponsoring organization, on the other hand, probably has a number of alternative investment opportunities. A better assumption would be that positive cash flows from our project are invested by the organization at their current cost of capital rate, which is probably less than our project internal rate of return (otherwise the project would probably not have been approved in the first place).

We will address this issue by using a Modified Internal Rate of Return, MIRR, as our next topic.

Footnotes

(1) XIRR was introduced in Excel 2013.

(2) When we colonize Mars, which has a 687 day year, will project managers need to specify Earth annual percentage rate (EARP?) or Mars annual percentage rate (MAPR?), or will Excel come up with a nifty Earth/Mars APR conversion function?

Modified Internal Rate of Return

Unlike the Internal Rate of Return function, IRR, the Modified Internal Rate of Return function, MIRR, assumes positive cash flows are not reinvested at the project internal rate of return, but at the organizations' cost of capital. That's the up side. The down side is that the cash flows must be at fixed intervals. Win some, lose some.

Discussion

MIRR offers another benefit over IRR. Sometimes, with a complex sequence of incomes and expenses, the IRR function in Excel can return multiple "correct" solutions. You may get one IRR and the PMO may get another for the very same project! MIRR avoids that touchy situation.

As we discussed, our sponsoring organization will probably have multiple investment opportunities; like cannabis futures. If nothing else, they can put the money in a savings account at the credit union. Also, as we mentioned earlier, a project is not really well suited to invest funds over and above what was included in the original project plan.[1]

Scenario

Your project will require an initial investment of $5,000 and another investment of $6,000 at the end of year 3. It will return $3,000 at the end of year 1, $2,000 at the end of year 2, $5,000 at the end of year 4 and $4,000 at the end of year 5. What is the internal rate of return of your project? First, we will use the IRR function, then compare it to MIRR output.

	A	B
1	Year	Cashflow
2	0	-$5,000
3	1	$3,000
4	2	$2,000
5	3	-$6,000
6	4	$5,000
7	5	$4,000
8	IRR	15.18%

Process

We will consider the initial investment at the start of year one to be the same as the end of year zero. This keeps all cash flows at the end of the years, and we are only fudging by one day. The formula in cell B8 is =IRR(B2:B7).

Based on the IRR output, it looks like the project will return at the rate of 15.18% over the course of the six years. The problem, as we discussed, is that the IRR assumes the revenue received at the end of years 1, 2, 4 and 5 will all be reinvested at the rate of 15.18%, which is highly unlikely.

Scenario

Checking with our project management office, PMO, we learn that the organization uses 10% APR as their standard cost of capital and 12% APR as their standard reinvestment rate. (Our project was probably approved because it offered a rate of return greater than 12%.) The initial $5,000 and the $6,000 at the end of year 3 will be borrowed at 10% APR. The revenues of $3,000, $2,000, $5,000 and $4,000 will be reinvested by the organization at 12% APR. Given that, what is the modified rate of return, MIRR, for our project?

Process

The organizational finance rate of 10% is shown in cell B8 and the reinvestment rate is shown in cell B9. The syntax for the Modified Internal Rate of Return is =MIRR(list of values, finance rate, reinvestment rate). The interest rates must be for the same time periods used between the values. The formula in cell B10 is =MIRR(B2:B7, B8, B9).

	A	B
1	Year	Cashflow
2	0	-5000
3	1	3000
4	2	2000
5	3	-6000
6	4	5000
7	5	4000
8	Finance rate	10.00%
9	Reinvestment	12.00%
10	MIRR	12.50%
11		

Results

Our modified internal rate of return, MIRR, is 12.50%, compared to the internal rate of return of 15.18% we got using the flawed IRR function. This is more realistic and a better indicator of what will probably happen in the real world.

Practice

Your project will require an initial investment of $10,000, followed by annual revenues of $1,000, $2,000, $3,000, $4,000, and $10,000. What is the internal rate of return using the IRR function?

Your organization uses a finance rate of 8% and a reinvestment rate of 10%. What is the modified internal rate of return for your project using the MIRR function?

Process

Expense and revenue data are entered in cells B2:B7, with your initial expense shown as negative. The formula in cell B8 is =IRR(B2:B7).

The organizations' standard finance rate of 8% is entered in cell B9 and their standard reinvestment rate of 10% is entered in cell B10. Both of these are given, not calculated by us. The modified internal rate of return of 17.25 is shown in cell B11 using the formula =MIRR(B2:B7,B9,B10).

	A	B
1	Year	Cashflow
2	0	-$10,000
3	1	$1,000
4	2	$2,000
5	3	$3,000
6	4	$4,000
7	5	$10,000
8	IRR	19.69%
9	Finance rate	8.00%
10	Reinvestment	10.00%
11	MIRR	17.25%
12		

Results

Both the IRR of 19.69 and the MIRR of 17.25 are above the reinvestment rate, so all else being equal, the project will probably be approved.

If we were asked what the actual return on investment for the project would be, we should use the more conservative and realistic MIRR rather than the IRR.

Earlier we discussed ballpark estimates. "Around 17%" (MIRR) would be a much safer estimate than "A little under 20%" (IRR).

Discussion

The MIRR function is really superior to the IRR function as it overcomes the multiple results problem and it takes a more realistic approach as to where and how revenue generated from the project will be reinvested.

MIRR does, however, require two additional assumptions, the cost of capital (finance rate) and the reinvestment rate. If these values are available, we should use MIRR. If we have to estimate them, with no help from the organization, we may be better off sticking with IRR.

Remember that our objective is to compare multiple project opportunities, so whichever function we decide to use, we must use the same function on all projects under consideration.

Comparing the IRR of one project to the MIRR (or XIRR) of another project would be like comparing apples to kumquats.

Footnote

(1) Some projects are designed to be self-funding. The project is expected to generate revenue prior to project completion, and that revenue will be reinvested back into the project.

If your project is intended to be self-funded, then the Internal Rate of Return, IRR, function is appropriate. If, on the other hand, your project was not designed to be self-funded, then the Modified Internal Rate of Return, MIRR, function is your best bet.

Filler:

The International Space Station, ISS, was built in 1994 on Earth and assembled in space. Fourteen countries worked together to complete the project. With a total cost of $150 billion, it is considered one of the most expensive projects in human history.

After 26 years of service, the ISS is reaching the end of its useful life and is scheduled to be crashed into the ocean in 2020. Sad.

Number of Periods

We have discussed solution to problems for present value, future value, and interest rates. It's about time we talked about time.

Scenario

You need to borrow $50,000 and you can afford to make monthly payments of $1,500 on the first of each month. The current annual interest rate is 12%. How many months will it take to repay the loan?

Process

We will use the Number of Periods function in Excel. The syntax is =NPER(interest rate per period, payment amount per period, present value, future value, and type). The result is the number of periods as defined by the interest rate. Future value and type are both optional with defaults of zero. As we have seen before, a type 0 means that payment is due at the end of the period, and a type 1 means payment is due at the start of the period.

Cell B1 is our APR of 12% and cell B2 translates that to a monthly rate with =B1/12. Cell B3 is our monthly payment of $1,500, entered as a negative since it represents outbound money. Cell B4 is the amount of the loan, $50,000, which is inbound money. Cell B5, future value, is zero because loans have no future value.

	A	B
1	Rate per year	12%
2	Rate per month	1%
3	Payment	-$1,500
4	PV	$50,000
5	FV	0
6	TYPE	1
7	NPER	40.25261
8		

Cell B6 is type. We entered 1 here because payments will be due at the start of each month. Cell B7 is =NPER(B2, B3, B4, B5, B6).

Results

Because we used a monthly interest rate, our output of 40.25 is in months. This would be rounded to an integer. If our maximum monthly payment is $1,500, we would round the number of periods up to reduce the monthly payment. For example, rounding the number of periods up to 42 months (3 ½ years) would give us a monthly payment of $1,449.29.

Scenario

Here's an interesting use of the NPER function that you probably won't find in a finance text, or a project management text either for that matter.

Your project will have an initial cost of $1,000,000 plus a monthly payroll of $5,000 payable at the end of each month until the project is completed. The project deliverable will have a value to the organization of $2,000,000. The organization expects all projects to return a minimum of 18% on their investment. You estimate the project will be completed in 3 years. Should the organization approve your project?

Process

We have entered the data in our spreadsheet. Cell B1 is the organizational required rate of return, RRR, of 18% per year. Cell B2 translates that to a monthly rate of 1.5% with =B1/12. Cell B3 is our monthly payroll expense of $5,000 and cell B4 is our initial investment of $1,000,000. Cell B5 is the future value of our project deliverable,

	A	B
1	Rate per year	18%
2	Rate per month	1.5%
3	Payment	-$5,000
4	PV	-$1,000,000
5	FV	2,000,000
6	TYPE	0
7	NPER	37.59
8	Years	3.1

$2,000,000. Cell B6, type, is zero because our project payroll will be paid at the end of each month. Cell B7 is = NPER(B2, B3, B4, B5, B6). The output of 37.59 months is converted to years in cell B8 with =B7/12.

Results

If you can complete the project in 3 years, in 36 months, your project will have a return on investment greater than 18%, but if it takes you longer than 37.59 months, your project ROI will be less than 18%.

Practice

Your project will cost $5,000,000 up front plus $7,500 a month (end of month). The future value is $10,000,000 and the organization requires a 24% ROI. How much time do you have to complete the project?

90

Answer

The organizational required rate of return of 24% is in cell B1 and cell B2 translates that to a monthly rate with =B1/12.

Cell B3 has your monthly expenses of $7,500 and cell B6 indicates they are payable at the end of each month.

Your initial investment of $5,000,000 is shown in cell B4 and the future value of your project deliverable, $10,000,000 is shown in cell B5.

Cell B7 is =NPER(B2, B3, B4, B5, B6), giving a value of 33.21 months, and cell B8 translates that to 2.77 years with =B7/12.

Discussion

If approved, you will have only 33 months to complete your project. Can it be done in two years and 9 months?

	A	B
1	Rate per year	24%
2	Rate per month	2.0%
3	Payment	-$7,500
4	PV	-$5,000,000
5	FV	$10,000,000
6	TYPE	0
7	NPER	33.2098
8	Years	2.77

How do we estimate how long it will take to complete something that, by definition, we have never done before?

That is the subject of our next chapter, "In Time." But first, we have a couple more topics to wrap up our discuss of project cost management.

Filler:

Work on the California High Speed Rail began in 2015 and is scheduled to be completed in 2029 (originally 2025). The high speed "bullet train" will eventually stretch between San Francisco and Los Angeles, with rails that can support travel up to 220 mph.

The project is over its original budget. The current budget at completion, BAC, is $77 billion. High and low estimates have also been planned "based on potential risks." The current pessimistic estimate is $98.5 billion.

What-If Analysis

"What if?" might be one of the first questions posed by our earliest ancestors. What if I ate that plant? What if I used that rock to protect myself from that animal? Today, computers, and specifically electronic spreadsheets like Excel, have given us the ability to quickly and economically perform a complex what-if analysis. What if I changed this? What if I changed that?

Discussion

Because values in Excel cells are often linked to each other, we can change one value and immediately see the results. For example, we can change the interest rate or the number of periods and immediately see the change in the payment amount. That's a working model.

Books have been written on spreadsheet modeling, so we are not going to get into too much detail here. The basic idea is that we clearly label our input and output.

What do I mean by clearly labeled input? Here's an example. Many of the Excel functions we have discussed include the variable "type" with 0 indication payment at the end of the period and 1 meaning payment at the start. If you are building a model, do not hide the type inside the function. The function should refer to a cell that contains the type and is so labeled. That way it is easy to see what the current type is, and easy to change the type if we want to see what happens when we do.

The next step is to enter the correct formulas and functions, with no errors. That might be easier said than done. "To err is human…" Now we could start changing things, but what if we forget where we started?

I recommend creating a baseline model that you do not change. Once it is working properly, make clones of it and perform your experiments on the clones.[1]

For a small model, we can place copies on the same spreadsheet. For a large model that fills a spreadsheet, we can make duplicate spreadsheets to play with, without altering the original.[2]

Process

About 40 pages ago when we were talking about payments, I asked you to keep a copy of your spreadsheet. It should look like this:

	A	B	C	D
1	Crawler excavator payment analysis	Adams Equipment	Earthmovers Incorporated	
2	Interest rate (per year)	14.4%	18.0%	
3	Interest rate (per month)	1.2%	1.5%	
4	Years	2	3	
5	Months	24	36	
6	Loan amount	$60,000	$55,000	
7	Future value	$0	$0	
8	Due (0 = end of period, 1 = start)	0	1	
9	Monthly payment	-$2,892	-$1,959	
10	Total cost	-$69,411	-$70,524	
11				

For each of the practice problems below, make a copy of the original baseline model and make your changes on the copy. If you do not get the expected answers, check your formulas, referring back to the payment topic as needed. Remember to start with a fresh copy of your baseline for each practice problem; the activities below are not cumulative.

Practice

What if Earthmover lowered their annual interest rate from 18% to 16%, what would the total cost be? (Answer: $68,695)

What if the Adams offer was for 3 years rather than 2, what would the total cost be? (Answer: $74,244)

What if Earthmover allowed payments at the end of each month, what would the total cost be? (Answer: $71,582)

What if Adams dropped their price from $60,000 to $57,500, what would the total cost be? (Answer: $66,519)

What if Earthmover dropped their interest rate from 18% to 16% but raised their price from $55,000 to $57,500? What would the total cost be? (Answer: $71,817)

What if Adams lowered their interest rate from 14.4% to 12%, but demanded payment at the start of each month rather than at the end of the month? What would the total cost be? (Answer: $67,115)

What if Earthmover increased their interest rate from 18% to 20% and required payoff in 2 years rather than 3, but lowered their price from $55,000 to $52,500? What would the total cost be? (Answer: $63,077)

What if Adams lowered their interest rate from 14.4% to 10% but raised their price from $60,000 to $62,500 and required payment at the start of the month rather than at the end? What would the total cost be? (Answer: $68,645)

Both firms have made their final offer. Adams is offering a purchase price of $52,000 at 11.25% for 3 years with payments due at the start of each month. Earthmover is offering a purchase price of $53,000 at 10.75% for 2.5 years (30 months) with payments due at the end of each month. What is the total cost for each firm? (Answer: $60,937 and $60,676)

Footnotes

(1) I do the same for downloads. When I have a large data set that I need to analyze, I keep the original data as is and do all my work on copies of it.

(2) I have a very large model that contains 36 spreadsheets and over 160,000 formulas. When I want to do a what-if on it, I make a copy of the entire file and do my work there. If I like the change, the new file becomes the primary model and I save the old model for historical reference. If my what-if does not work as planned, I scrap the new file and revert back to my original version.

Cost Benefit Analysis

The purpose of this book is to understand the mathematical tools and techniques available to us to help make better decisions. Recognizing that our ultimate goal is better decisions, I am going to wrap up our discussion of project costs with a little philosophy.

We have looked at different ways to determine the costs and benefits of projects. If the total benefits are greater than the total costs, accounting for risk, the project will probably be approved; but this was always from the perspective of the sponsoring organization, not society at large.

A true cost-benefit analysis looks at a proposed project from the combined perspective of all stakeholders. Because for-profit organizations focus on adding value for the owners, the stockholders, they may fail to consider the impact of a project on less obvious stakeholders such as the general public or local governments.

Scenario

Your company has purchased a mostly vacant, bankrupt shopping mall in a low-income residential district. Your project is to convert the mall into a factory. Before issuing a permit, the city planning department has requested a full cost-benefit analysis of the proposed project.

Discussion

It is obvious that we have a bias; our company purchased the mall with the intent of converting it into a factory so we could make stuff, including a bunch of money. We should expect our cost-benefit analysis to undergo considerable scrutiny by the planning department.

Process

Step one is to identify all of the project stakeholders. The usual stakeholders are obvious: stockholders, employees, suppliers, and customers. Other stakeholders would include the current businesses in the mall and their owners, employees, customers, and suppliers.

Other stakeholders include the nearby residents, some of whom may be future employees, their property values as local traffic changes from cars to trucks, and traffic patterns shift as our factory workers all arrive and depart at the same time each day. The city might experience additional costs for road maintenance, utility infrastructure expansion, or emergency response equipment and personnel.

Don't forget to include potential environmental issues like noise, air pollution or ground water contamination. Also include positive or negative company goodwill in your list.

Accidentally or intentionally excluding a stakeholder who may be negatively impacted by the project is probably our biggest concern for avoiding a charge of bias, so we need to list every possible stakeholder in our analysis. If in doubt about a stakeholder or group of stakeholders, include them in the list. There is no such thing as a stakeholder register that is too long.

Step two is to identify all of the possible costs and benefits to each group of stakeholders over a relevant time period. Qualitative costs and benefits should be expressed in quantitative units, dollars and dates, whenever possible. Qualitative considerations that are difficult to quantified can be dealt with in a factor weighted table. More on that later.

Step three is to convert these future costs and benefits into present values. Use the Present Value, Net Present Value, and other tools discussed in this chapter.

Step four is to conduct a sensitivity analysis that includes the likelihood of uncertain costs and benefits occurring. See the Expected Monetary Value and the Risk Analysis topics for more about sensitivity analysis.

Step five is to present our findings, in both summary and detail form, first to the project sponsor and senior management, and then, with their approval, to the city planning department. If the total value of the benefits exceeds the total value of the costs; the net benefits (benefits less costs) are positive; the benefit/cost ratio is greater than one, then the project should be approved.

<u>Discussion</u>

Suppose the factory will make solar panels. How would you address the issue of global climate change? Is Earth a stakeholder? Are future generations stakeholders of current projects? Are species other than humans stakeholders in our projects?

In the Flood Control Act of 1936, the Federal Government required that the total benefits "to whomsoever they may accrue" should be in excess of the total estimated costs for projects undertaken by the U.S. Army Corps of Engineers. The Corps of Engineers developed methods for estimating benefits and costs. Since the 1950's economists have improved and standardized methods for cost-benefit analysis in public decision-making.

Today, a proper cost benefit analysis should include both tangible and intangible costs and benefits. It should include both short-term and long-term costs and benefits. It should include both one-time or fixed costs and benefits, and ongoing, or variable costs and benefits.

The results of the analysis should be objective. Any equally-skilled business analyst would have reached the same conclusion, even if the conclusion was not what senior management wanted to see.

Remember that our objective is to improve the quality of our decisions, not to influence the decision with biased information.

Don't confuse a business analysis with a sales pitch. If the project is approved, there will be ample opportunity for vision statements and other promotional material. For now, our objective is to present a non-biased assessment leading to the correct decision, whatever it may be.

<u>Filler:</u>

The total cost of the Apollo program to put a man on the moon was $25.4 billion. That equates to about $145,000 billion today. Benefits are a bit harder to calculate. In addition to everything we learned about space travel, money spent on the space program enabled development of the microprocessor; which lead to personal computers, smart phones, the Internet, and video doorbells. Not a bad investment, if you ask me.

In Time

My favorite things in life don't cost any money. It's really clear that
the most precious resource we all have is time.

Steve Jobs

The future ain't what it used to be.

Yogi Berra

Better three hours too soon than a minute too late.

William Shakespeare

The only reason for time is so that everything doesn't happen at once.

Albert Einstein

There cannot be a crisis next week. My schedule is already full.

Henry A. Kissinger

The key is not to prioritize what's on your schedule, but to schedule
your priorities.

Stephen Covey

If I could save time in a bottle, the first thing that I'd like to do,
is to save every day 'til eternity passes away, just to spend them with you

Jim Croce

Does anybody really know what time it is? Does anybody really care?

Chicago

He had a pickup truck, and the devil's eyes.
He stared at me and I felt a change.
Time meant nothing, never would again.

The Time Warp
The Rocky Horror Picture Show

Never put off 'till tomorrow what you can do today.

Philip Stanhope, 4th Earl of Chesterfield

Never put off 'till tomorrow what you can do the day after tomorrow.

Mark Twain

Basic Scheduling

How long will it take to complete the project? Is the project progressing at a suitable pace to finish on time? When should each activity begin and end? When should purchased items be ordered? Project management is time management.

Scenario

Your project consists of three activities. Activity A will cost $20,000 and will take 2 weeks to complete. Activity B will cost $30,000 and will take 3 weeks to complete. Activity C will cost $50,000 and will take 5 weeks to complete. What is the total cost of your project and how long will it take to complete?

Process

This looks simple, right? The total cost is $20,000 + $30,000 + $50,000 = $100,000. But what is the total time? Is it 2 weeks + 3 weeks + 5 weeks = 10 weeks? Maybe, but maybe not.

Results

If activities A, B and C must be done sequentially, then 10 weeks is the correct answer, but that's a big "if." Can we finish the project earlier?

Suppose activities A and B could be done concurrently, followed by activity C. The total time would be the longer of activity A or B, plus the time for activity C; 3 weeks + 5 weeks = 8 weeks.

Now suppose activities B and C could be done concurrently after activity A is completed. The total time would then be time for activity A plus the longer of activity B or C; 2 weeks + 5 weeks = 7 weeks.

Lastly, suppose all three activities could be done at the same time. In that case, the total project time is equal to the longest activity time of 5 weeks.

Determining project cost is easy compared to determining project time.

Discussion

The obvious key here is if our project activities can be performed concurrently or must they be performed sequentially, and if so, in what sequence?

There are three types of constraints that we must consider; natural, resources and cost.

A natural constraint is usually beyond our control. For example, we cannot install asphalt in the new parking lot until the land is graded. We cannot train the staff until after we hire them and develop the training material. We could, however, develop the training material while we are hiring the staff.

Resource constraints may require sequential activities even if there is no natural constraint to concurrent scheduling. For example, we only have one bulldozer, so we cannot grade the front parking lot and the rear parking lot at the same time. If we had two bulldozers, we could grade both parking lots concurrently.

The third constraint is money. We could grade both parking lots at the same time if we rented a second bulldozer, but the time we would save does not justify the additional expense, or the additional cost is just not in the budget.

A required sequence in project management is usually referred to as a precedence. If activity B has a precedence of activity A, then B cannot begin until A is complete. If there is no precedence specified for activity B then it can be done whenever we want, including concurrently with activity A.[1]

Practice

Going back to our original scenario, your project consists of three activities. Activity A will take 2 weeks to complete and has no precedence. Activity B will take 3 weeks to complete and has a precedence of activity A. Activity C will take 5 weeks to complete and also has a precedence of activity A. How long will it take to complete?

Answer

Since both activity B and activity C have a precedence of activity A, and B is not a precedence of C, we can perform activities B and C concurrently as soon as activity A is done. Our total project time is therefore the time for activity A plus the longer of activity B or C. In this case, our total project time is 2 weeks + 5 weeks = 7 weeks.

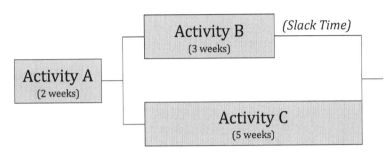

Discussion

For simplicity, we will say that our project will begin on the first day of week 1. Activity A will take place during weeks 1 and 2. Activity C, the longer of B and C, should begin on the first day of week 3, and should conclude at the end of week 7.

Let's think about activity B for a moment. It will take 3 weeks to complete and will be performed concurrently with activity C. Activity B cannot start until activity A is finished, so the earliest activity B can start is the first day of week 3 and the earliest it can finish is the last day of week 5.

Our total project time is 7 weeks, so activity B must be completed by week 7 if our project is to finish on time. For activity B to finish on week 7, it would have to start by week 5.

Activity B can start any time between weeks 3 and 5. This flexibility is called slack time or float.[2] Activity B has slack time. Because activities A and C must start and finish on specific weeks, they have no slack time.

Activities with no slack time are on the critical path. Activities A and C make up the critical path. Activity B is not on the critical path. The length of the critical path is what determines the total time for our project.

<u>Footnote</u>

(1) This activity precedence relationship is known as finish-to-start. Activity A must finish before activity B can start. It is the most common precedence relationship, but not the only one.

Other relationships include start-to-start (activity B cannot start until activity A has started), finish-to-finish (activity B cannot finish until activity A has finished), and start-to-finish (activity A cannot finish until activity B has started).

The start-to-finish relationship is rarely used. Here's an example: the night security guard (A) cannot leave until the day guard (B) arrives.

We will assume a finish-to-start relationship for all of the project examples in this book.

(2) Both "slack" and "float" are used in project management literature. They mean exactly the same thing. The activity has been allocated more time between the early start and the late finish than it needs to complete the assigned work. This additional time is slack or float.

<u>Filler</u>

My first job was at a foreign car parts company is Santa Ana, California. I was a junior in high school and would ride my bicycle there after school. My assignment was to post receipts and sales on inventory cards. Every day the manager would phone orders into Los Angeles, about an hour away, and every afternoon, one of our drivers would pick up the orders.

One day the owner told me he wanted to start buying from a company in New York. That would be a two week lead time, rather than two hours. He asked me if I had any ideas. I said I would think about it. After a few days, I came up with the idea of setting ideal inventory levels for each item we stocked. On a two-week rotating schedule, we would count the items on hand and order enough to get us up to the ideal level.

Years later I learned this is called a periodic replenishment system.

Critical Path Method

As we just saw, the critical path determines the shortest possible time for a project. Although project management software can determine the critical path for us, a manual graphical method has been around forever and should be understood by every project manager. It is known as the critical path method, or CPM.

Scenario

We have a very simple project consisting of four activities: A, B, C, and D. Activities B and C cannot begin until activity A is finished, and activity D cannot begin until both activities B and C have finished.

Activities A and B will each take 5 days to complete; while activities C and D will each take 8 days to complete.

When should each activity start and finish, and when will the project finish? We will draw a network diagram to better understand the project.

Process

There are several methods of illustrating a project network. We will use a very common one called "activity on node."

Early Start	Activity Name	Early Finish
Late Start	Activity Duration	Late Finish

Each activity node (rectangle) will include a short name for the activity, the expected duration of the activity (we'll use days) the early start, early finish, late start, and the late finish for the activity. We'll use the above format.

Arrows connecting the nodes will indicate the precedence relationships between each of the activities.

The first step is to draw the network with activity names and durations, but without start and finish data. Adding the arrows indicates that the project begins with activity A and it ends with activity D.

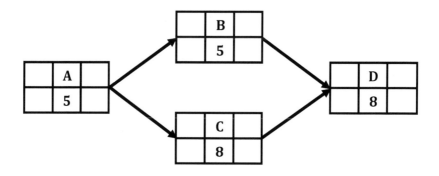

Next, we will calculate the early starts and early finishes. The early start for activity A is day zero.[1] Activity A has a duration of 5 days, so the early finish for activity A is day 5 (0 + 5 = 5). This means the earliest we can begin activities B and C is day 5, so we enter 5 as the early start for those activities. Activity B takes 5 days, so it has an early finish of 10 (5 + 5 = 10). Activity C will take 8 days, so it has an early finish of 13 (5 + 8 = 13).

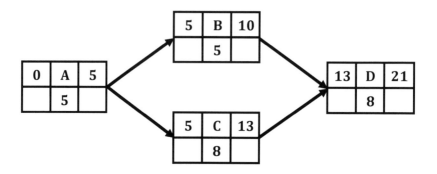

Activity D cannot begin until <u>both</u> B and C have finished, so it cannot start until day 13 (we take the largest of 10 and 13). Activity D takes 8 days, so the early finish for activity D, and for the project, is day 21 (13 + 8 = 21).

This process of calculating the early starts and the early finishes, for each activity from the first to the last, is known as the "forward pass." We moved from start to finish, we added durations to early starts to get early finishes, and when we had a choice of early finishes, we used the larger value as the start of the dependent activity, such as we did with activity D.

As you probably guessed, in the backward pass, we will move from finish to start. If the earliest the project will finish is day 21, than we will use that as our goal and set the late finish for activity D to 21.

In the backward pass, we subtract the duration from the late finishe to get the late start. For activity D, we subtract 8 from the late finish of 21 and get 13 as the late start. The late start for activity B is 8 (13 – 5 = 8) and the late start for activity C is 5   (13 – 8 = 5).

When we get to activity A, we have a choice of late starts; activity B is 8 and activity C is 5. Which should we use? The rule in the backward pass is that we use the smaller value, so we use the late start of 5 from activity C as the late finish for activity A.

Finally we subtract the duration of activity A from its late finish to get the late start of 0 (5 – 5 = 0).

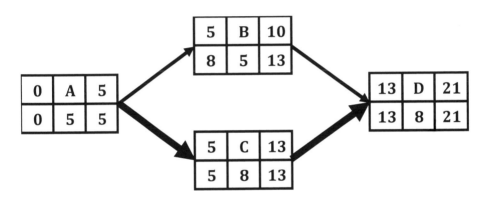

Results

We have constructed the critical path network diagram. It's a useful tool to help us understand the relationships and dependencies between the activities, and to explain them to others.

In the process, we determined that the project should finish on day 21, we determined the early start and early finish for each activity.

Repetitive summarize: In the forward pass, we <u>add</u> durations to early starts to get early finishes, and we use the <u>largest</u> early finish when given a choice. In the backward pass, we <u>subtract</u> durations from late finishes to get late starts, and we use the <u>smallest</u> early finish when given a choice.

Discussion

For any activity, if the early start equals the late start and the early finish equals the late finish, the activity has no slack time.

If the early start does not equal the late start and the early finish does not equal the late finish, the activity has slack time.

Early Start	Activity Name	Early Finish
Late Start	Activity Duration	Late Finish

The difference between the early start and the late start will be the same as the difference between the early finish and the late finish, and that amount is the slack time for the activity.

If your differences are not the same, go back and check your work.

Remember our definition of the critical path? The critical path is the series of activities that have no slack time. Our simple rule: activities without slack time are on the critical path, activities with slack time are not on the critical path. All projects have a critical path, and some have more than one critical path.

In our example, activities A, B, and D are the critical path; activity B is not.

Practice

Your project consists of six activities with durations, in weeks, and predecessors, as shown in the table below.

Draw the network diagram.

When will the project finish?

Which activities have slack time?

What is the critical path?

Activity	Duration	Predecessor
A	3	(none)
B	5	A
C	4	A
D	7	B
E	9	C
F	2	D & E

Answer

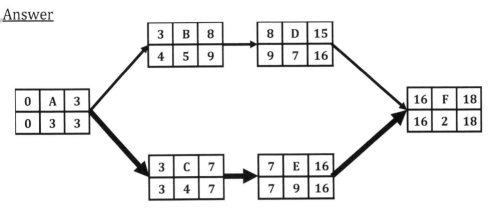

Your project should finish in week 18. Activities B and D have slack time, so the critical path is ACEF.

Actually, activities B and D share one week of slack time. If activity B starts in week 3 and finishes in week 8, activity D has a week of slack, but if activity B uses the slack and does not finish until week 9, activity D must start in week 9. If this happened, the critical path becomes ACDEF. This is a good example of the critical path changing as the project proceeds. In addition to focusing on the critical path, the project manager must be aware of what's happening at non-critical path activities.

Practice

Your project consists of 8 activities, as described in the table. The durations are in months. Activity A can begin as soon as the project is approved. Other activities cannot begin until their predecessor activities have been completed. Draw the network diagram; complete with early start, early finish, late start, and late finish, for each activity. When will the project be finished? What is the critical path?

Hint: Start with a simple sketch of letters and lines only. After you see the general layout, you can produce a better looking diagram with all the data. Defining the critical path is the last step. Take your time, this one is challenging.

Activity	Duration	Predecessor
A	2	(none)
B	5	A
C	3	A
D	2	A
E	5	B & C
F	6	B, C, & D
G	5	C & D
H	2	E, F, & G

Answer

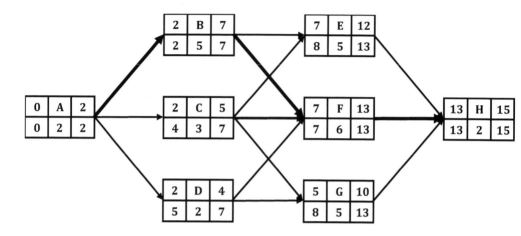

The project will finish in month 15. Activities C, D, E, and G all have slack time. The critical path is ABFH.

Discussion

If you are using project management software, it can produce a professional looking network diagram for you, complete with dates and output suitable for presentations. If not, you can make a nice looking network drawing using Excel, as I did with these examples.

Footnote

(1) Some people start with day 1 rather than day 0, and/or they assume that a subsequent activity will start on the following day (for example, if an early finish is day 5, the dependent activity would start on day 6. There is nothing wrong with this approach, as long as you are consistent. I prefer the method I used in these examples.

Filler:

Critical Path methodology was developed by E. I. du Pont de Nemours and Company (DuPont) between 1940 and 1943 and contributed to the success of the Manhattan Project.

Activity Duration

We find the all-important project duration by summing the durations of the activities on the critical path; adding a few integers with little opportunity for error. The critical path method even gives us a built-in check for errors. If the difference between the early start and the late start for any activity does not match the difference between the early finish and the late finish for that activity, we made a mistake. But, what if our input is wrong? How confident are we of our activity durations?

<u>Discussion</u>

Activity durations are only estimates. We researched prior projects that included similar activities, we asked experts in the respective fields, and we asked the people we will hold responsible for conducting these activities.

Let's say we ask our experts for the most likely duration of an activity, and they come up with a value of 15 days. This is a point estimate. We could enter it in our project management software or spreadsheet and calculate start and finish times for subsequent activities and a finish date for the project. But, we are missing something very important. How confident were the experts about the point estimate of 15 days? We didn't give them the opportunity to tell us.

Three-Point Estimating

Rather than asking our experts for a single point estimate, we will ask them for a "most likely" plus an "optimistic" and a "pessimistic" estimate.

Does this sound familiar? I hope it does because we introduced three-point estimating when we estimated activity costs. Three-point duration estimating is exactly the same three-point cost estimating, except that we are working with time rather that money.

The pessimistic estimate includes everything that could go wrong with the activity. (We'll keep a copy of that go-wrong list for our risk register.) The optimistic estimate assumes everything will go right, and the most likely is the best guess considering everything we know at this time.

So which estimate do we use to schedule our activities? The answer is all of them. As with cost estimation, we have two ways to estimate activity durations, triangular distribution and a beta distribution.

Triangular distribution is a simple average of our three estimates:

$$Duration = (Optimistic + Most\ Likely + Pessimistic)/3$$

Triangular distribution assumes our three estimates are equally likely, but are they? Imagine a bell curve with optimistic and pessimistic tails and the most likely somewhere near the mean. We would expect most random samples to cluster around the mean.

Beta distribution places more emphasis on the most likely value than it does on the optimistic or pessimistic values.

Beta distribution is a weighted average of our three estimates:

$$Duration = \frac{Optimistic + 4(Most\ Likely) + Pessimistic}{6}$$

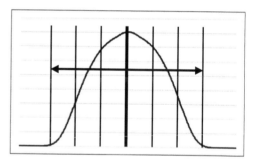

Why the 6? In statistics, the empirical rule states that 99.7% of random observations will fall within 6 standard deviations, 3 on either side of the mean, and 68% will fall within 1 standard deviation of the mean. Beta distribution says that, if we have not made a mistake, our outcomes will be within our optimistic – pessimistic range, and two thirds of them, 66.7%, will cluster around our most likely estimate.

Which method should we use, beta distribution or triangular distribution? If we have good optimistic and pessimistic estimates, we should use the beta distribution unless the sponsoring organization preference otherwise. Both methods, however, are superior to simply using point estimates, which should only be used when that's all we have.

Triangular distribution comes from the Critical Path Method (CPM) of project scheduling. It assumes deterministic times; the times are known. Beta distribution, on the other hand, comes from Program Evaluation and Review Technique (PERT) and assumes stochastic times; the times are estimated with some degree of uncertainty.

Practice

You have been assigned as the project manager on a simple, three-activity project. The organization has no prior experience with projects, and does not have a project management office. You gather estimates and ask your project sponsor if he has a preference for the method used to estimate activity duration. He replies he has no idea what you are talking about.

You offer to schedule the project using three different techniques and, with your result in hand, explain the difference to him.

Activity	Predecessor	Optimistic	Most Likely	Pessimistic
A	-	18	24	36
B	A	24	28	32
C	B	20	22	30

What is the estimated duration for each of the above activities using single point (using the most likely estimates only), triangular distribution, and beta distribution?

Filler:

Three-point estimating comes from Program (or Project) Evaluation and Review Techniques, PERT. The technique was developed to manage uncertainty and improve scheduling in large complex projects. It was developed for the U.S. Navy Special Projects Office in 1957 to support the Polaris nuclear submarine project. DuPont's critical path method was invented at roughly the same time as PERT.

Answers

Single point:

$$Duration\ A = 24$$
$$Duration\ B = 28$$
$$Duration\ C = 22$$

Triangular distribution:

$$Duration\ A = \frac{18 + 24 + 36}{3} = \frac{78}{3} = 26$$

$$Duration\ B = \frac{24 + 28 + 32}{3} = \frac{84}{3} = 28$$

$$Duration\ C = \frac{20 + 22 + 30}{3} = \frac{72}{3} = 24$$

Beta distribution:

$$Duration\ A = \frac{18 + 4(24) + 36}{6} = \frac{150}{6} = 25$$

$$Duration\ B = \frac{24 + 4(28) + 32}{6} = \frac{168}{6} = 28$$

$$Duration\ C = \frac{20 + 4(22) + 30}{6} = \frac{138}{6} = 23$$

Scenario

To show the impact on the project, prepare three project network diagrams, one for each of the activity duration estimates.

What is the expected project duration using each of the activity duration methods?

Answers

Single point (most likely):

0	A	24
0	24	24

24	B	52
24	28	52

52	C	74
52	22	74

Triangular distribution:

0	A	26
0	26	26

26	B	54
26	28	54

54	C	78
54	24	78

Beta distribution:

0	A	25
0	25	25

25	B	53
25	28	53

53	C	76
53	23	76

Note that the three methods produce three different results; 74 days, 78 days, and 76 days.

Also note that we used the same estimation method for all activities within each network model. This is probably best unless you are prepared to spend a lot of time explaining why you used one method for one activity and another for another.

Which will be the better estimating method? That all depends upon the quality of our three-point estimates.

If we have good estimates, beta distribution will tend to be the most accurate over the long run, but of course, any given activity could fall anywhere within the optimistic – pessimistic range.

If we get actual activity durations outside our optimistic – pessimistic range, or if single point or triangular distribution tend to produce better estimates, then there is something systematically wrong with the way we estimate activity durations, not in our choice of methods. We need to find out what it is, fix it, and document it in our lessons learned register.

Project Duration

A project duration of 75 days, plus or minus 5 days, is not the same as a project duration of 75 days, plus or minus 25 days.

We start with rich detail from experts regarding optimistic, most likely, and pessimistic durations for each activity. Then we identify which activities are on the critical path and which are not. Then we take all that beautiful detail and condense it into a single number. What a waste!

<u>Discussion</u>

In the prior topic we used triangular and beta distributions to estimate the duration of activities, but then we added the expected durations of the critical path to get a point estimate of the duration of the total project. A point estimate tells us nothing about our confidence in the number.

When we discussed Total Project Cost, we learned how we could use a calculator and beta distribution to improve the quality of our project cost estimates. We will now use beta distribution and Excel to improve the quality of our estimate for the project duration. We could use triangular distribution (O+M+P)/3 if that was preferred by the organization, but as we have said before, given a choice, beta is better.

Since project duration is the sum of the activities on the critical path, we will use project models that consist only of a single critical path. Our results would be the same if our project included non-critical path activities; in other words, activities with slack time.

<u>Scenario</u>

Our project consists of four sequential activities. The expected

Activity	Optimistic	Most Likely	Pessimistic	Expected
A	39	52	83	55
B	49	58	91	62
C	42	48	72	51
D	56	74	86	73

activity durations in the table are beta distributions. What are the optimistic, most likely and pessimistic durations for the project?

Process

The expected duration for the project is the sum of the expected duration for each activity on the critical path. That's the same rule we have been using for the project duration all along. For the optimistic duration, we square the difference between the optimistic and the expected duration for each activity and add the squares. Then we subtract the square root of the sum of the squares from the expected duration of the project. For the pessimistic duration, we square the difference between the pessimistic and the expected duration for each activity and add the squares. We then add the square root of the sum of the squares to the expected project duration.

Results

	A	B	C	D	E	F	G	H	I
1	Activity Data					Optimistic		Pessimistic	
2	Activity	Optimistic	Most Likely	Pessimistic	Expected	Range	Squared	Range	Squared
3	A	39	52	83	55	16	256	28	784
4	B	49	58	91	62	13	169	29	841
5	C	42	48	72	51	9	81	21	441
6	D	56	74	86	73	17	289	13	169
7	Totals:				241		795		2235
8	Square roots:						28.20		47.28
9									
10	Project Duration Estimates				Roundup				
11			Optimistic	212.80	213				
12			Expected	241.00	241				
13			Pessimistic	288.28	289				
14									

Cells E3:E6 are our beta distributions for each activity. For example, the formula in cell E3 is =(B3+(4*C3)+D3)/6. Cell E7 is the total of the activity durations on the critical path, =SUM(E3:E6). That is our point estimate for the duration of the project, 241 days, and that is, sadly, where most project management literature stops. But not us.

The formula in F3 is =E3 – B3. This is the difference between the optimistic estimate and the expected duration of activity A (55 – 39 = 16). Cell G3 is the square of F3 (16^2 = 256). We repeat this for all activities and show the sum of the optimistic squares in cell G7. Below that, in cell G8, we calculate the square root with the formula =SQRT(G7). Repeat the process for the pessimistic estimates. H3 is D3 – E3 (83 – 55 = 33).

The sum of the pessimistic squares is in I7 and its square root is in cell I8, =SQRT(I7). The expected project duration, 241 days, has not changed; cell D12 is the same as cell E7. The optimistic project duration in cell D11 is the expected duration minus the optimistic square root (241.0 – 28.20 = 212.80). The pessimistic project duration in cell D13 is the expected duration plus the pessimistic square root (241.0 + 47.28 = 288.28).

We should round these values to full days, so we don't imply a level of accuracy we cannot justify. Output is never more accurate than input. For project durations, I recommend always rounding up. Tuesday at 8:05 AM is still Tuesday; there is no logic in rounding it off to Monday.

The syntax for the Roundup function is =ROUNDUP(value, decimals) Cell E11 is =ROUNDUP(D11,0) and was copied into cells D12 and D13.

Discussion

Why not just add the optimistic or pessimistic estimates for each activity?

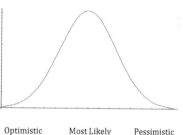

Optimistic   Most Likely   Pessimistic

Think of our estimates as a bell curve. In statistics, distances from the mean are measured in standard deviations, and the addition rule for independent variables[1] is that we must convert standard deviations to variances[2] by squaring them, adding the variances, then take the square root of the sum of the variances to convert back to the original unit of measure. The squaring process ensure that optimistic and pessimistic estimates far away from their expected value are weighted heavier than optimistic and pessimistic estimates close to their expected values.

Practice

Your project sponsor has requested an estimate of the project duration using both the most likely activity estimates and beta distribution expected durations. Start by calculating the beta distribution for the four activities.

Activity	Predecessor	Optimistic	Most Likely	Pessimistic
A	-	4	6	14
B	A	6	8	40
C	A	8	10	18
D	B & C	5	8	17

Answer

We calculated the expected durations using beta distribution. We entered =(C2 + D2*4 + E2)/6 in cell F2 and then copied it into F3:F5.

	A	B	C	D	E	F
1	Activity	Predecessor	Optimistic	Most Likely	Pessimistic	Expected
2	A	-	4	6	14	7
3	B	A	6	8	40	13
4	C	A	8	10	18	11
5	D	B & C	5	8	17	9

Scenario

Draw the network diagram using the most likely activity durations. What is the critical path?

Answer

We produced the network diagram using the most likely activity durations of 6, 8, 10, and 8. The project will finish on day 24 and the critical path is ACD.

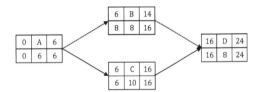

Scenario

Draw the network diagram using the beta distribution activity durations. What is the critical path?

Answer

We produced the network diagram using the beta distribution activity durations of 7, 13, 11 and 9. The project will finish on day 29 instead of day 24 and the critical path has changed from ACD to ABD.

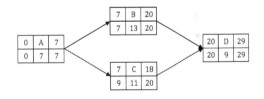

Practice

What is the optimistic, pessimistic, and most likely duration for this project? Use the beta distribution estimates with a critical path of ABD.

Answer

We did not include activity C because it is not on the critical path.

		Activity Data			Optimistic		Pessimistic	
Activity	Optimistic	Most Likely	Pessimistic	Expected	Range	Squared	Range	Squared
A	4	6	14	7	3	9	7	49
B	6	8	40	13	7	49	27	729
D	5	8	17	9	4	16	8	64
Totals:				29		74		842
Square roots:						8.60		29.02

Project Duration Estimates	Expected	Diff	Sum	Roundup	Rough
Optimistic	29.00	-8.60	20.40	21.00	20
Expected	29.00	0.00	29.00	29.00	30
Pessimistic	29.00	29.02	58.02	59.00	60

Rounding up, we expect the project to take 29 days, but it might finish as early as day 21, or as late as day 59 days; or we could provide rough estimates of 20 days, 30 days, and 60 days.

Reporting just the expected duration of 29 days to the decision makers would deny them the critical knowledge that the project could take twice as long to complete; or, with a little luck, it might finish in just two-thirds the expected time. The pessimistic estimate also opens the door to discussing the negative risks associated with activity B.

Footnote

(1) We consider our activity duration estimates to be independent variables. Assuming no bias in our estimating process, the accuracy of our duration estimate for one activity should have no effect on any other activity, hence our estimates are independent.

(2) I used the statistical terms standard deviation and variance; the variance being the square of the standard deviation and vice versa.

In project management the term variance frequently has a very different meaning. In most project management literature, the term variance is used to describe the difference between the baseline or the expected value and the actual value. It is a measurement of historical data and not a device for predicting the future.

It is perfectly acceptable to add real variances. For example, if two activities are on the critical path, and both took 10 days longer to complete than planned, we can say the project is 20 days behind schedule. But back in the planning process, we would not have assumed that both variances would be positive any more than we would not have assumed that both would be negative.

Date and Time Functions

Microsoft Excel includes many date and time functions. We will discuss a few of them here, and include them in our problem solutions later.

Discussion

Excel uses a sequential serial number that represent dates and time. The integer is the day and the decimal is the time. January 1, 1900 was day 1. Four digit years are required, as "25" could mean "1925" or "2025."[1] The maximum year is 9999.[2]

Process

Open Excel and enter the following functions. Use the function wizard (f_x) for help. Let Excel format the results, then format them as numbers to see the date/time serial number.

- Enter =TODAY to get the current date. The value will automatically change tomorrow, driven by the date in your computer.
- Enter =NOW to get the current date and time. The value will change every time you recalculate the spreadsheet.
- The syntax for the Date function is =DATE(year, month, day). Enter the Date function for April 12, 2020 in cell B5, then in cell B6, enter =B5+1. The result will be April 13, 2020. Remember that the date/time serial number uses integers for days, so "1" means 1 day.
- In most cases, you can simply enter the date directly, without using a function, as long as you use the format: month/day/year.
- You should never have to enter a date/time serial number.
- If prompted for a date when entering a function, try to point to a cell that contains the date you want.

Scenario

Working in days and using a bottom-up method, you have calculated that your project will take 220 days to complete. If the project begins on April 1, 2020, when will it finish? We will use the WorkDay[3] function

Answer

	A	B	C	D	E	F
1		Non-stop	Not weekends	Not holidays		Holidays
2	Start date	4/1/2020	4/1/2020	4/1/2020		11/26/2020
3	Days	220	220	220		12/25/2020
4	Finish	11/7/2020	2/3/2021	2/8/2021		1/1/2021

Cell B4 is =B2 + B3. Yes, Saturday, November 7, 2020 is exactly 220 days after April 1, 2020, but who wants to work 220 non-stop? Not me!

Cell C4 uses the Workday function. The syntax is =WORKDAY(start date, number of days, holidays)[4]. Cell C4 is =WORKDAY(C2, C3). Holidays are optional and were not used in cell C4. Working 5-day weeks, our 220-day project will finish on Wednesday, February 3, 2021.

But wait, what about holidays. Do we expect our team to work through Thanksgiving, Christmas, and New Year's day? Don't be a grinch!

We entered a list of holidays in cells F2:F4. Cell D4 is = WORKDAY(D2, D3, F2:F4). Giving our team Thanksgiving, Christmas, and New Year's day off, plus weekends, allows our project to finish on Monday, February 8, 2021.

Discussion

How did I know that November, 7, 2020 was a Saturday and that February 8, 2021 was a Monday? No functions needed, I simply formatted the cells as long dates.

	A	B	C	D	E	F
1		Non-stop	Not weekends	Not holidays		Holidays
2	Start date	Wednesday, April 1, 2020	Wednesday, April 1, 2020	Wednesday, April 1, 2020		Thursday, November 26, 2020
3	Days	220	220	220		Friday, December 25, 2020
4	Finish	Saturday, November 7, 2020	Wednesday, February 3, 2021	Monday, February 8, 2021		Friday, January 1, 2021

Scenario

Your project will start on August 31, 2020 and must end by January 29, 2021. Holidays are 11/26/2020, 12/25/2020, and 1/1/2021. How many workdays are available for your project? Use the NetWorkDays function.

120

Answer

	A	B	C	D	E
1		Dates		Holidays	
2	Start date	Monday, August 31, 2020		11/26/2020	
3	Finish date	Friday, January 29, 2021		12/25/2020	
4	Finish	107		1/1/2021	
5					

The syntax for the NetWorkDays function is =NETWORKDAYS(start date, end date, holidays)[5]. Holidays are optional, we entered ours in D2:D4.

The formula in cell B2 is =DATE(2020, 8, 31) and the formula in cell B3 is =DATE(2021, 1, 29). The formula in cell B4 is = NETWORKDAYS(B2, B3, D2:D4). Excluding holidays, there are 107 workdays available for our project between Monday, August 31, 2020 and Friday, January 29, 2021,

Footnotes

(1) Many software programs written in the mid-twentieth century only used the last two digits of the year. Near the end of the century, the world faced the year 2000 crisis, or "Y2K." Under the old system, a 5 year note taken out on 1/1/90 would be due on 1/1/95, but how could a 5 year note taken out on 1/1/98 be due on 1/1/03? Every computer on earth knew that 1903 happened 95 years before 1998.

(2) We assume that Microsoft and other software vendors will address the year 10,000 crisis, Y10K, in time to avoid a global catastrophe.

(3) This unusual form of capitalization is known as CamelCase. It is used to make words created from multiple words more readable.

(4) Use the WorkDay function when Saturday and Sunday are non-work days. Use the WorkDay.Intl function for other non-work day options.

(5) Similar to the WorkDay function, use the NetWorkDays function when Saturday and Sunday are non-work days. Use the NetWorkDays.Intl function for other non-work day options.

Gantt Chart

The Gantt chart has been around since 1920. Today, you will probably use something like Microsoft Project to create Gantt charts, but it can be done with Excel. If you are comfortable with Excel, try this exercise to expand your skillset. On the other hand, if you will always have access to project management software, or don't care for Excel, feel free to skip this topic.

<u>Process</u>

Enter the data at right into a blank spreadsheet. Merge and center the "Predecessor" heading into two columns. Cell E2 is =DATE(2020,6,1).

Task	Description	Predecessor		Start	Duration	Finish
0	Start			6/1/2020	1	
1	Develop project plan	0			3	
2	Hire staff	1			15	
3	Order hardware	1			2	
4	Write software	1			10	
5	Install hardware	3			10	
6	Test software	4			5	
7	Test system	5	6		4	
8	Document process	7			3	
9	Train staff	2	8		5	
10	Go live	9			1	

Select the entire table, including the column headings. In the Excel menu bar, select Formulas and then Name Manager. Click New to create a new name. Use "TaskTable" as the name. The Scope should be the Workbook. "Refers to" should be your table cell range, A1:G12. Click OK and then Close when you are done.

Cell G2 is =WORKDAY(E2, F2). We are not going to enter holidays because the only holiday in this timeframe, July 4th, falls on a Saturday in 2020. Copy the formula in cell G2 to cells G3:G12.

A task cannot start until all of the specified predecessors have finished. We will use the Vlookup function to determine when each task can start. The syntax for Vlookup is =VLOOKUP(lookup value, table array, column). The lookup value is the predecessors task number, the table array is "TaskTable" and the column index is 7 because the finish dates are in column 7 of our TaskTable. Cell E3 is =VLOOKUP(C3, TaskTable,7). But, some tasks may have more than one predecessor.

Task	Description	Predecessor		Start	Duration	Finish
0	Start			6/1/2020	1	6/2/2020
1	Develop project plan	0		6/2/2020	3	6/5/2020
2	Hire staff	1			15	1/20/1900
3	Order hardware	1			2	1/3/1900
4	Write software	1			10	1/13/1900
5	Install hardware	3			10	1/13/1900
6	Test software	4			5	1/6/1900
7	Test system	5	6		4	1/5/1900
8	Document process	7			3	1/4/1900
9	Train staff	2	8		5	1/6/1900
10	Go live	9			1	1/2/1900

Before we copy our formula in cell E3 into cells E4:E12, we will edit the formula to look for the later (larger) finish date for a predecessor in column C or in column D.

	A	B	C	D	E	F	G
1	Task	Description	Predecessor		Start	Duration	Finish
2	0	Start			6/1/2020	1	6/2/2020
3	1	Develop project plan	0		6/2/2020	3	6/5/2020
4	2	Hire staff	1		6/5/2020	15	6/26/2020
5	3	Order hardware	1		6/5/2020	2	6/9/2020
6	4	Write software	1		6/5/2020	10	6/19/2020
7	5	Install hardware	3		6/9/2020	10	6/23/2020
8	6	Test software	4		6/19/2020	5	6/26/2020
9	7	Test system	5	6	6/26/2020	4	7/2/2020
10	8	Document process	7		7/2/2020	3	7/7/2020
11	9	Train staff	2	8	7/7/2020	5	7/14/2020
12	10	Go live	9		7/14/2020	1	7/15/2020
13							

We do this with the Max function. The syntax for the Max function is =MAX(numbers...). The formula in cell E3 is MAX(Vlookup(C3,TaskTable,7), VLOOKUP(D3,TaskTable,7)), and we copy this formula into E4:E12. Note that task 7 cannot begin until both tasks 5 and 6 are complete. Task 5 will finish on 6/23/2020 but task 6 will not finish until 6/26/2020. The formula in cell E9 correctly identifies the later finish date of task 6 and uses it for the start date of task 7.

We are now ready to create our Gantt chart. Select the headers and data for Task thru Duration (not including Finish column) and insert a Stacked Bar Chart on your current worksheet. In the Chart Styles menu, select Layout 1; this includes a title at the top of the chart. Edit the title, changing it from "Duration" to "Schedule."

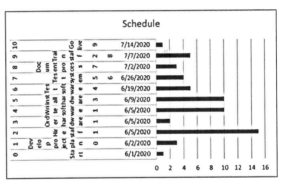

Right-clicks the chart and click Select Data. In Legend Entries (Series), remove Duration. Click on Add to add a new series with Series Name "Start." For the Series values, select the dates in your "Start" column, then click "OK." Click on Add again to add a new series, with Series Name "Duration" and select your Duration values for the Series values, then click "OK."

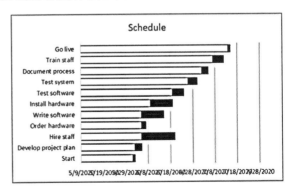

In the "Horizontal (Categories) Axis Labels" click "Edit" and select the task descriptions names (but not the column header or the task numbers) for the "Axis label range." Click "OK" and then "OK" again to close the Select Data Source dialog box.

In the chart, right-click on the y-axis (the task names), select Format Axis, and check the box "Categories in reverse order" to put the rows in Start date sequence. Click "Close" to close the dialog box, or click the close "X" in to top right corner. Right-click on the left portion of any stacked bar (Start dates) and choose Format Data Series. Choose Fill, then click No Fill to make those parts of the stacked bar invisible, and then click "Close."

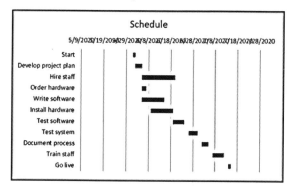

To start the chart at the project's start date, we need to format the horizontal axis. Right-click on the x-axis at the top of the chart, and select Format Axis. Change the "Minimum" to "6/1/2020." Select "Number" and select the short date format (3/14). Change the Major Units to 7 and then click "Close." Finally, delete any legends.

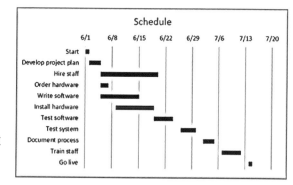

Scenario

We ran into some problems and the system test took 10 days rather than 4 days. Change this in your table. The chart should adjust automatically.

Answer

With this delay, our finish date changed from 7/15/2020 to 7/23/2020.

Discussion

Change some activity durations and see how your Gantt chart reacts.

Filler

Our next topic is procurement lead time, so here's an example of it; and another story of how difficulty and challenges lead to innovation.

When I was the materials manager at SOLA Optical in Petaluma California, we needed to keep our finished goods inventory in balance; not an easy task given almost 100,000 stock keeping units, SKU's. Fortunately, we could produce a monomer lens in about one day, and a polymer lens a few minutes, allowing us to react quickly to unexpected spikes in demand for any particular SKU.

Transitions® lenses automatically adapt to changing light conditions. Even though the transitions process was developed and owned by our competitor, they were willing to imbibe our lenses for us and that allowed us to offer a line of transition lenses; but at a big price.

The "price" we had to pay was not the cost, it was the time. The demand for transitions-enables lenses was sufficient to support a price that included the additional manufacturing cost. The problem was that the Transitions factory was in Florida, and we were in California. The margin would not cover airfreight, so we shipped our lenses to and from Florida by truck. Our manufacturing lead time went from days to weeks.

We needed to anticipate our needs weeks in advance. We eventually did this with a technique I called Inventory Profile Analysis, based on another technique called Pyramid Forecasting.

Pyramid Forecasting is included, appropriately enough, in the Forecasting topic, in about 20 pages. We will cover Inventory Profile Analysis as our final topic in this text.

Procurement Time Management

We find procurement[1] in all three of our constraints. The materials we need to purchase are in Scope, what we will pay for the materials is in Cost, and when we need to order the materials is here in Time.

Bill of Material

What materials? A bill of materials (BOM) is a list of the raw materials and semi-finished goods necessary to build one finished goods item. For example, a toy wagon (finished goods) may require two axles (semi-finished), each of which requires two wheels (semi-finished) each of which requires one rim and one tire (raw materials). Lead times associated with the BOM tell us how long it takes to receive purchased items once they are ordered, and how long it takes to assemble semi-finished and finished goods once we have the required material on hand.

Material Requirements Planning

Material requirements planning, MRP, begins with finished goods requirements at a future date, deducts on-hand inventory (finished goods, semi-finished, and raw material), considers the bill of materials and lead times, and back-schedules to tells us when we need to order purchased items and when we need to begin assembly processes.

Work Breakdown Structure

The work breakdown structure, WBS, is the decomposition of the project deliverable into logical and measurable activities. The lowest level activities for which cost and duration can be identified and managed are called work packages. The WBS includes activity durations, but does not necessarily specify the sequence in which the activities are performed.

Sequencing

Sequencing is the process of identifying logical relationships between the activities that would require one to be completed before another could begin, or would allow both to be performed simultaneously.

Project Procurement Schedule

The output of the sequencing process is a project schedule that includes the planned start date, duration, and finish date for each activity. Unfortunately, a very important item, the theme of this topic, may be missing from the project schedule; and that is the purchase date.

We need to ensure that purchased items are available when needed for each activity. This is especially important for items with long lead times, such as things that have to be custom manufactured by our vendor.

Another consideration is that activity start times may change during the execution of the project. If purchase dates are not linked to their respective activity dates, the purchased material may arrive too early or too late, resulting is additional costs and possible a late project finish.

Scenario

As part of the Nature Trail restoration project, we plan to build a restroom adjacent to the parking lot. The completion date for the restroom is May 1st. When should we order the materials? All times are in workdays, with 5-day workweeks.[2]

	A	B	C	D
1	Activity	Duration	Purchase	Lead-time
2	Construct frame	5	Order lumber	8
3	Install siding	4	Order siding	12
4	Install roof	4	Order roofing	15
5	Install plumbing	3	Order plumbing	4
6	Install electrical	2	Order electrical	5
7	Install drywall	3	Order drywall	10
8	Paint restroom	2	Order paint	1
9				

Process

The first step is to plan the project with the assumption that all materials will be available when needed. We start with the completion date of May 1st in cell D8. The formula in cell C8 is =WORKDAY(D8,-B8). Note that we subtract the duration from the finish date to get the start date, a process known as backscheduling.

The formula in cell D7 is =WORKDAY(C8,-1). We copy cell D7 into cells D3:D6, and we copy cell C8 into cells C2:C7.

	A	B	C	D
1	Activity	Duration	Start	Finish
2	Construct frame	5	23-Mar	30-Mar
3	Install siding	4	31-Mar	6-Apr
4	Install roof	4	7-Apr	13-Apr
5	Install plumbing	3	14-Apr	17-Apr
6	Install electrical	2	20-Apr	22-Apr
7	Install drywall	3	23-Apr	28-Apr
8	Paint restroom	2	29-Apr	1-May
9				

Now that we know activity start dates, we can use the purchase lead-times to find when to place each of our purchase orders. The formula in cell G2 is

	A	B	C	D	E	F	G
1	Activity	Duration	Start	Finish	Purchase	Lead-time	Order
2	Construct frame	5	23-Mar	30-Mar	Order lumber	8	11-Mar
3	Install siding	4	31-Mar	6-Apr	Order siding	12	13-Mar
4	Install roof	4	7-Apr	13-Apr	Order roofing	15	17-Mar
5	Install plumbing	3	14-Apr	17-Apr	Order plumbing	4	8-Apr
6	Install electrical	2	20-Apr	22-Apr	Order electrical	5	13-Apr
7	Install drywall	3	23-Apr	28-Apr	Order drywall	10	9-Apr
8	Paint restroom	2	29-Apr	1-May	Order paint	1	28-Apr
9							

=WORKDAY(C2,-F2). We then copy our G2 formula into cells G3:G8.

Discussion

Even though construction does not begin until March 23rd, we have three purchase orders to place prior to that date.

Practice

Our painter recommends we allow 3 days for painting. Create the spreadsheet as described, and then change the duration for Paint restroom from 2 to 3 days.[3]

Answer

All of our dates change, including all of our order dates. We must now place our order for lumber on March 10th rather than on March 11th.

Footnotes

(1) The purchasing function falls within the procurement function. Procurement includes sourcing, which is identifying and qualifying vendors. Purchase involves placing and managing purchase orders once the vendors approved.

(2) To keep things simple, there are no holidays in this schedule. We could have included holidays as non-work days using the method we discussed in the Date and Time Functions topic.

(3) Does paint dry on weekends and holidays? Yes, of course it does. If that was a concern, rather than using =WORKDAY(D8,-B8) in cell C8, we could have simply used =D8-B8. That would give us the start date, the finish date minus the duration, regardless of the day of the week.

Agile Scheduling

Agile methodologies, such as Scrum, Extreme Programming (XP), Lean, Feature-Driven Development, and Crystal, use a different scheduling concept than traditional, waterfall, project management. The following is a *very brief* overview of agile scheduling, focusing on the mathematics.

Discussion

Two differences between agile and waterfall are the roles of key players and the use of iterations. In agile, the project manager becomes a facilitator; the product owner, or customer, takes on a more active role; and the team is empowered to make the scheduling decisions. In most agile methodologies, the iterations have a fixed length of about three weeks. The scope, not the duration of the iteration, is the variable.

Meetings are also much more common in agile than in waterfall, but they tend to be a lot shorter in duration. The daily stand-up, for example, should last no longer than 15 minutes. A planning meeting is held at the start of each iteration. At the end of the iteration, an iteration review meeting is conducted where the product owner accepts or rejects the product. A retrospective meeting is also held to discuss what went right, what went wrong, and what changes should be made in the next iteration.

User Stories

The product owner divides the project deliverable into a number of features, or stories. The idea is to start delivering value to the organization as soon as possible, rather than waiting until the end of the project. The product owner prioritizes the stories so, once developed, they can be implemented by the organization at once.

Story Points

The team reviews the stories and, based on prior experience, assigns story points to each story. The more challenging a story, the more points it gets. Based on experience, the team knows how many story points it can complete in one iteration, so the team selects the top priority stories that, in total, do not exceed their story point per iteration maximum.

Velocity

Velocity is the number of story points the team has demonstrated that they can complete in one iteration. Historical data is reviewed and a velocity, points per iteration, is agreed upon. Agile iterations are not frantic races; they should be sustainable work pace, and the velocity should reflect that. The Scrum term "sprint" is not what it implies.

During the retrospective meeting, the team can decide to adjust their velocity or story point awarding logic, based on experience.

Scenario

Your team has established a velocity of 100 story points per iteration. The product owner has prioritized the stories in the backlog; the stories to be completed.

Backlog	
Story	Points
F	20
J	10
K	50
E	25
G	20
L	40
M	15
P	60
N	35

Process

The product owner and the team meet during the iteration planning meeting. The team says they can accept stories F, J and K because they total 80 points, but they cannot include E as that would total 105 points. The team offers some suggestions to the product owner:

1. Deescalate story J and work on F, K and E (95 points).
2. Deescalate E and work on F, J, K and G (100 points).
3. Split story E into two parts, either of which could be included with stories F, J and K in the upcoming iteration.
4. Split story F, J, or K into two parts, deescalating one of the parts.

This is an example of the team and the product owner working together to provide the maximum value to the organization as soon as possible.

In the end, it is the product owners' decision as to which stories are included in the next iteration, up to the maximum velocity set by the team, but it is the teams' decision as to how many story points they can confidently commit to completing within the iteration.

In Scope

The beginning is the most important part of the work.

Plato

In God we trust, all others must bring data.

W. Edwards Deming.

If you don't know where you are going. How can you expect to get there?

Basil S. Walsh

If you tell people where to go, but not how to get there,
you'll be amazed at the results.

Gen. George S. Patton

You can't manage what you can't measure.

Peter Drucker

A fixed deadline and a flexible scope are the crucial combination.

Jason Fried

Working on new projects gives you the opportunity to learn
and absorb new things.

Michelle Ryan

Working hard and working smart sometimes can be two different things.

Byron Dorgan

Probable impossibilities are to be preferred to improbable possibilities.

Aristotle

The only thing that is constant is change

Heraclitus

Setting goals is the first step in turning the invisible into the visible.

Tony Robbins

Down scope. Fire one.

Clark Gable, *Run Silent, Run Deep* (1958)

131

Setting Goals

Projects are initiated to accomplish goals. The first step to a successful project, therefore, is a well-defined goal. A traditional (waterfall) project scope statement should include quantitative characteristics for the deliverable. If this cannot be done, because the deliverable is not yet clearly understood, then agile methodologies would be more appropriate.

<u>Discussion</u>

Two popular methods for ensuring our goals include everything they should are SMART and CLEAR. Nothing wrong with using both of them.

SMART = Specific, Measurable, Attainable, Realistic, and Timely.

- Set **specific** goals by answering the questions: who, what, where, when, how, and, most importantly in my opinion, why.
- Criteria that can be used to **measure** the attainment of a goal.
- Set **attainable** goals, and provide the necessary resources.
- Set **realistic** goals that can be achieved with resources provided.
- Create a **time** frame to achieve the goal.

CLEAR = Collaborative, Limited, Emotional, Achievable, and Refinable.

- The goal should encourage people to **collaborate** with each other.
- The goal should be **limited** in scope and time.
- The goal should tap into the passion of your people and be something they can form an **emotional** connection with.
- Break larger goals into smaller tasks that can be quickly **achieved**.
- As new situations arise, be flexible and **refine** goals as needed.

I have no math exercises to share with you on this topic, but I wanted to include this in the book because it is critical that we have a clear and measurable goal for our project. If the project scope statement includes vague references to things like "the biggest" or "the best" we need to have a serious talk with the project sponsor. As project managers, we have an obligation to the organization, and to our team, to resolve any ambiguities before we break-ground on the project deliverable.

Displaying Data

This topic describes two types of data, the appropriate tools to be used on each, and ways we can summarize and present our data to stakeholders.

Continuous or Discrete

Data can be continuous or discrete. The amount of current flowing thru a power line, the temperature in our vineyard, or the amount of sugar in a box of breakfast cereal are examples of continuous data. If measured, continuous data may have many decimal places, depending on the accuracy of our measuring instrument.

Discrete data are[1] categorical. The number of power poles required to get electricity from the road to our factory, the number of grapevines in our vineyard, or the number of cases of breakfast cereal we produced last week. Discrete data are integers, they do not have decimals.

Scenario

Unfortunately, your last project included a few worker injuries. You decide to review data from prior projects that the organization keeps in their lessons learned repository:

Year	2008	2009	2010	2011	2012	2013	2014	2015	2016	2017	2018	2019
Injuries	11	15	24	33	38	42	51	53	56	58	63	65

Which is more appropriate for this data, the bar chart or the line chart?

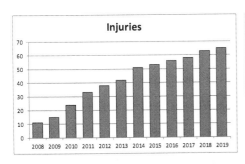
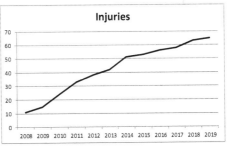

Discussion

Interesting question. Injuries are discrete, a person is either injured or they are not. One might assume that years are also discrete. If I am preparing the year-end financial statements, it makes a big difference if an expense was incurred in December of one year or in January of the following year. On the other hand, is there really any difference between a person injured on December 31st while driving to the project team party, or being injured on January 1st while driving home after the party? In this case, years may be seen as artificial aggregations of months, weeks, or days. In reality, time is continuous.[2] Which chart to use? Since neither is misleading, either one will do. I prefer the line chart for the reasons given, but you may prefer the bar chart, and that is fine too.

Scenario

Based on the data in the table, and the charts, it certainly looks like injuries are increasing since the company was founded in 2008, but we have grown a lot since then too, with more projects, and larger teams.

Let's look at the data by worker days (number of workers times number of days worked), and then calculate injuries per worker day.

Year	2008	2009	2010	2011	2012	2013	2014	2015	2016	2017	2018	2019
Injuries	11	15	24	33	38	42	51	53	56	58	63	65
Worker/days	104	154	265	369	425	463	560	688	741	784	863	884
Injuries/Worker day	0.106	0.097	0.091	0.089	0.089	0.091	0.091	0.077	0.076	0.074	0.073	0.074

Results

Injuries per worker day have actually declined since 2008. We plot the data in a line graph to better visualize the trend. It looks like there was a significant decline in 2014. Why was that?

Discussion

With a little research, we learn that a safety incentive bonus program was initiated in January 2014. We decide to include a safety discussion in our initial team meetings on all projects, with a reminder about the safety incentive bonus. Nothing like offering a little cash to get people's attention.

Scenario

In addition to safety concerns, finishing projects on time is a serious issue. While we have access to all this data, we decide to do a little more research.

We select 100 projects at random from the organizations' lessons learned repository, comparing their actual finish date to their original planned finish date. We find that 85% of our sample projects finished late. We plot the data in a histogram.

On time or early	15
1 week late	20
2 weeks late	24
3 weeks late	18
4 weeks late	11
5 weeks late	8
6 or more late	4
Total	100

Results

A histogram is the appropriate tool to use to display continuous data that has been grouped into categories.

From a practical standpoint, there is not much difference in a project that finished

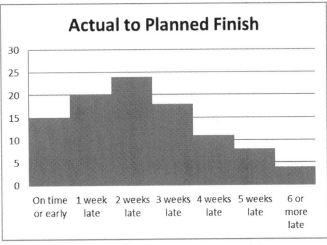

on Friday of one week and another that finished on Monday of the following week. Weeks are an arbitrary time measurements anyway. Why 7 days? Why not 5 or 10 days? A histogram is actually just a vertical bar chart with no gaps between the bars, indicating that the underlying data are continuous.

Scenario

Why do some projects finish on time and some late? We reviewed the documentation for each of our 100 random-sample projects and we noticed that some have relatively few approved change requests while others have a lot of approved change requests. To see if there is a correlation between the number of approved change requests and a late project finish, we plot the data on a scatter chart and add a trendline.

Process

The number of approved change requests for each project is shown on the horizontal (X) axis and the number of weeks late for the project is shown on the vertical (Y) axis.

A scatter chart is also known as an XY chart, for obvious reasons, and also as a cause and effect chart.[3] The idea is that a change in X, the independent variable, may cause a change in Y, the dependent variable. Looking at the dots, there does not appear to be a correlation

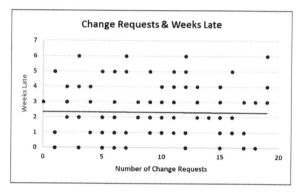

between X and Y. As X gets bigger, we don't see Y getting bigger (positive correlation) or smaller (negative correlation).

By the way, if we just want to see if there is a correlation, and don't need the fancy chart, we can use the Excel function =CORREL(array 1, array2).

Back to our scatter chart, the trendline is the "vertical average" of the dots. Technically, it's called the linear least-squared line as it represents the straight line, of all possible straight lines, with the least square vertical difference between each dot and the line; it's the best fit. Our trendline does not appear to have a significant positive or negative slope; as X increases, Y does not appear to increase or decrease. Regardless of the number of change requests, all of our projects tend to be about 2.3 weeks late. Why is that?

Scenario

We notice that the number of subcontractors per project fluctuates significantly. We don't see a relationship to late finish, but there does seem to be a relationship to change requests. Let's have a deeper look.

Process

We have plotted the number of subcontractors on our X axis and the number of change requests on our Y axis. Visually, both the dots and the trendline indicate that the number of change requests increases as the number of subcontractors increases[4].

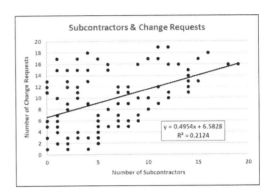

We have also included the equation for the trendline and the R^2 value.

The equation $y = 0.4954x + 6.5828$ tells us that Y tends to increase 0.4954 units (change requests) for every one-unit increase in X (subcontractors). The value 0.4954 is known as the slope of the trendline. With a slope of about 0.5, we will add one more change request for every two subs we add. Our slope is positive; a negative slope would indicate that Y decreases as X increases. The value 6.5828 is known as the y-intercept. If X equals zero, Y will be 6.5828; if a project has no subcontractors, we should still expect it to average about 6.6 change requests.

The coefficient of determination, R^2 is a value between zero and one. An R^2 of zero says there is no correlation between X and Y. An R^2 of one says there is a 100% correlation between X and Y. Our R^2 value of 0.2124 says about 21% of the change in Y (change requests) can be attributed to a change in X (subcontractors) and that about 79% (100 – 21 = 79) of the change in Y is caused by some something other than X. If we reversed the input, with change requests as the X variable and subcontractors as the Y variable, our R^2 would still be the same, 0.2124, proving that a "cause and effect" chart does not prove a cause and effect. Increasing change requests causes an increase in subcontractors? Really? I don't think so.

Practice

Does rain delay outdoor projects? You randomly selected ten outdoor projects and gathered data regarding the average daily rainfall, in inches, during the project and the number of days the project was late.

Rain	Late
0.76	6
0.49	9
0.67	8
0.59	3
0.77	4
0.43	7
0.80	9
0.34	7
0.08	1
0.18	4

Enter the data into Excel and construct a scatter chart. Include a trendline with equation and R^2.

How could you use this information to improve on-time performance of future projects?

Process

Enter the data into Excel, then select the entire table and insert a scatter chart. Choose a layout that includes the chart title and both X and Y axis titles. If the layout includes a legend, delete it. Edit the titles as appropriate. Right click any one of the data points and select Add Trendline. Select Linear and checkmark to display the equation and the r-squared.

Answer

Your chart should look something like the example below. An inch of rainfall adds about 5 days to the project, but with only 23% confidence, there is a lot more going on besides the rain.

How could you use this in the future? We could use historical data to predict the average daily rainfall during the outdoor portion of planned projects, and then add additional days to compensate for the rain delays. You might even add some contingency reserve days for above average rainy spells.

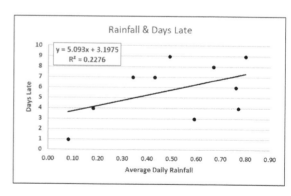

138

Scenario

Your organization completed 53 projects in the last three years; 16 for the government, 29 commercial, and 8 internal. Construct a pie chart to better understand, and graphically communicate, this distribution.

Process

A table was constructed in Excel for the three values. The total is not included. The table was then used to insert a pie chart. Slices were edited to change the default colors. The font used for "Internal 15%" was changed from black to white. The percentages shown for the pie slices are automatically included by default.

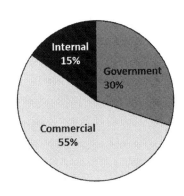

Scenario

Not all projects are profitable. Only 10 of the 16 government projects were profitable, only 22 of the 29 commercial projects were profitable, and only 2 of the 8 internal projects were profitable.

Account Type	Profit	Loss
Government	10	6
Commercial	22	7
Internal	2	6

Create a stacked column chart with profit and loss by account types.[5]

Results

Like our pie chart, the stacked column chart shows us the relative proportion of each account type, but it also includes information about project profitability. Loss appears to be about the same in all three types of projects.

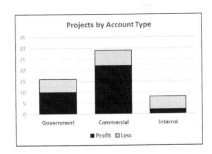

Scenario

Change the chart type from stacked column to 100% stacked column.

139

Results

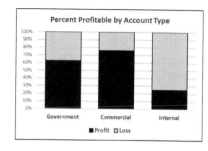

With the click of a button, Excel changes the chart type from stacked column to 100% stacked column. The Y axis automatically changes from units to percent of total for each account type. Comparing the two charts, the stacked column indicated that the number of unprofitable projects was about the same for each account type, but the percent chart clearly shows that the percent of unprofitable projects was much higher for internal projects.[6]

Scenario

Let's look at our profit and loss data using the Data Analysis feature in Excel.[7] It's not a chart, but it produces a nice table. We will only look at the eight Internal projects, but we could follow the same steps to look at all three account types, side by side, if we wanted to. The table at right displays the profit or loss for each of our eight internal projects.

Profit (Loss)
(3,830)
62,240
(42,660)
(45,700)
74,480
(15,930)
(32,680)
(6,960)

Process

On the Data menu tab, select Data Analysis > Descriptive Statistics > OK. The Input Range is our profit and loss data, including the column heading.

Check "Labels in first row." Select a cell on your spreadsheet as the top left corner of your Output Range. Checkmark Summary Statistics and click OK. Excel produces this table. Adjust your column width as needed.

	A	B
1	Profit (Loss)	
2		
3	Mean	-1380
4	Standard Error	16201.3426
5	Median	-11445
6	Mode	#N/A
7	Standard Deviation	45824.317
8	Sample Variance	2099868029
9	Kurtosis	-0.4471947
10	Skewness	0.99513759
11	Range	120180
12	Minimum	-45700
13	Maximum	74480
14	Sum	-11040
15	Count	8
16		

Our eight internal projects lost an average of $1,380 with a net loss of $11,040. The most profitable was $74,480 and the biggest loser was –$45,700, giving a range of $120,180. The median was a loss of $11,445. Standard deviation, variance, and skew are also given.

Footnotes

(1) The word data is the plural form of the word datum. "Data are…", not "data is…". But, the word police are very lacks. Don't be surprised to see "data is…" in the real world; just don't you be the one saying it.

(2) It may be that time is not continuous. Time may come in units of "Planck time" equal to about 10^{-43} seconds. That is the time, at the speed of light, to travel one Planck length, which is 1.6^{-36} meters. Think of a digital clock that jumps instantly from one second to the next. With our digital clock, there is no such thing as a half second.

(3) A "cause and effect" chart does not actually prove cause and effect, it only shows a correlation between the two variables. It may be that a change in X is actually causing a change in Y, or it may be that some other variable we have not considered is changing both X and Y.

(4) I am using this hypothetical example of subcontractors and change requests to illustrate the use of a scatter chart. I am not aware of any real-world studies that show a statistically significant relationship between subcontractors and change requests.

(5) The exact steps to create a chart in Excel are different depending on the version of Excel you have. Check your Excel help file.

(6) It is not unusual for internal projects to be unprofitable in the short term. Organizations frequently use projects to implement strategic initiatives, which may take many years, if ever, to become profitable, but they are considered necessary for the long-term benefit of the organization and its' stockholders. Compliance with regulations, long-term research and development, or acquisition of a competitor are all examples of strategic projects that may not yield immediate profits.

(7) If "Data Analysis" is not visible on your Data tab, go to File > Options > Add-ins > Excel Add-ins > Go. Checkmark Analysis ToolPak and OK. While you are at it, I recommend you also add Analysis ToolPak – VBA and Solver Add-in if they are available. We will play with Solver later on. If some of your projects take place in Europe, you will probably want to add the Euro Currency Tools while you are in there.

Factor-Weighted Analysis

We have looked at several quantitative tools that could be used to decide between competing projects, such as present value, future value, and internal rate of return. Our assumption when using these tools was "all things being equal" we want to select the option that will return the most money, or the highest return on investment (ROI) to the organization. But in the real world, all things are never equal. There may be important qualitative factors, things other than money, that we need to consider when deciding between competing options.

Scenario

Your project is to build a new distribution center and phase 1 is to select the location. You have narrowed the search down to three locations: A, B, and C.

Important non-financial factors include local infrastructure, weather, and workforce availability and skill level. You have gathered data on each factor for each location, but how can you organize the data to make an intelligent decision?

Process

We need a scoring system to compare different locations, let's say a score between 0 (unacceptable) and 100 (perfect) for each factor. Infrastructure, for example could be a score resulting from a formula that includes the number of miles to the nearest interstate highway, the nearest rail terminal, and the nearest sea port. The quality of the roads could also be considered. The reliability of the power grid would also be an infrastructure consideration. The score for weather could be based on the average number of days per year that local roads are closed due to the weather related problems, or the anticipated cost of heating and air conditioning. The workforce score could be based on the local unemployment rate for the appropriate skill level. A high unemployment rate would make it easy to staff our distribution, while a low unemployment rate would make it more difficult and more costly. Low skill levels, compared to our needs, could be compensated for with training, but that would be an additional expense.

We calculate a value for each location and factor based on our objective formulas. But, are the three factors of the same importance? A great highway system, for example, is useless if it is buried under six feet of snow.

We need to weight each of our factors. After a discussion with the project sponsor we decide that infrastructure is most important, followed by weather, with workforce in last place because the goal of the distribution center is to distribute stuff, not to pay low wages. Though not required, it's customary to express each of the weights as a percent, totaling 100 percent. We agree to make infrastructure 40%, weather 35% and workforce 25%.[1]

Results

The first step is to create the table with the factors, locations and weights.

	A	B	C	D	E	F	G	H	I
1	Factor	Weight	Location A		Location B		Location C		
2			Score	Weighted	Score	Weighted	Score	Weighted	
3	Infrastructure	40%							
4	Weather	35%							
5	Workforce	25%							
6	Totals	100%							
7									

Next we enter the scores. For infrastructure, Location A scored 25 points, Location B scored 90, and Location C scored 20. For Weather, Location A got 40, Location B got 60 and Location C got 40. For Workforce, Location A scored 80, while Location B scored 20 and Location C scored 60.

	A	B	C	D	E	F	G	H
1	Factor	Weight	Location A		Location B		Location C	
2			Score	Weighted	Score	Weighted	Score	Weighted
3	Infrastructure	40%	25		90		20	
4	Weather	35%	40		60		40	
5	Workforce	25%	80		20		60	
6	Totals	100%						
7								

Finally, multiply each score by its respective weight and total the weighted scores for each location. For example, cell D3 is B3*C3, cell F3 is = B3*E3 and cell H3 is =B3*G3. Cell D6 is = Sum(D3:D5), Cell F6 is = Sum(F3:F5), Cell H6 is = Sum(H3:H5). Location B has the highest weighted score of 62 and is our choice for the new distribution center.

	A	B	C	D	E	F	G	H
	Factor	Weight	Location A		Location B		Location C	
1			Score	Weighted	Score	Weighted	Score	Weighted
2								
3	Infrastructure	40%	25	10	90	36	20	8
4	Weather	35%	40	14	60	21	40	14
5	Workforce	25%	80	20	20	5	60	15
6	Totals	100%		44		62		37
7								

Practice

Your company is opening a manufacturing facility in Europe. The first phase of your project is to select a suitable location. Working with your team and selected area experts, you have identified relevant factors, assigned weights to them, developed an objective scoring algorithm for each factor and determined the scores for three potential locations.

Complete the factor-weighted table below. What are the weighted total scores for each location? Which location do you recommend?

Factor	Weight	Location A		Location B		Location C	
		Score	Weighted	Score	Weighted	Score	Weighted
Climate	5%	79		85		44	
Construction cost	10%	82		96		95	
Culture	5%	98		61		50	
Currency exchange risk	5%	74		68		59	
Environmental regulations	5%	43		41		80	
Government incentives	5%	83		95		71	
Labor availability	8%	90		55		69	
Labor cost	10%	86		91		44	
Land cost	10%	94		60		71	
Political risk	8%	98		95		91	
Proximity to customers	5%	84		84		87	
Proximity to suppliers	5%	88		62		56	
Taxes	8%	88		86		76	
Unions	6%	69		71		77	
Utilities	5%	63		66		74	
Totals	100%						

Answer

Location A, with a score of 83.02 is your first choice, followed by location B with a score of 75.94. Location C, with a score of 70.55 in last place.

Factor	Weight	Location A		Location B		Location C	
		Score	Weighted	Score	Weighted	Score	Weighted
Climate	5%	79	3.95	85	4.25	44	2.20
Construction cost	10%	82	8.20	96	9.60	95	9.50
Culture	5%	98	4.90	61	3.05	50	2.50
Currency exchange risk	5%	74	3.70	68	3.40	59	2.95
Environmental regulations	5%	43	2.15	41	2.05	80	4.00
Government incentives	5%	83	4.15	95	4.75	71	3.55
Labor availability	8%	90	7.20	55	4.40	69	5.52
Labor cost	10%	86	8.60	91	9.10	44	4.40
Land cost	10%	94	9.40	60	6.00	71	7.10
Political risk	8%	98	7.84	95	7.60	91	7.28
Proximity to customers	5%	84	4.20	84	4.20	87	4.35
Proximity to suppliers	5%	88	4.40	62	3.10	56	2.80
Taxes	8%	88	7.04	86	6.88	76	6.08
Unions	6%	69	4.14	71	4.26	77	4.62
Utilities	5%	63	3.15	66	3.30	74	3.70
Totals	100%		83.02		75.94		70.55

Discussion

Using a spreadsheet like Excel is the best choice for tables like this because all of the output is automatically recalculated whenever the input is changed.

Suppose the Labor Party gains control of the government in Location A and they promises major revisions in employer/worker regulations. You can easily change the weights or scores for Political risk and Unions with a few keystrokes and the location totals are instantly updated.

Suppose the local government of Location B offers free land and no-interest financing to encourage you to locate the factory in their jurisdiction, and provide much-needed employment opportunities for their citizens. A few clicks at the keyboard and your factor weighted analysis is updated.

Footnote

(1) These are just examples. You would decide, for your project, what factors are important and their relative weight. That's one of the nice things about a factor-weighted table, it is extremely flexible. You choose the factors and you choose the relative weights.

Filler

I was the inventory manager at ComputerLand Corporation from 1974 to 1978, when they were the world's largest retailer of personal computers. We would purchase products from manufacturers in huge quantities and sell them to our franchisees at cost. High technology products are subject to Moore's Law, which states that the number of transistors on a silicon chip will double every two years. The practical implication is that technology gets better and cheaper over time. So, how does a computer manufacturer get retailers to stock their products, when everyone knows better and cheaper products are on the way?

The answer is "price protection." When the new computer is introduced, the manufacturer gives a rebate to all retailers holding the old models, allowing them to discount the old machines and make room for the new models. This was new to everyone at the time, and every manufacturer came up with their own set of rules and requirements to qualify for the rebates. My department was responsible for administering the various price protection rebates, and we treated them as unique projects.

Our stakeholders were over 700 ComputerLand franchisees, and effective stakeholder communications was critical. About that time, ComputerLand Corporation was hosting a vendor fair for the franchisees in San Francisco. Our department rented a booth with a sign overhead reading: "We gave away over $19,000,000 last year. Did you get your share?" We had easy chairs in our booth. We would invite the franchisees to sit down, relax, and share their concerns with us. All conversations were documented. The following week, we resolved all of the issues, around 400 as I recall, and communicated the results back to the franchisee, along with any price protection money due them.

A good example of proactive stakeholder engagement.

Forecasting

The only thing that matters is the future; the only thing we know is the past, and the only thing we can change is the present. Forecasting is the tool we use to learn from the past and to prepare for the future.[1]

<u>Discussion</u>

A common use of forecasting in business is to forecast demand for our product or service. Historical sales data are readily available and a good forecast allows us to produce, or procure, the goods needed to meet future demand. But there is one problem, sales and demand are not the same thing. Sales and demand are only equal as long as we have sufficient inventory to meet demand. Sales are the lessor of demand and inventory.

If we ran out of inventory, our historical sales data do not truly reflect demand. The first step, therefore, in any forecasting technique is to review our data. If we ran out of inventory in any period, then we need to replace the sales number with an educated guess of what we could have sold if sufficient inventory had been available.

Naïve Forecasting

<u>Scenario</u>

Your project is to increase the capacity of our factory so we can meet future demand. The first step is to find the best forecasting technique for predicting future demand. We will define the "best" forecasting technique as the technique with the least average error.[2]

Your customer service data base includes information on unfilled orders. Combining this with our sales data, we are able to build a set of historical demand by month for the past year. (See next page)

The first forecasting technique we will look at is naïve forecasting. Naïve forecasting is the simplest of all forecasting techniques. It assumes the future will be the same as the past. Demand in February will be what we sold in January. If it is raining today, it will probably rain tomorrow.

Process

Combining our sales data with our unfilled orders data, we are able to produce an estimated demand value for each month of last year. Naïve forecasting says that the future will be the same as the past, so we forecast each month to be the same demand as the prior month. The formula in cell C3 is =B2, and this was copied to cells C4:C13.

	A	B	C
1	Month	Demand	Forecast
2	Jan	498	
3	Feb	412	498
4	Mar	537	412
5	Apr	492	537
6	May	522	492
7	Jun	500	522
8	Jul	529	500
9	Aug	503	529
10	Sep	553	503
11	Oct	509	553
12	Nov	539	509
13	Dec	507	539
14			

Results

We have a forecast. It's easy to use, but is it the best we can do? Nope!

Discussion

We need to try some other forecasting techniques, but first, we need a way to compare the different techniques. We could use statistics, specifically standard deviations, but to keep things simple, we will use mean absolute deviation. It's much easier to calculate, and much easier to explain to non-statisticians (like senior management).

Mean Absolute Deviation

Scenario

We intend to try several different forecasting techniques with our data to see which produces the least error. We will do this by calculating the mean absolute deviation, MAD,[3] for our naïve forecast. The mean absolute deviation is just like it sounds. We calculate the deviation (difference) between each of our forecasts and the actual amounts. We don't want negative and positive differences to offset each other, so we convert the differences to absolute values. The negatives become positive. The Excel function =ABS(...) does this for us very easily. We then calculate the average, the mean, of the absolute deviations. The smaller the MAD, the better our forecast. Just like in life, little mad is better than big mad.

148

Process

We have retained our naïve forecasts. The absolute deviation between demand and forecast is in column D. The formula in cell D3 is =ABS(B3 – C3) and the formula was copied into cells D4:D13. Cell D14 is =AVERAGE(D3:D13).

	A	B	C	D
1	Month	Demand	Forecast	MAD
2	Jan	498		
3	Feb	412	498	86
4	Mar	537	412	125
5	Apr	492	537	45
6	May	522	492	30
7	Jun	500	522	22
8	Jul	529	500	29
9	Aug	503	529	26
10	Sep	553	503	50
11	Oct	509	553	44
12	Nov	539	509	30
13	Dec	507	539	32
14				47.18
15				

Results

The MAD value of 47.18 is meaningless until we compare it to something else, so let's move on.

Moving Average

Scenario

Do we want to bet all of our chips on one value? How about averaging our bet over the last three months? Let's try a three-period moving average.[4] We will forecast each month, beginning with April, by averaging the three prior months. We will then compare our forecasts to the actual demand and use mean absolute deviation, MAD, to compare our three-period moving average to our naïve forecast.

Process

Our forecasts are in column C and our MAD is in column D. We entered the formula =AVERAGE(B2:B4) in cell C5 and copied it down into cells C6:C13. To summarize, the forecast for each month is the average of the three preceding months. The formula in cell D5 is =ABS(B5-C5) and this was copied into cells D6:D13. Our Mean Absolute Deviation, MAD, is in cell D14, with the value of 23.56.

	A	B	C	D
1	Month	Demand	Forecast	MAD
2	Jan	498		
3	Feb	412		
4	Mar	537		
5	Apr	492	482	10
6	May	522	480	42
7	Jun	500	517	17
8	Jul	529	505	24
9	Aug	503	517	14
10	Sep	553	511	42
11	Oct	509	528	19
12	Nov	539	522	17
13	Dec	507	534	27
14				23.56
15				

149

Results

We then compare our naïve forecast MAD of 47.18 to our three-period moving average forecast MAD of 23.56, remembering smaller is better. For our data and our marketplace volatility, it appears that a three-period moving average has less forecast error than a naïve forecast.[5]

Discussion

Will it rain tomorrow? If it is raining today then there is a good probability of rain tomorrow, but if the last rain we had was a week ago, then the probability of rain tomorrow is a lot less. The near past is usually a better indicator of the future than the distant past. So why did we value each of our three months equally in our moving average forecast? Let's do it again, with more weight on the near past and less on the distant past.

Weighted Moving Average

Scenario

Use a weighted moving average, with weights of 3, 2, and 1 to forecast April thru December, then calculate the mean absolute deviation.

Process

To forecast April demand, March demand will be multiplied by 3, February demand by 2, and January demand by 1 and then the total will be divided by 6. Regardless of the number of periods or the weights, the largest weight is always applied to the most recent period, and we work backward and downward from there. The most distant period will be assigned the lowest of the weights. The formula in cell C5 is =ROUND((B4*3+B3*2+B2)/6, 0).

	A	B	C	D
1	Month	Demand	Forecast	MAD
2	Jan	498		
3	Feb	412		
4	Mar	537		
5	Apr	492	489	3
6	May	522	494	28
7	Jun	500	515	15
8	Jul	529	506	23
9	Aug	503	518	15
10	Sep	553	511	42
11	Oct	509	532	23
12	Nov	539	523	16
13	Dec	507	531	24
14				21.00
15				

This formula is copied into cells C6:C13. We included the Round function in our formula, with zero decimal places, because we cannot sell a fraction of a unit and because decimals would imply an unjustified level of accuracy. The syntax for the Round function is =ROUND(Number, decimal places). Excel also includes ROUNDUP and ROUNDDOWN. Your organizational policies may specify to use ROUNDUP when forecasting demand, to be sure of always having enough stock on hand.

Results

We use the same MAD calculation we used before, but with a result of 21.00 rather than 25.33. For our data, a weighted (3,2,1) forecast is better than a 3-period moving average, and both are better than a naïve forecast.

Discussion

Why did we only look back three periods? Why not more? It's a compromise between accuracy and resources, specifically computer memory in this case. Believe it or not, years ago computer memory used to be very expensive. (You smartphone today has more memory, and faster computing power, than a multi-million dollar super computer of the 1970's or 1980's.) Back then, forecasters wanted a way to include a lot of historical information in a single value that would require very little computer memory. Their solution was exponential smoothing.

Exponential Smoothing

Discussion

If each forecast is based, to some degree, on the forecast for the prior period, then each of our forecasts include some historical information, all embedded in a single number. The formula for exponential smoothing is the prior forecast plus the actual minus the forecast times a constant called *alpha* (α) which is a value between 0 and 1. Subtracting the prior forecast from the actual demand will result in either a positive or negative number.

$$New\ forecast = Prior\ forecast + \alpha(Actual\ demand - Prior\ forecast)$$

In other words, the new forecast is the old forecast plus an adjustment for the error in the last forecast. If actual demand was greater than forecasted, actual less forecast will be positive, and we will add an amount to the old forecast. If the actual demand was less than the forecast, then actual less forecast will be negative and we subtract an amount from the old forecast. If demand is going up, our new forecast goes up by a proportionate amount (depending on our *alpha*) and if demand is going down, our forecast goes down with it.

Suppose we decide to use an *alpha* of 0.25. What we are saying is that 75% of our new forecast is based on historical data and 25% of it is based on the current forecast error, the difference between the forecast and the actual observed value.

Scenario

Forecast February through December using exponential smoothing with an *alpha* of 0.50. Use 500 as the forecast for January. For your mean absolute deviation, only include April thru December to keep our MAD comparable to the other forecasting techniques we have used.

Process

Our *alpha* of 0.50 is in cell E2 and we entered a value of 500 in C2.

The formula in cell C3 is =ROUND(C2+(B2 – C2)*E2,0). Before we can copy C3 into other cells, we need to make the reference to cell E2 absolute rather than relative. If I copied the above formula into cell C4, the E2 reference in it would change to E3.

That would obviously cause a problem. When we copy cell C3 to C4, we want the B2 to change to B3, and we want C2 to change to C3, but we do not want E2 to change to E3.

	A	B	C	D	E
1	Month	Demand	Forecast	MAD	Alpha
2	Jan	498	500		0.50
3	Feb	412	499		
4	Mar	537	456		
5	Apr	492	497	5	
6	May	522	495	27	
7	Jun	500	509	9	
8	Jul	529	505	24	
9	Aug	503	517	14	
10	Sep	553	510	43	
11	Oct	509	532	23	
12	Nov	539	521	18	
13	Dec	507	530	23	
14				20.67	
15					

152

To prevent this from happening, we change the reference to cell E2 in the formula from relative to absolute, by including a dollar sign before the row or column I want to freeze, to make absolute. The revised formula in cell C3 looks is =ROUND(C2+(B2 – C2)*E$2,0). I can now copy it into cells C4:C13 and the resulting formulas will always refer to E2. Use the function 4 (F4) key to edit formulas and quickly toggle between the four relative and absolute reference choices.

Results

The mean absolute deviation for our exponential smoothing ($\alpha = 0.50$) forecast is 20.67. That is a whole lot better than the 47.18 we got with our naïve forecasts, the 23.56 we got with our 3-period moving average forecast, and even slightly better than the 21.00 we got with our weighted (3,2,1) moving average forecast.

Discussion

In the above example, we used an *alpha* value of 0.50. Why? Where did that come from, other than being a safe comprise between zero and one?

The truth is that it was a guess.

We could replace it with another guess, 0.25, 0.75, whatever, until we found the *alpha* value that gives us the lowest MAD for our data.

Since there are an infinite number of numbers between zero and one, we should probably look for some help in our pursuit of the ultimate *alpha*.

That help is an Excel Add-in called Solver.

Filler:

Exponential smoothing, like naïve, moving average, and weighted moving average, does not do well if there is a trend in our data. Double exponential smoothing, or second-order exponential smoothing, may be used for trends; but we will use seasonality, which is easier to explain.

But first, let's look into Solver and single-order exponential smoothing.

Solver

Discussion

Solver is included in Excel, but it might not be visible. If you don't see it in the Analyze box on the right side of your Data menu: select File > Options > Add-ins > Excel Add-ins > Go. Checkmark Solver Add-in and click Go. Solver should now be in the Analyze box on your Data menu. By the way, you can use the same menu path to add the Data Analysis ToolPak to the Data menu.

Process

We want to change our *alpha* in cell E2 until we find the smallest value for MAD, in cell D14. All of the formulas are as described in the last section. When you click Solver, a blank Solver Parameters box appears.

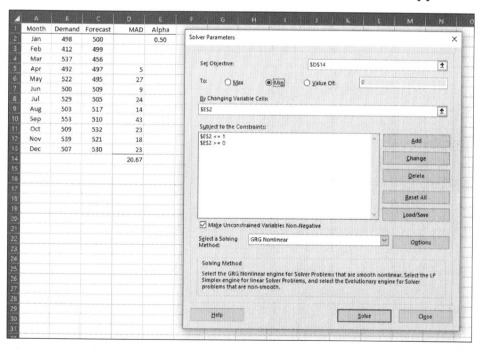

Set the object to cell D14, our mean absolute deviation. The dollar signs are not necessary, but Excel will probably add them to your entry. We want to minimize our MAD, so check Min. We want to do this by changing *alpha*, the value in cell E2. We need to add some constraints to the changes made to cell E2. Click Add, and follow the directions to make E2 less than or equal to 1. Click Add again and follow the directions to make E2 greater than or equal to 0. Finally, checkmark "Make Unconstrained Variables Non-Negative" and click Solve. Excel will announce that it found a solution, and ask if you want to keep it. Click OK.

Your output should look like this example, with an *alpha* of 0.17 and a MAD of 16.67. If you did not get these results, the problem is probably not with Solver, but with the formulas in your spreadsheet. In particular, the formulas in C3:C13 should refer to cell E2. If you entered "0.50" in the formulas rather than referring to cell E2, changing the value in E2 will have no effect on the formulas or the value of our MAD in cell D14.

	A	B	C	D	E
1	Month	Demand	Forecast	MAD	Alpha
2	Jan	498	500		0.17
3	Feb	412	500		
4	Mar	537	485		
5	Apr	492	494	2	
6	May	522	494	28	
7	Jun	500	499	1	
8	Jul	529	499	30	
9	Aug	503	504	1	
10	Sep	553	504	49	
11	Oct	509	512	3	
12	Nov	539	512	27	
13	Dec	507	516	9	
14				16.67	
15					

Results

Exponential smoothing (α = 0.17) is the best technique for our data.

Practice

You have gathered demand data for last year. Use this data to forecast demand for April thru December using naïve forecasting, three-period moving average, weighted moving average (3,2,1) and exponential smoothing (α = 0.50) and exponential smoothing (α = Solver). Use a January forecast of 467 to prime the exponential smoothing forecasts. Remember to only compare MADs from April through December as the three-period moving average and the weighted moving average (3,2,1) did not forecast demand for January, February, or March.

	A	B
1	Month	Demand
2	Jan	467
3	Feb	479
4	Mar	402
5	Apr	442
6	May	415
7	Jun	451
8	Jul	434
9	Aug	458
10	Sep	477
11	Oct	441
12	Nov	478
13	Dec	459
14		

Round up each of your forecasts to the next whole number. Calculate the mean absolute deviation for each of the five forecasting technique. For this data, which technique produces the lowest mean absolute deviation?

Process

See the proceeding pages for the correct layout and formulas. You could recreate the examples. When they are working properly and showing the correct results, simply change the forecast formulas from ROUND to ROUNDUP and replace the original demand data with the practice data.

Results

- Naïve forecasting produced a MAD of 21.56.
- Three-period moving average produced a MAD of 18.00.
- Weighted moving average (3,2,1) produced a MAD of 17.44.
- Exponential smoothing ($\alpha = 0.50$) produced a MAD of 18.00.
- Exponential smoothing (α = Solver) produced a MAD of 17.00 with a Solver generated *alpha* of 0.35.

Given our data set, exponential smoothing ($\alpha = 0.35$) would be our preferred forecasting for future periods.

Seasonality

Discussion

Seasonality is a characteristic of a time series in which the data experiences regular and predictable changes every cycle. It is usually associated with a calendar year, but the same concept can apply to any time series. A restaurant may experience daily seasonality with heavy demands for breakfast, lunch, and dinner, and slow periods in between.

Filler:

My first job after graduating from college was a department sales manager in a department store. We had daily seasonality. To make our day, we had to sell more than the department sold that day of the week last year. Long before Dirty Harry said "Go ahead, make my day," my divisional sales manager was asking me "Jim, did you make your day?"

Scenario

Your organization manufactures both snow skis and water skis using the same facility. Demand is seasonal with total monthly demand for last year as shown.

Annual demand is expected to increase at the rate of 15% a year. Forecast monthly demand for the next five years.

	A	B
1	Month	Demand
2	Jan	6,000
3	Feb	3,000
4	Mar	2,000
5	Apr	3,000
6	May	4,000
7	Jun	5,000
8	Jul	4,000
9	Aug	3,000
10	Sep	2,000
11	Oct	4,000
12	Nov	6,000
13	Dec	8,000
14		50,000
15		

Process

We don't expect the relative proportion between the months to change, just the annual total. The first step is to calculate the monthly percentages of the annual total. The formula in cell B14 is =SUM(B2:B13).

The sum function is used so much in Excel that there are a couple "Autosum" buttons available to you, one on the Home menu and one on the Formulas menu. Just select the cell and click the Autosum button. Excel guesses at the cells you want to include. Confirm or edit as needed.

	A	B	C
1	Month	Demand	Percent
2	Jan	6,000	12%
3	Feb	3,000	6%
4	Mar	2,000	4%
5	Apr	3,000	6%
6	May	4,000	8%
7	Jun	5,000	10%
8	Jul	4,000	8%
9	Aug	3,000	6%
10	Sep	2,000	4%
11	Oct	4,000	8%
12	Nov	6,000	12%
13	Dec	8,000	16%
14		50,000	100%
15			

The formula in cell C2 is =B2/B$14. The dollar sign tells Excel, when you copy the formula into cells C3:C13, that you have made an absolute reference to row 13 and Excel is not allowed to change it. We copy cell B14 into cell C14, which becomes =SUM(C2:C13), or we could use that Autosum button, and we format cells C2:C14 as a percent with no decimals.

We now know the percent of the annual total that each month represents. The rest is a slam-dunk.

We will start with our total annual demand. Cell D14 is = B14 * 1.15. Cell E14 is = D14 * 1.15 and that formula we can copy into cells E14:H14. A 15% annual increase is the same as multiplying the prior year by 1.15.

	A	B	C	D	E	F	G	H
1	Month	Demand	Percent	Year 1	Year 2	Year 3	Year 4	Year 5
2	Jan	6,000	12%	6,900	7,935	9,125	10,494	12,068
3	Feb	3,000	6%	3,450	3,968	4,563	5,247	6,034
4	Mar	2,000	4%	2,300	2,645	3,042	3,498	4,023
5	Apr	3,000	6%	3,450	3,968	4,563	5,247	6,034
6	May	4,000	8%	4,600	5,290	6,084	6,996	8,045
7	Jun	5,000	10%	5,750	6,613	7,604	8,745	10,057
8	Jul	4,000	8%	4,600	5,290	6,084	6,996	8,045
9	Aug	3,000	6%	3,450	3,968	4,563	5,247	6,034
10	Sep	2,000	4%	2,300	2,645	3,042	3,498	4,023
11	Oct	4,000	8%	4,600	5,290	6,084	6,996	8,045
12	Nov	6,000	12%	6,900	7,935	9,125	10,494	12,068
13	Dec	8,000	16%	9,200	10,580	12,167	13,992	16,091
14		50,000	100%	57,500	66,125	76,044	87,450	100,568

We doubled our sales, from 50,000 to over 100,000 in only five years! Nice!

The next step is to calculate the monthly demands. The formula in cell D2 is = $C2*D$14. The dollar sign in $C2 says that column C is an absolute reference and not to change it if we copy the formula to other columns. The dollar sign in D$14 says that row 14 is an absolute reference and not to change it if we copy the formula to other rows. We now copy the formula in cell D2 into cells D2:H13. Our absolute references ensured that all 60 of our formulas referred to the percentages in column C and to the annual totals in row 14. Is that cool, or what?

Results

With very little effort, we have forecasted the expected demand for the next 60 months.

Discussion

To keep things simple, we did not round our forecasts to integers, but we could have easily done so with ROUND or ROUNDUP. Suppose we wanted to round our forecasts to the nearest 10 units, or the nearest 100 units.

No problem. For example, the formula in cell H13 is =$C13*H$14 and the result is 16,091. The formula =ROUND(($C13*H$14)/10,0)*10 would give us 16,090. The formula =ROUND(($C13*H$14)/100,0)*100 would give us 16,100. And the formula =ROUND(($C13*H$14)/1000,0)*1000 would give us 16,000. Check with your project sponsor, or the project management office, regarding organizational preferences in forecasting.

Pyramid Forecasting

We wrap-up our discussion of forecasting with a brief discussion of pyramid forecasting.[6] I say brief because if you understood seasonality, pyramid is the same, but with stock keeping units rather than time units.

Scenario

Your organization manufactures skis in six sizes: children's small, medium and large, and adult small, medium and large. The ratio between sizes appears to be constant year after year, however total annual demand is expected to grow at the rate of 15% per year over the next five years. What is the annual demand for each size for the next five years?

Process

The percent for each size has already been calculated. The formula in cell B8 is =SUM(B2:B7) and it was copied into cell C8. The formula in cell C2 is =B2/B$8. This formula was then copied into cells C3:C7. Finally, cells C2:C8 were formatted as percent with no decimal places.

	A	B	C
1	Size	Demand	Percent
2	Child-Sm	1,500	3%
3	Child-Med	3,500	7%
4	Child-Lg	5,000	10%
5	Adult-Sm	10,000	20%
6	Adult-Med	20,000	40%
7	Adult-Lg	10,000	20%
8		50,000	100%

We used the same formulas that we used for seasonality, except that we rounded to the nearest ten units for both the annual totals and the sizes. For

	A	B	C	D	E	F	G	H
1	Size	Demand	Percent	Year 1	Year 2	Year 3	Year 4	Year 5
2	Child-Sm	1,500	3%	1,730	1,980	2,280	2,620	3,020
3	Child-Med	3,500	7%	4,030	4,630	5,320	6,120	7,040
4	Child-Lg	5,000	10%	5,750	6,610	7,610	8,750	10,060
5	Adult-Sm	10,000	20%	11,500	13,230	15,210	17,490	20,120
6	Adult-Med	20,000	40%	23,000	26,450	30,420	34,980	40,230
7	Adult-Lg	10,000	20%	11,500	13,230	15,210	17,490	20,120
8		50,000	100%	57,500	66,130	76,050	87,460	100,580

example, the formula in cell D8 is =ROUND((B8*1.15)/10,0)*10 and the formula in cell D2 is =ROUND($C2*D$8/10,0)*10.

Due to rounding, the totals for years 1, 4 and 5 are off by 10 units. Year 5 rounds up 10 while years 1 and 4 round down 10. The total for the five years is therefore off by 10 units. What can I say? Rounding has its ups and downs.

Footnotes

(1) Most project management literature defines forecasting as estimating the cost and time of the completion of the project. We will cover that in detail when we discuss Earned Value Management, EVM. For now, we are going to discuss forecasting tools in a more generic sense.

(2) The term "forecast error" does not imply you made a mistake. In statistics, an error is the difference between the expected value and the actual value. It's similar to how project management uses the term variance to define the difference between the expected value and the actual value. So don't be offended when told your forecast contains errors. I would be highly suspect of a perfect forecast with no forecast error.

(3) (Actually, this is more filler than footnote.) Many years ago I was preparing for a lecture the following day on Mean Absolute Deviation. The textbook I was using said that one MAD equaled 4 standard deviations. This made no sense to me and I didn't want to tell my students something I could not defend. There was a phone number in the book, so I called it and explained my dilemma. The receptionist said she would forward my message. I should mention that I live in California and the publisher was in New York, because at 5:00 AM the next morning I got a call from the author of the text. Actually, my wife got the call as the phone was on her side of the bed, and we were both sound asleep. She said it was for me and stretched the handset over to me. The well-known author, whom I will not name, was furious that I would challenge something in his book. When I explained my concern, he said he meant MAD was "approximately" equal to 4 standard deviations. I said no, the book clearly said "equal," not "approximately equal." His parting comment was "well, I meant approximately equal." I thanked him for returning my call, said goodbye and handed the phone back to my wife, asking her to hang it up. She did, but I could tell she was mad about being woken up so early in the morning. In fact, she was really mad, and when I tried to explain the conversation she got really, really mad. To this day, whenever I discuss Mean Absolute Deviation, MAD, I remember how mad my wife was because of that early morning phone call.

(4) Three periods is quite common, but you could use more than three to smooth out big fluctuations between the periods. The use of moving averages to smooth out data can be traced back to 1901. That was well before computers, and they did the calculations by hand.

(5) Your real-world data may indicate a different forecasting technique is a better fit for your specific needs. Please try all the techniques described in this topic, and then choose the best one for you. It would also be a good idea to periodically reconfirm your chosen technique is still the best for your particular needs. Perhaps an annual review would be warranted. If nothing else, the review should reassure the many users of your forecasts that you are keeping an eye on things.

(6) I developed a multi-level forecasting technique when I was the materials manager at SOLA Optical, and I later described it in a 1998 article for APICS. I needed a name for the technique and, since I was using a triangle to visually depict it, I decided to call it "pyramid forecasting." Today pyramid forecasting is an established forecasting technique and is included in many forecasting articles and textbooks. This is that original 1998 triangle; the first pyramid.

Filler

Here's another story from ComputerLand. Despite our best efforts, we accumulated a lot of brand new but obsolete inventory; another casualty of Moore's Law. Our franchisees did not want any of it, and, by contract, we were not allowed to sell it to directly the public.

My solution was to auction it to our employees, with all proceeds going to charity. We raised over $13,000 for charities, got rid of a lot of obsolete inventory, and many of our employees got their first personal computer.

I got my first PC that way, a brand new IBM PCJr. Are you old enough to remember the PCJr? It was only produced from March 1984 to May 1985.

Regression Analysis

Regression analysis is the prefect topic to follow forecasting because, among its many uses, regression can be used for forecasting. We touched on regression while discussing ways to display data when we created a scatter chart with a trend line Now we will use that trendline to predict the future.

Scenario

Your project is to upgrade the e-commerce web site for your company, with the objective of increasing sales. You begin by reviewing data from the legacy system.[1] Like many e-commerce web sites, products are described on separate pages, with links to similar or related products. Shoppers can add products to a shopping cart from any page. When ready, they select the cart and begin the checkout process. Is there a relationship between the number of pages visited and the total value of the purchase?

Discussion

The regression equation is: $y = a + bx$

X is the "cause" or input, in our case, the number of pages visited, and y is the "effect" or output, the dollar value of the purchase. The "y-intercept," a, is the value of y if x equals zero. This is not important to us because we know that people who do not visit our pages did not purchase anything. The "slope" of the regression, b, is what we are really interested in. The slope, b, is the approximate increase in y for a one unit (one page) increase in x. In other words, if someone visited x pages, we would expect them to purchase $b(x)$ worth of products.

It's important to understand "known x's" and "known y's" because several functions in Excel will need to use them. The known x's is a list of the observed values of our independent variable, pages viewed. The known y's is a corresponding list of the observed values of our dependent variable, purchases. They must match, meaning that there must be the same number of values in each list, or Excel will give us an error message.

Process

We selected 10 customers at random[2] and entered the data into Excel. Of course you would include all available data in your analysis, (or at least a very large sample) but we will limit our illustration to ten, or $n = 10$.

	A	B	C
1	Pages visited	Purchased	
2	4	$30.73	
3	3	$16.35	
4	12	$82.04	
5	8	$44.68	
6	9	$35.31	
7	8	$52.47	
8	5	$75.69	
9	3	$20.18	
10	7	$53.59	
11	6	$39.86	
12			
13	Slope	$5.02	
14	R^2	0.446	
15			

We will use the Slope function in Excel. The syntax is =SLOPE(known y's, known x's). Remember, x is the input and y is the output. In or hypothesis, more pages (x) causes larger sales(y). The formula in cell B13 is = SLOPE(B2:B11,A2:A11)

The R squared (R^2) is a value between 0 and 1 that tells us approximately what proportion of a change in Y can be attributed to a change in X. The syntax for the R squared function in Excel is =RSQ(known y's, known x's). The formula in cell B14 is = RSQ(B2:B11,A2:A11).

Results

In our example, our customers purchased about $5.00 for every page they visited, but only about $0.446 = 45\%$ of the purchase can be attributed to the number of pages visited. Other factors, currently unidentified, were responsible for about 55% of the amount purchased.

Scenario

You have discovered that as customers visit more pages, there is about a 45% chance they will spend more. So, how can we get them to visit more pages?

One of the reasons we are upgrading the web site is to increase the speed at which pages are loaded, the response time to user input. Our legacy system frequently gets overloaded and response times become very slow. Perhaps some customers get tired of the slow response times and stop visiting new pages? Will faster response times increase page visits, and thus increase sales?

Process

We selected 10 hours at random from our legacy data. We calculated the average response time, in seconds, and the total pages visited by all shoppers during the hour. What is the relationship between response times and pages visited?

We entered the average response times and the total number of customer page visits for each of the ten randomly selected hours.

The formula in cell B13 is =SLOPE(B2:B11,A2:A11) and the formula in cell B14 is =RSQ(B2:B11,A2:A11).

	A	B	C
1	Time (Sec)	Pages	
2	0.68	814	
3	2.72	145	
4	2.82	151	
5	1.67	566	
6	1.62	672	
7	1.35	719	
8	2.71	172	
9	1.27	789	
10	2.50	482	
11	2.57	447	
12			
13	Slope	-320	
14	R^2	0.86	
15			

Results

The slope (-320) has a negative relationship to time. As response times get longer, the page visits gets smaller. For every additional second of response time, the average number of pages visited decreases by 320.

The R squared value tells us that about 86% on the reduction in pages visited can be attributed to the increase in response time.

Just for fun, let's add a Chart. Select A1:B11, then insert a scatter chart. Add a trendline with equation and R^2.

The equation shows the slope as -319.76 (-320) and the R^2 as 0.8576 (86%). The y-intercept implies that 1132.4 pages would be visited if our response rate was zero, instantaneous. But that is not totally accurate.

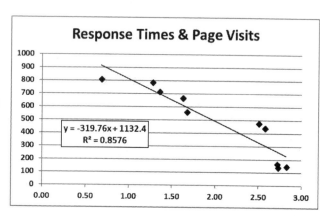

Response Times & Page Visits

$y = -319.76x + 1132.4$
$R^2 = 0.8576$

164

An important rule in regression analysis is that we can only use it to make predictions within the input range. Our response rates are approximately 0.50 to 3.00 seconds. We cannot make predictions outside that range.

We do need the y intercept, however, to make predictions within the valid range. For example, we could estimate page views if the response rate was 2.00 seconds as: $y = -319.76(2.00) + 1132.4 = 494.88$.

Scenario

If we could lower our average response rate by one seconds, how many more pages would be visited per hour and, more importantly, what would be the increase in sales?

Process

Our equation for response rate was $y = -320(x)$. If we are reducing the response rate by one second, the change in x is -1. Substituting -1 for x in our equation gives us $y = -320(-1) = 320$ page visits. Our equation for sales was $y = \$5.02(x)$. If page visits are 320, $y = \$5.02(320) = \$1,606$.

Results

We could use the $1,606 per hour increase in sales to cost justify a project to lower the average response time by one second.

Practice

We can cut out the middleman, page visits. You selected another 10 hours at random and calculated the average response time, in seconds, and the total sales during the hour.

What is the relationship between response time and sales?

	A	B	C
1	Time (Sec)	Sales	
2	1.03	$1,569	
3	0.51	$2,755	
4	2.95	$607	
5	1.18	$1,461	
6	2.10	$861	
7	1.27	$1,131	
8	2.07	$1,054	
9	2.83	$922	
10	0.52	$2,039	
11	0.98	$2,233	
12			

Results

Cell B13 is =SLOPE(B2:B11,A2:A11) and cell B14 is =RSQ(B2:B11,A2:A11).

It costs us $670 in sales per hour for every second of average response time. This is in line with what we would expect, given that sales are positively related to pages viewed, but pages viewed are negatively related to response time.

The relatively high R^2 value of 75% indicates that about 75% of the change in sales is caused by a change in average response time.

	A	B	C
1	Time (Sec)	Sales	
2	1.03	$1,569	
3	0.51	$2,755	
4	2.95	$607	
5	1.18	$1,461	
6	2.10	$861	
7	1.27	$1,131	
8	2.07	$1,054	
9	2.83	$922	
10	0.52	$2,039	
11	0.98	$2,233	
12			
13	Slope	-$670	
14	R^2	0.75	
15			

Practice

Insert a scatter chart with equation and R^2.

Results

In this scatter chart, response time, in seconds, is shown on the horizontal axis (the X axis) and sales are shown on the vertical axis (the Y axis). The trendline clearly shows that an increase in response time correlates to a

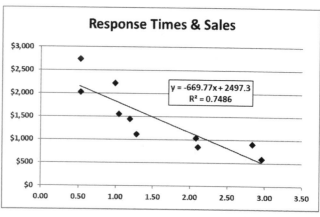

reduction in sales. For every one second increase in average response time, we lose about $670 every hour.

As in our previous example, we could use this to justify the expense of a project to reduce response time down to 0.50 seconds, but not lower.

166

Footnotes

(1) In computer configuration management, the old system is called the legacy system, whether it's being upgraded or replaced.

(2) We are using a sample size of ten ($n = 10$), but it really should be a lot larger. In statistics, a sample size of 30 or more is preferred. The larger the sample size, the more confidence we can have in our results. Regardless of sample size, it is important that our samples be randomly selected so they are representative of the entire population.

(3) The trendline follows the formula and is sometimes called a "least squares error" line. The distance of each data point from the line is called an "error." If all the errors were squared, then added together, they would result in some value. Of all possible linear trendline, this is the one with the least squared error; it is the best fit.

Filler

As director of production control for a manufacturing company, I had a problem. We needed to expedite jobs in the shop, but the output from the work centers was entered into the computer the following morning, which meant that the job locations were obsolete by noon, if not earlier.

We were using ASK MANMAN, a manufacturing management system developed in the late 1970's. The problem was that the system displayed the cost of each item, and senior management did not want cost information to be available to the heavily-unionized workforce.

So I took on the role of project sponsor, project manager, and chief programmer. I wrote a simple BASIC program to act as a user interface to MANMAN. Without a password, the user could not get past the interface. The interface displayed all the required information to indicate workorder status or completion, but none of the costing information.

I then purchased ten computers and had them installed throughout the workshop. With very little training, the work center operators could report completion of their workorders and we had real-time information regarding the progress and location of every workorder in the building.

Trend Analysis

Trend analysis uses a time series of historical data to predict future outcomes. In project management, we can use it mid-way through our project to predict if we will finish on time and in budget.

Discussion

When we discussed regression analysis we learned about the regression equation: $y = a + bx$ where x was the independent variable, y was the dependent variable (we suspect a portion of a change in y was dependent upon a change in x), b was the slope (which indicated the relationship between x and y, and a was the y-intercept (which we did not use). For trend analysis, we will begin with the regression equation, but will include the y-intercept, and we'll explore a couple more Excel functions.

Scenario

Your project is to upgrade the e-commerce web site for your company. We began by reviewing data from the legacy system. We found that sales increased as more pages were viewed, but that response time slows when a lot of customers visited the site at the same time. We need to increase the capacity of the system, but by how much? How many page visits should we expect in each of the next five years?

Process

We gathered total page visits for the last ten years, rounding to the nearest 1,000. Is the number of page visits increasing? Is there a trend? Can we extend this trend into the future?

The formula in cell B13 is =AVERAGE(B2:B11). The average number of page visits was 4,717,000, but looking at the data there certainly appears to be an increasing number of visits year after year.

The slope in cell B14, =SLOPE(B2:B11,A2:A11), tells us the annual visits are increasing by about

	A	B
1	Year	Visits (000)
2	2011	947
3	2012	1,606
4	2013	2,553
5	2014	3,493
6	2015	4,301
7	2016	5,192
8	2017	5,999
9	2018	6,890
10	2019	7,692
11	2020	8,496
12		
13	Average	4,717
14	Slope	852.3
15	Intercept	-1,709,776
16	R^2	0.9995
17		

852,300 every year, and the R^2 value of 0.9995 gives us a lot of confidence in our analysis. The formula in cell B16 is =RSQ(B2:B11,A2:A11).

We can use the Intercept function to determine the y-intercept. The syntax is =INTERCEPT(known y's, known x's). The formula in cell B15 is =INTERCEPT(B2:B11,A2:A11).

Now that we have both the slope and the y-intercept, we can use the regression equation $(y = a + bx)$ to estimate demand for the next five years.

We entered the formula =B$15+(B$14*A19) in cell B19 and then it was copied into cells B20:B23. Because we made rows 14 and 15 absolute (with the dollar sign), they did not change when we copied the formula, but because row 19 was a relative reference, it changed to 20, 21, 22 and 23.

	A	B
1	Year	Visits (000)
2	2011	947
3	2012	1,606
4	2013	2,553
5	2014	3,493
6	2015	4,301
7	2016	5,192
8	2017	5,999
9	2018	6,890
10	2019	7,692
11	2020	8,496
12		
13	Average	4,717
14	Slope	852.3
15	Intercept	-1,709,776
16	R^2	0.9995
17		
18	Year	Visits (000)
19	2021	9,405
20	2022	10,257
21	2023	11,109
22	2024	11,962
23	2025	12,814
24		

Discussion

We used the regression equation to estimate the future based on the past. The results were fine, but the process was a bit clumsy. First we had to determine and display the slope and the y-intercept, and then write a formula that included them. Now that we understand the process, we can bypass this middle step with the Forecast function.

Scenario

Organizational process assets and environmental factors are both a resource and a constraint to the project team. Let's suppose we have just presented our estimates of future web site page visits to our project sponsor. When questioned, we reply that we used the slope and the y-intercept to perform the calculations.

The sponsor says that organization policy is to use the forecast function. Are the results the same? We better check to be sure.

Process

Using the same historical data, we skip the slope, intercept, R^2 and average output and go right to our desired output: the future forecast.

The syntax is =FORECAST(x, known y's, known x's). Cell B14 is =FORECAST(A14,B$2:B$11,A$2:A$11), and this formula was copied into cells B15:B18.

Results

We obtained the same results as before, but in less time and with fewer steps; and with fewer human interactions, less opportunity for human errors.

	A	B
1	Year	Visits (000)
2	2011	947
3	2012	1,606
4	2013	2,553
5	2014	3,493
6	2015	4,301
7	2016	5,192
8	2017	5,999
9	2018	6,890
10	2019	7,692
11	2020	8,496
12		
13	Year	Visits (000)
14	2021	9,405
15	2022	10,257
16	2023	11,109
17	2024	11,962
18	2025	12,814

Discussion

Since we are talking about trend analysis, we should mention the Trend function in Excel. I consider this function optional because it is rather complicated and provides little added value for us. There are some operations in Excel that require an array formula, but forecasting a linear growth trend is not one of them. Someone once said that you cannot consider yourself an Excel power user unless you understand array formulas, so here's my two-page tribute to array formulas and the Trend function.[1]

The trend function is one of several array functions in Excel that use input from an array of cells and, if desired, can display output in a multi-cell array. If it helps, think of an array as a manual version of a pivot table.

	A	B
1	Year	Visits (000)
2	2011	947
3	2012	1,606
4	2013	2,553
5	2014	3,493
6	2015	4,301
7	2016	5,192
8	2017	5,999
9	2018	6,890
10	2019	7,692
11	2020	8,496
12		

Scenario

Use the Trend function to forecast web site page visits for the next five years.

170

Process

The syntax for the function is =TREND(known y's, known x's, new x's). Array functions are entered into Excel using a very specific, two-handed technique. Select the entire range B14:B18 and type the following: "=TREND(B2:B11,A2:A11,A14:A18)" and then, while holding down both the control (Ctrl) key and the shift key with your left hand, press the Enter key with your right hand. Is that crazy or what!

	A	B
1	Year	Visits (000)
2	2011	947
3	2012	1,606
4	2013	2,553
5	2014	3,493
6	2015	4,301
7	2016	5,192
8	2017	5,999
9	2018	6,890
10	2019	7,692
11	2020	8,496
12		
13	Year	Visits (000)
14	2021	9,405
15	2022	10,257
16	2023	11,109
17	2024	11,962
18	2025	12,814

Results

The results in cells B14:B18 are the same we obtained with the SLOPE and INTERCEPT functions and with the FORECAST function, but with the single formula in cells B14:B18 {=TREND(B2:B11,A2:A11,A14:A18)}.

Try this in Excel. It's not difficult once you get the hang of the Control + Shift + Enter technique. Select any cell in the B14:B18 range and you will see the above formula, brackets and all. Try to edit one cell in the range and you will get an error message saying you cannot change part of an array. You can, of course, delete it and start over if you need to change it.

Practice

While reviewing the legacy data, you decide to forecast future demand for some of your major product categories.

Use the SLOPE and INTERCEPT functions, the FORECAST function, or the TREND function to estimate demand for the next five years.

	A	B	C	D	E
1	Year	Books	Houseware	Electronics	Sports
2	2011	980	520	260	730
3	2012	1,030	580	340	820
4	2013	1,100	620	430	910
5	2014	1,140	650	500	920
6	2015	1,200	700	590	1,000
7	2016	1,240	760	650	1,100
8	2017	1,280	780	710	1,160
9	2018	1,340	800	780	1,240
10	2019	1,400	840	860	1,280
11	2020	1,470	860	920	1,340

Answer

Regardless of the method you used, you should get the results below.

	A	B	C	D	E
1	Year	Books	Houseware	Electronics	Sports
2	2011	980	520	260	730
3	2012	1,030	580	340	820
4	2013	1,100	620	430	910
5	2014	1,140	650	500	920
6	2015	1,200	700	590	1,000
7	2016	1,240	760	650	1,100
8	2017	1,280	780	710	1,160
9	2018	1,340	800	780	1,240
10	2019	1,400	840	860	1,280
11	2020	1,470	860	920	1,340
12					
13	Year	Books	Houseware	Electronics	Sports
14	2021	1,507	919	1,005	1,423
15	2022	1,559	956	1,078	1,490
16	2023	1,612	994	1,150	1,558
17	2024	1,664	1,032	1,223	1,626
18	2025	1,717	1,070	1,296	1,694
19					

Footnote

(1) This is the only array function we are going to discuss, but there are many more in Excel. In the Function Wizard (*fx*) dialog box, enter "array" in the search function box and click Go. The functions listed may all be entered as array functions, using the control + shift + enter technique. You too can impress your coworkers as an Excel power user.

Probability

Much of project management involves planning for the future; but what will the future hold? If we don't know the future, how can we plan for it? Risk management, the topic after this, relies heavily on the rules of probability, so let's briefly discuss them before we move on.

- The probability of an event happening is expressed as a value between 0 and 1. If an event will never happen, it has a probability of 0. If an event will always happen, it has a probability of 1. For example, the probability of our supplies being delivered next week is 0.75 based on our experience with this particular supplier.

- The probability of an event not occurring is 1 minus the probability of the event occurring. The probability of our supplies not being delivered next week is 1.00 – 0.75 = 0.25, or 25%.

- The probability of the set of all possible outcomes is 1. Our supplies will either be delivered next week or they won't: 0.75 + 0.25 = 1.00.

- If we know our supplies will be delivered on one of our five workdays next week, the probability our supplies being delivered on Tuesday is 1/5 or 0.20. The probability of the supplies being delivered in the morning of any day is 0.50 or 50%, since each day is ½ morning and ½ afternoon.

- For two independent events, the probability of both events occurring is the probability of one multiplied by the probability of the other. The probability of our supplies being delivered Tuesday morning is the probability of a Tuesday delivery multiplied by the probability of a morning delivery is 0.20 × 0.50 = 0.10.

- The probability of two mutually exclusive (one or the other, but not both) events is the probability of one plus the other. The probability of a Tuesday or Wednesday delivery is 0.20 + 0.20 = 0.40.

- If two events are not mutually exclusive (one or the other, or both), the probability of one or the other is the probability of one plus the probability of the other, minus the probability of both. The probability of our supplies being delivered on Tuesday or in any morning is 0.20 + 0.50 – 0.10 = 0.60. Tuesday morning is included in both sets, so we need to subtract it once from the total to avoid counting it twice.

- Conditional probability is when the probability of one event is influenced by another event. The probability of a morning delivery is 0.50, and the probability that Maria is the driver is 0.25, but, we have observed, the probability of a morning delivery and Maria is the driver is 0.20. The probability of a morning delivery given that Maria is driving is therefore 0.20/0.25 = 0.80. Maria has a positive influence on morning deliveries, increasing the probability from 0.50 to 0.80.

Scenario

Our supplies have finally arrived, 240 boxes in all and 60 of them contain bolts. What is the probability that a box picked at random contains bolts?

Results

The probability that a box picked at random contains bolts is 60/240 = 0.25. There is a 25% chance that a box picked at random contains bolts.

Scenario

Thirty-six of the 240 boxes contain metric nuts or metric bolts. What is the probability that a box picked at random contains metric nuts or bolts.

Results

The probability that a box picked at random contains metric nuts or metric bolts is 36/240 = 0.15, or 15%.

Scenario

What is the probability that a box picked at random contains metric bolts? Note that we have two events here, bolts and metric.

Results

The probability that a box picked at random contains bolts is 0.25 and the probability of a box picked at random contains either metric nuts or metric bolts is 0.15, so the probability of a box picked at random contains metric bolts is $0.25 \times 0.15 = 0.0375$ or 3.75%.

Practice

1. Of the 240 boxes, 72 contain nails. What is the probability that a box picked at random contains nails?

2. What is the probability that a box picked at random does not contain nails?

3. Of the 240 boxes, 36 contain washers. What is the probability that a box picked at random contains washers?

4. What is the probability that a box picked at random does not contain washers?

5. What is the probability that a box picked at random contains nails or washers?

6. There is a 0.25 probability that a box picked at random contains nuts, and there is also a 0.25 probability that a box picked at random contains bolts. What is the probability that of two boxes picked at random, one contains nuts and the other contains bolts?

7. The probability of a morning delivery is 0.50, and the probability that Tony is the driver is 0.25. We have observed that the probability of a morning delivery driven by Tony is only 0.10. What is the probability of a morning delivery given that Tony is the driver?

Answers

1. The probability that a box picked at random contains nails is 72/240 = 0.30, or 30%.

2. The probability that a box picked at random does not contain nails is 1 – 0.30 = 0.70, or 70%.

3. The probability that a box picked at random contains washers is 36/240 = 0.15, or 15%.

4. The probability that a box picked at random does not contain washers is 1 – 0.15 = 0.85, or 85%.

5. The probability that a box picked at random contains nails or washers is 0.30 + 0.15 = 0.45, or 45%.

6. The probability that of two boxes picked at random, one contains nuts and the other contains bolts? is 0.25 X 0.25 = 0.0625.

7. The probability of a morning delivery given that Tony is the driver is 0.10/0.25 = 0.40. Tony has a negative influence on morning deliveries, decreasing their probability from 0.50 to 0.40.

   One final question, what's the probability that Tony stops off for a long breakfast when should be making his morning deliveries?

Filler

A physics professor, a chemistry professor, and a statistics professor are called into the deans' office. But as soon as they are seated, the dean looks down, and then jumps up and runs out of the office. Upon investigation, the professors find a fire in the waste basket behind the deans' desk.

The physics professor says it is a physical reaction and they can put it out by removing the fuel. The chemistry professor says no, it is an oxidation reaction and they need to eliminate the source of oxygen. As they are arguing, they look up and see the statistics professor running around the office starting more fires. What are you doing! They yell in unison.

The statistics professor replies: "I'm trying to get a larger sample size."

Project Risk Management

Risks are uncertain events that, if they occur, have a positive or negative impact on our project. When we discussed probability we saw that the assignment of a delivery driver, an uncertain event, could have a positive or negative influence on the timely delivery of our much-needed supplies.

Discussion

Projects do not take place in a vacuum. There is a significant overlap between project risks and organizational risks. The first step in project risk management is to recognize it as a subset of organizational risk management, and to coordinate risk management between the two.

Strategic planning for an organization frequently includes a SWOT analysis; identification of internal Strengths and Weaknesses, and external Opportunities and Threats.

Opportunities are positive risks and threats are negative risks. We want to maximize the probability of opportunities, and be prepared to exploit them when they occur. Conversely, we want to minimize the probability of threats, and be prepared to deal with them when they do occur.

We used historical information and expert opinions to identify all potential risks and recorded them in the risk register. The opportunities and threats identified in the SWOT analysis should be included in our list of identified risks. These are called the "known unknowns" because we know of them, but we do not know if they will materialize. Risks that we have not identified are called the "unknown unknowns." A negative risk that has occurred is often called an issue, and documented in the issues log, whereas a positive risk that has happened might be considered a windfall. They should also be entered in the issues log to be sure we do not miss the opportunity to exploit them.

Strategies for negative risks include avoidance, transfer, mitigate, and accept. Avoidance might involve changes to the project plan, such as not breaking ground until after the rainy season. Transferring the risk might involve purchasing insurance or adding performance provisions to a procurement contract.

Mitigating a risk involves actions to lower the probability of occurrence and/or lower the impact if the risk does occur. Anti-virus software and automatic data backup are examples of risk mitigation. Acceptance of the risk happens when the team is unable to avoid, transfer, or mitigate the risk. An example is to establish a contingency reserve of time or money to be used if the risk occurs. Purchasing a first aid kit for the project worksite is another example of risk acceptance.

Strategies for positive risks include exploit, enhance, share, and accept. Exploiting a risk could involve identifying a cause and effect relationship and devoting resources to enhance the cause, to improve the likelihood of the risk occurring. Enhancing the risk is to take full advantage of an opportunity if it happens. An example would be a purchasing agent on the project team monitoring the daily market for a commodity and placing a purchase order when the price appears to have bottomed out rather than waiting to purchase the commodity when the work schedule dictates. Sharing the risk involves transferring some of the benefit to a third party. An example would be a purchase agreement with a vendor that encouraged them to monitor the daily commodity price and share any savings with us. Accepting a positive risk is the only option when the project team is unable to do anything to influence or exploit it.

Acceptance may be the best option when a cost-benefit analysis indicates that the cost to avoid, transfer, mitigate, exploit, or enhance the risk is greater than the negative or positive impact of the risk.

Risk appetite is the amount of risk an organization will accept in return for the potential reward. This is different for each organization and will probably be different for any given organization over time. If the last project was very successful, the organization may be eager to try a high risk, high reward project. But if the last project was marginal or failed, only low risk projects might be considered in the near future.

Whatever the situation, it is the organization that decides how much risk it can accept. Therefore, the project risk management plan must fall within the guidelines of the organizational risk management plan.

A good start would be to develop a risk probability and impact matrix that meets organizational guidelines, strategy, and philosophy.

Risk Probability and Impact Matrix

Scenario

Meeting with your project sponsor or project management office, you learn that the organization has set standard definitions for risk probability and risk impact. This allows risks to be compared using either qualitative or quantitative evaluations.

Risk probabilities less than 20% are very unlikely, 20% to 40% are unlikely, 40% to 60% are moderate, 60% to 80% are likely, and over 80% are very likely.

Risk impacts less than $200,000 are very low, $200,000 to $400,000 are low, $400,000 to $600,000 are moderate, $600,000 to $800,000 are high, $800,000 to $1,000,000 are very high, and impacts over $1,000,000 are extreme.

The same rules apply to both positive and negative risks. Construct a Risk Probability and Impact Matrix for the organization.

Results

You construct your matrix using, for example, increments from 0.10 for very low impact and very unlikely risks to 1.00 for extreme impact and very likely risks, showing positive and negative values for each category.
Scenario

		Impact				
	Very Low <$200 K	Low $200 - $400 K	Moderate $400 - $600 K	High $600 - $800 K	Very High $800 K - $1 M	Extreme >$1 M
Very Unlikely < 20%	0.10 (0.10)	0.20 (0.20)	0.30 (0.30)	0.40 (0.40)	0.50 (0.50)	0.60 (0.60)
Unlikely 20% - 40%	0.20 (0.20)	0.30 (0.30)	0.40 (0.40)	0.50 (0.50)	0.60 (0.60)	0.70 (0.70)
Moderate 40% - 60%	0.30 (0.30)	0.40 (0.40)	0.50 (0.50)	0.60 (0.60)	0.70 (0.70)	0.80 (0.80)
Likely 60% - 80%	0.40 (0.40)	0.50 (0.50)	0.60 (0.60)	0.70 (0.70)	0.80 (0.80)	0.90 (0.90)
Very Likely > 80%	0.50 (0.50)	0.60 (0.60)	0.70 (0.70)	0.80 (0.80)	0.90 (0.90)	1.00 (1.00)

Probability (row axis label)

Two competing projects have been proposed and their project managers have identified the risks. Prioritize the risks for each project. Which project has the greater negative risk?

Project A	Probability	Impact	Pos/Neg
Risk A1	Likely	Very low	Negative
Risk A2	Very unlikely	Moderate	Positive
Risk A3	Likely	Low	Positive
Risk A4	Unlikely	Very low	Negative
Risk A5	Very likely	High	Negative
Risk A6	Likely	Moderate	Positive
Risk A7	Moderate	Very high	Positive
Risk A8	Likely	Extreme	Negative

Project B	Probability	Impact	Pos/Neg
Risk B1	25%	$300,000	Negative
Risk B2	90%	$1,200,000	Negative
Risk B3	75%	$750,000	Positive
Risk B4	10%	$1,500,000	Positive
Risk B5	50%	$350,000	Negative
Risk B6	50%	$500,000	Positive

Results

Don't panic. This is not a challenging as it appears, even though we have qualitative estimates from Project A and quantitative estimates from Project B.

All we need to do is look up each risk in our Risk Probability and Impact Matrix and record the positive or negative score.

We then prioritize the risks for each project in descending absolute order, ignoring their positive or negative signs. Priority 1 is our most important risk.

Finally we total the risk signed scores, not their absolute values, to get the

Project A	Probability	Impact	Pos/Neg	Score	Priority
Risk A1	Likely	Very low	Negative	-0.40	6
Risk A2	Very unlikely	Moderate	Positive	0.30	7
Risk A3	Likely	Low	Positive	0.50	5
Risk A4	Unlikely	Very low	Negative	-0.20	8
Risk A5	Very likely	High	Negative	-0.80	2
Risk A6	Likely	Moderate	Positive	0.60	4
Risk A7	Moderate	Very high	Positive	0.70	3
Risk A8	Likely	Extreme	Negative	-0.90	1
Known project risk				-0.20	

Project B	Probability	Impact	Pos/Neg	Score	Priority
Risk B1	25%	$300,000	Negative	-0.30	6
Risk B2	90%	$1,200,000	Negative	-1.00	1
Risk B3	75%	$750,000	Positive	0.70	2
Risk B4	10%	$1,500,000	Positive	0.60	3
Risk B5	50%	$350,000	Negative	-0.40	5
Risk B6	50%	$500,000	Positive	0.50	4
Known project risk				0.10	

relative risk for each project. In our example, Project A has a negative score of -0.20, but Project B had a positive score of 0.10. All else being equal, we would want to go with Project B.

<u>Discussion</u>

We prioritized the risks by absolute value, assuming that negative and positive risks with the same score are equal. That is your call. If the organization has a very low risk tolerance, we might want to prioritize negative risks before positive risks.

Actually, risk prioritization is not that critical. You will have assigned risk owners to each identified risk, with the responsibility to develop an appropriate risk mitigation plan and monitor the risk during project execution. To each risk owner, their assigned risk is priority number one. It's only at the project manager level and above that people may need to separate the "vital few from the trivial many" (Vilfredo Pareto, 1848-1923.)

Tornado Diagram

Another way to visually prioritize your risk management activities is with a tornado diagram. It's also a good way to explain the risks to various stakeholders; pictures rather than words and numbers.

	A	B
1	Risk	Score
2	Risk A4	-0.20
3	Risk A2	0.30
4	Risk A1	-0.40
5	Risk A3	0.50
6	Risk A6	0.60
7	Risk A7	0.70
8	Risk A5	-0.80
9	Risk A8	-0.90

 <u>Scenario</u>

Create a tornado diagram for the risks in Project A.

<u>Process</u>

We begin with a table of risks, sorted in ascending order by their absolute value. Select the table and insert a horizontal bar chart. It looks like a tornado, except that our concern is at the top, not the bottom.

The tornado diagram displays prioritized risks, based on their score in the Risk Probability Impact Matrix. Negative risks are on the left and positive risks are on the right, high priority risks are at the top and low priority risks are at the bottom.

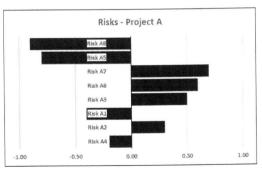

Risks - Project A

Expected Monetary Value of Risks

Discussion

A third way to prioritize and compare risks is with Expected Monetary Value, EMV; not to be confused with Earned Value Management, EVM.

Risk probability and impact are difficult to estimate, so our Risk Probability and Impact Matrix may have been as precise as we needed. If, on the other hand, we can estimate probabilities and impacts more accurately, it would be a shame to not take advantage of the improved quality of our information.[1] Expected Monetary Value has many uses in project management, and comparing risks is one of them.

Scenario

We compared Project A and Project B, and selected Project B. Now a third project, Project C, has been suggested. We decide to compare Project B and C using Expected Monetary Value.

Process

The process is super simple. Rather than looking up scores in a matrix, we calculate values by multiplying the probability times the impact, expressed in dollars. We will further simplify things by listing negative impacts as negative dollar amounts, thus avoiding the positive/negative descriptions.

Project B	Probability	Impact	EMV	Priority
Risk B1	25%	-$300,000	-$75,000	6
Risk B2	90%	-$1,200,000	-$1,080,000	1
Risk B3	75%	$750,000	$562,500	2
Risk B4	10%	$1,500,000	$150,000	5
Risk B5	50%	-$350,000	-$175,000	4
Risk B6	50%	$500,000	$250,000	3
Expected Monitory Value:			-$367,500	

Project C	Probability	Impact	EMV	Priority
Risk C1	75%	-$1,250,000	-$937,500	1
Risk C2	95%	$500,000	$475,000	2
Risk C3	65%	$340,000	$221,000	5
Risk C4	15%	-$180,000	-$27,000	7
Risk C5	30%	-$1,100,000	-$330,000	4
Risk C6	10%	$900,000	$90,000	6
Risk C7	50%	$700,000	$350,000	3
Expected Monitory Value:			-$158,500	

Results

First, please note that our priority sequence for Project B changed for risks B4, B5 and B6. That was due to using the actual probability and impact estimates rather than "rounding" them into the scores in our Risk Probability and Impact Matrix.

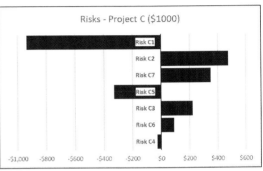

Project B has an expected risk monetary value of negative $367,500 while Project C has an expected risk monetary value of only negative $158,500. All else being equal, we would prefer Project C over Project B. A tornado diagram for Project C is included for your viewing pleasure.

Three-Point Risk Estimating

Three's the charm. We used three-point estimating to improve our cost estimates and our time estimates. We will now use it, for the third and last time, to improve our risk estimates.

Scenario

You asked the risk owner for the estimated probability and impact, but you specified you wanted three estimates for each, optimistic, most likely, and pessimistic. For a negative risk, low probabilities and low impacts are optimistic estimates. For a positive risk, low probabilities and low impacts would be pessimistic estimates.

Your risk owner provided an optimistic probability of 25%, a most likely probability of 40%, and a pessimistic probability of 70%. They also gave you an optimistic impact cost of $240,000, a most likely of $450,000, and a pessimistic of $750,000. This is obviously a negative risk.

Using both a triangular distribution and a beta distribution, what is the expected probability and impact for this risk?

Results

Triangular distribution:

$$Probability = \frac{0.25 + 0.40 + .70}{3} = 0.45$$

$$Impact = \frac{240,000 + 450,000 + 750,000}{3} = 480,000$$

Beta distribution:

$$Probability = \frac{0.25 + 4(0.40) + .70}{6} = 0.425$$

$$Impact = \frac{240,000 + 4(450,000) + 750,000}{6} = 465,000$$

Discussion

Should we use the triangular distribution or the beta distribution?

First, we should follow organizational guidelines. If the decision is ours, then whichever we choose, we should discuss the logic of our decision in our risk management plan.

Generally the beta distribution tends to be more accurate but, without any guidance from the project sponsor, the project management office, or the lessons learned repository, it's our call. As stated earlier, it's a matter of how confident we are that the most likely is, in fact, more likely than any other value between the optimistic and pessimistic estimates. The more confidence we have in the most likely estimate, the more we are inclined to use a beta distribution.

Scenario

You are discussing risk management issues with your project sponsor during your weekly status update meeting. You begin with a brief review of three-point estimating techniques and your sponsor approves your suggestion to use beta distributions for risk analysis. Next you present and discuss your Risk Probability and Impact Matrix, your sensitivity analysis with your tornado diagram, and your expected monetary value, EMV, for the total project risk.

The sponsor is impressed with your analysis, but has some concerns as to how you intend to implement actions to avoid, transfer, or mitigate the negative risks and exploit, enhance, or share the positive risks.

Before you can discuss that, you have a few questions about the organization's risk appetite, risk tolerance, and risk threshold. You explain the three:

Risk appetite is a qualitative statement of how much uncertainty the organization is willing to accept in anticipation of a positive benefit. A very profitable organization, with lots of financial reserves, will probably have a larger risk appetite than an organization without deep pockets.

Risk tolerance is a quantitative statement. For example, an organization might be willing and able to accept a specific cost overrun of X dollars or schedule delay of Y weeks, as long as the scope is intact.

Risk threshold is a specific limit to what the organization can accept. The organization, for example, might not have the resources to deal with a million dollar cost overrun, and would have to cancel the project if such as risk could not be avoided, transferred, or mitigated.

You and your sponsor agree that the organization has a moderate risk appetite; and has the resources to tolerate the net (EMV) project risk of $68,500. Your sponsor cautions, however, that a total cost overrun greater than $100,000 would be over their threshold and would be unacceptable.

Discussion

You discuss each of your five risks. Some can be best managed with additional cash, while others best managed with additional time.

There are two places for additional cash: contingency reserves and managerial reserves. Contingency reserves are included in the cost baseline and might be controlled by the project manager. They are the "known unknowns" from the risk register and are frequently related to a specific time and activity. If the risk materializes, the funds are available from the contingency reserve to mitigate or exploit the risk. If the risk does not materialize, the funds usually revert back to the organization.

A managerial reserve is for the "unknown unknowns," the unexpected things that may develop during the execution of the project. Managerial reserves are not in the cost baseline and are not controlled by the project manager. In our story, we will say that the sponsor includes $31,500 (the threshold of $100,000 less the net project risk of $68,500) in the project budget as managerial reserve, but not in the project cost baseline.

The sponsor might include a "managerial time reserve" by adding some time to the completion date shown in the project schedule. For example, the project schedule may indicate the project will be completed on April 10th, but the sponsor may use April 30th for planning purposes outside of the project.

There are two places to include additional risk-management time in the project schedule baseline, both from the critical chain method, a technique developed by Eliyahu Goldratt, and both under the control of the project manager. Think of the project as a critical path with several non-critical paths feeding into it. Additional time, known as a feeding buffer, can be scheduled at the end of each non-critical path where it feeds into the critical path, so that an unexpected delay on a non-critical path does not delay the subsequent activities on the critical path. The other location for additional time is at the end of the critical path, just before the completion date for the project and is known as a project buffer.

Practice

You have identified four risks in your project, one positive (D3) and three negative (D1, D2 and D4).

	Probability Pessimistic	Most likely	Optimistic
Risk D1	0.70	0.30	0.20
Risk D2	0.80	0.40	0.30
Risk D3	0.20	0.60	0.70
Risk D4	0.90	0.80	0.40

Use beta distribution to determine the expected probabilities and impact for each risk.

Impact	Pessimistic	Most likely	Optimistic
Risk D1	-$500	-$360	-$100
Risk D2	-$830	-$700	-$660
Risk D3	$200	$300	$700
Risk D4	-$700	-$660	-$500

Calculate the Expected Monetary Value for each risk. What is the total Expected Monetary Value for the project?

Answer

	Probability Pessimistic	Most likely	Optimistic	Expected
Risk D1	0.70	0.30	0.20	0.35
Risk D2	0.80	0.40	0.30	0.45
Risk D3	0.20	0.60	0.70	0.55
Risk D4	0.90	0.80	0.40	0.75

Impact	Pessimistic	Most likely	Optimistic	Expected
Risk D1	-$500	-$360	-$100	-$340
Risk D2	-$830	-$700	-$660	-$715
Risk D3	$200	$300	$700	$350
Risk D4	-$700	-$660	-$500	-$640

	Probability	Impact	EMV
Risk D1	0.35	-$340.00	-$119.00
Risk D2	0.45	-$715.00	-$321.75
Risk D3	0.55	$350.00	$192.50
Risk D4	0.75	-$640.00	-$480.00
Total			-$728.25

(1) Multiplying one estimate (probability) times another estimate (impact) only worsens our confidence level.

My general formula is:

Wild Guess X Wild Guess = Wild Ass Guess

Here's a definition I found online at the Urban Dictionary:

> "A Wild Ass Guess (WAG) is an estimate that is based upon experience, similarity and 'windage' and does not have immediately verifiable data that could be used to substantiate the estimate."

Their example:

> "Management requests a rough order of magnitude (ROM) cost estimate, and there isn't time to do all of the necessary research, so you offer a WAG (wild ass guess) estimate scaled off of a previous project that you consider to have a similar complexity."

This reference to "scaled off of a previous project" sounds a lot like a parametric estimate to me.

While browsing online, I also found SWAG on Wikipedia:

> "Scientific wild-ass guess (SWAG) is an American English slang term meaning a rough estimate made by an expert in the field, based on experience and intuition. It is similar to the slang word guesstimate, a portmanteau of guess and estimate."

Filler:

During World War II there was a critical shortage of artillery firing tables, which were calculated by hand by people called computers. The Electronic Numerical Integrator and Computer, ENIAC, was developed by the U.S. Army to calculate the firing table data. The ENIAC was the first multi-purpose programmable computer. The total cost was about $487,000, equivalent to about $7,000,000 today. It began work on December 10, 1945, about three months after the end of the war.

Make or Buy Analysis

The make or buy decision is one of the classics in decision science, and is encountered in both project management and operations management.

Scenario

One of the deliverables for your project is 100 steel worktables. You could make them with some additional resources from the sponsoring organization, or you could buy them from Standard Fixtures, Inc. You need all 100 in month 12. You can make 10 per month for 10 months, or take delivery of all 100 in month 12. Should you make them yourself, or buy them readymade?

Process

This is not complicated math; we will total the costs for each option and choose the one with the lowest cost. For our analysis, costs will be assigned to things like risk, quality, resource availability, workforce skills, and intellectual property. The hard part is identifying all the relevant costs, so for this topic, we will dispense with our usual math and formulas, and use this opportunity to discuss the various cost categories found in project management.

The future costs will need to be converted to present values; see the topic Net Present Value with Irregular Periods for more information on that. Non-financial considerations such as risk or quality should also be converted to present value dollars. See the Risk Management topic for a description of risk probability, and see the Quality Management topic for a discussion of the cost of quality.

We should not limit our consideration of costs to only items within the project budget. For example, assume the organizational procurement and accounts payable departments will handle the purchase order and invoice payment functions for us, and the project will probably not be charged directly for these services. We should still consider the anticipated number of purchase orders and invoices in our decision. Just because a cost is not in our project budget does not mean it is not a cost to our organization.

Along that same line, we may legitimately disregard some costs that are in the project budget. For example, if we make the worktables we will need floor space in the factory. Assume we would need 10% of the factory floorspace to make the tables. It would be reasonable to charge the project budget with 10% of the factory overhead. But if we decide to buy the tables, we will not be saving the organization any money, so we should not include the overhead burden in our make or buy decision.

Discussion

The costs that can impact a project are countless. To simplify our discussion we will put them in categories. Some costs may be in multiple categories, but that should not be a problem as our purpose is to identify areas to look into.

Direct costs are directly related to the activity. The cost of labor and materials, if we make the worktables; or the purchase price, if we buy the worktables, is direct. Direct costs do not have to be allocated.

Indirect costs cannot be traced directly to the activity. If we use the organizations' receiving department to receive and inspect our raw material and/or finished goods, then we should consider a portion of the cost of operating that department, perhaps allocated on a per-purchase order or per-invoice amount basis.

Fixed costs do not change as the quantity of an item changes. The cost to design the worktables is the same whether we make or buy one, a hundred, or a thousand.

Variable costs change with the quantity. The cost of labor and materials is a function of the quantity we make. The cost to purchase readymade worktables is a function of the quantity we buy. Freight for materials or finished goods is a variable cost.

Inventory holding cost is a variable function of cost, time, and the prevailing interest rate. If we make 10 worktables in month 3, but do not need them until month 12, we must carry them in inventory for 9 months, and must pay interest on the money used to produce them and safely store them. If, on the other hand, all 100 arrive in month 12, we pay the invoice at about the same time that the project "consumes" them.

190

Setup is the cost of the time and labor required to make the production area and equipment ready to begin producing our worktables. If we have a dedicated area in a corner of the main factory we may encounter setup costs only once. If, on the other hand, we convert a factory area to our needs every evening when the regular crew goes home, and then reconfigure it back to the normal layout at the end of our shift, we could encounter two setup costs every day. While labor costs are important, typically the largest setup cost is that the equipment is not available for use during the setup. Minimizing setup cost is a goal of every manufacturing manager in the world.

Ordering cost is the procurement version of setup cost. It is the total cost to place a purchase order, receive the goods, and pay the invoice. If we order 100 worktables from Standard Fixtures for a single delivery, we encounter one ordering cost. If we purchase ten a month for ten months, with ten receipts and ten payments, we have ten ordering costs.

Quality costs are discussed in greater detail in the Quality topic. For now, let's discuss two of them, inspection and prevention. If we purchase the worktables, we may need to inspect each upon receipt, a 100% inspection, or we could inspect a random sample. If we build the worktables, we could also inspect each one after it has been built, but it would be much more cost efficient to design a production process that prevents defects. The moral of this story is that it is usually cheaper to design a system that prevents errors before they occur than to inspect everything we build, and then rework or replace any defective units discovered in the inspection. This is sometimes called "quality at the source" and involves worker empowerment (again, see the Quality topic for more on this) and is very much in line with contemporary project management best practices.

Known risks must be converted to monetary values for inclusion in our make or buy analysis. We discussed this in the Risk Management topic, but for now let's consider one risk. Suppose we decide to buy the worktables and for some unforeseen reason (fire, earthquake, flood, tornado, disgruntled former employee, whatever) our vendor, Standard Fixtures, fails to deliver them on time. If we consider the cost to recover from this risk to be $100,000 and the probability of the risk actually occurring to be 5%, then we could add the cost of $5,000 ($100,000 X 0.05 = $5,000) to the Buy side of our make or buy analysis.

Sunk costs are irreversible costs associated with a make or buy decision, and many other project management decisions. Earlier we talked about the cost to design the worktables. Let's assume it cost $500 to come up with a set of specifications that we gave to vendors as part of our request for quotation (RFQ). We then invested an additional $1000 to convert the specifications into detailed manufacturing plans and drawings. So we have invented $500 in the Buy side of the equation and a total of $1500 in the Make side of the equation. So what? That money has been spent. We should not consider it in our make or buy decision. If we had held off with the manufacturing plans and drawings until after the make or buy decision, we could have included $1000 in the Make side of the equation, but we didn't, so forget it. To mix my metaphors, that ship has sunk.

If we make the worktables, we may need a specialized piece of equipment such as a sheet metal bender. This may be a very common item for companies like Standard Fixtures, but our organization does not have one and has no need for one when our project is complete, so for us, a sheet metal bender is specialized equipment and the entire cost, less any salvage value, should be charged to the project if we decide to make the tables.

This introduces another decision, should we buy one or rent specialized equipment? Assuming we have an option to rent one, we need to compare the total costs of buying to renting.

Buying costs might include the purchase price, delivery, installation, setup, training, and maintenance. If we expect to dispose of the machine at the conclusion of the project, the estimated salvage value and the potential resale market are also considerations.

If we rent the machine, delivery, setup, training, and removal will probably be included in the rental fee. Maintenance will probably still be our responsibility, but the uncertainty of the resale market is removed.

Renting or buying the equipment, and indeed, making or buying the worktables, may have depreciation or tax implication for the organization. If not clearly stated in the project charter, we will want to check with the project sponsor or possibly the organization accounting department regarding a preference to make or buy or rent.

Quantity flexibility is a valid consideration. As the project progresses, it may become apparent that one hundred workbenches is too few, or too many. If we are building them, we could continue building more, or we could halt production early. Do we have the same options if we purchase them? What would be the cost to change our contract with the vendor?

Design flexibility is also a consideration. If we make the worktables, we can test the first few units and modify the design for future units to meet unanticipated requirements or opportunities, a process called concurrent engineering. If we are buying a stock item, we could purchase one for testing and evaluation, but if we are purchasing custom-built units, we may not have the opportunity to make changes once the order is placed.

Finally, suppose some unique features in the worktables will enable the organization to produce their products at lower cost, or higher quality. This would give the organization a strategic competitive advantage. To sustain this advantage, we would want to make the worktables ourselves and not share the design with anyone, especially a vendor who could produce and sell similar worktables to our competitors.

Results

To summarize, make or buy decisions usually involves identifying all relevant issues, converting qualitative or subjective issues into costs, and using the total cost for each option, make or buy, to determine our best choice.

Discussion

If we have difficulty with subjective issues, we could use a factor weighted analysis to assign weights to different factors. Some strategic issues, such as the proprietary design of our worktables, may be so important to us, yet so difficult to quantify, that a factor weighted analysis may be preferable to a pure mathematical comparison of total costs.

Quality Management Tools

Many of our current quality management tools come from Japan. How they got there is a fascinating story, but more appropriate as a footnote than here in the main body of this book.[1]

Discussion

Project managers are concerned with the quality of the project management process and the quality of the project deliverables. We will discuss several common quality tools that may be used in either situation. The tools are cause and effect diagrams, flowcharts, storyboards, check sheets, scatter charts, histograms, Pareto diagrams, and control charts.

Scenario

You have called a meeting to discuss motor failure due to overheating in the prototypes you are building. Everyone has ideas; how do you organize them? How do you prioritize them? How do you ensure you have not left out something important? How will you know when you have found the cause of the problem and not just another symptom of an underlying and as yet undetected root cause?

Cause and Effect Diagrams

A cause and effect diagram, sometimes called a fishbone diagram or an Ishikawa diagram, is a good starting point. Take off your "boss" hat and put on your "facilitator" hat. Set up a large white board in your meeting room. Write the problem, the effect, on one side of the whiteboard and circle it. The circle will be the head of your fish. Then draw the spine of the fish as a single line from the circle to the other side of the board.

Next, you ask for major categories that could lead to the overheating problem. In the example on the next page, the motor, other components, the airflow, the case, the machine operator, the materials used, the load on the motor, and the environment were suggested as categories worthy of investigation; as potential sources of the cause of the overheating problem.

After the group agrees that all potential categories are on the board, ask them to suggest individual areas to investigate within each category. For example the case or body of the prototype that the motor sits in could be causing the overheating. Possibly it is the type of case, or the size of the grills (holes that allow air in and out of the case), if grills are located on the bottom of the case, the height of the legs could be an issue. Insulation might also be a factor; too much, too little, wrong type, whatever.

This is a brainstorming session. All ideas are placed on the board without challenge, although discussion is allowed as to where to place them. The process continues until the group agrees that all possible causes of the problem have been listed. The name of the person suggesting each idea is not recorded. All ideas go up on the board without review or challenge. As facilitator, your objective is to get all of the ideas written on the board, and that will require team leadership skills. Be sure everyone has a chance to talk.

Results

The completed cause and effect (fishbone) diagram is displayed below.

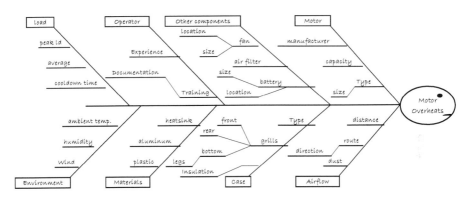

Your next step is to assign responsibility for investigating each of the potential causes to the appropriate individuals. You ask for time estimates and schedule a meeting to discuss the findings and plan the next step.

Discussion

Note the informal nature of the process. The important thing is to get all possible ideas about the causes of the problem up on the board. Starting with major categories will help the participants identify all potential problem areas within each category. All participants will be looking for all possible causes in all categories. Sometimes the "local expert" may be too close to the problem to see it, but an "outsider" may offer a different, and enlightening, perspective.

Don't allow the group to stop and discuss the merits of the suggestions until you are done. Criticizing ideas as they are suggested is a sure way to stiffly future suggestions.

A cause and effect diagram is part of a root cause analysis. The idea is to track each cause of the problem back to its "root cause." Fixing the root cause will fix all of the subsequent causes as well. Failure to identify the root cause of the problem will waste resources and delay the ultimate solution.

For example, the motor may have been overheating due to the amount and direction of the airflow, which was caused because not enough hot air was allowed to escape the case via the bottom grill, because the legs on the case were too short. Replacing them with longer legs solved the root cause of the problem. Adding fans, cleaning filters, and enlarging the intake grill or the exit grill will not solve the root problem.

Discussion

Using a cause and effect diagram in a root cause analysis is an example of a quality technique known as "5 Whys" (developed by Sakichi Toyoda for Toyota) or "3 Whys" or "7 Whys" proposed by other quality gurus. Regardless of the name or number, the idea is to keep digging until you find the root cause of the problem.

Scenario

Your project is to create the e-commerce software for Captain Hook, an online retailer of fishing gear. To better understand the various activities, and the relationships between the activities, you decide to a create flowcharts for each module, and you select the checkout module as a relatively simple place to start. Activities will include displaying the content of the creel (fishing basket, shopping cart) allowing the customer to remove items, update the ship-to address, update their billing information, complete the sale, or continue shopping.

Flowcharts

A flowchart is a diagram of an existing or a proposed process.[2] Activities are depicted as various shapes and their relation, or sequence, is shown with arrows. Some common activity shapes are:

Ovals are used as terminals and frequently include the word "start" or "end."

Circles may be used to connect multi-page flowcharts.

Rectangles represent processes.

Diamonds are used for decisions, with one input arrow and two or three output arrows.

Parallelograms are used to indicate input or output of data.

Data is in storage.

Data is displayed to the user.

Data is available for printing.

Plastic templates are available for hand-drawn flowcharts. For computer generated reports, both Microsoft Word and Excel include these and more flowchart shapes. Go to Insert > Shapes and scroll down to the flowchart shapes, which are labeled with their usage. The example on the next page was created with shapes in MS Word.

Results

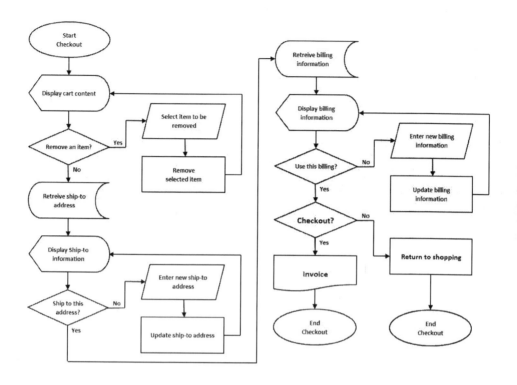

The example above is simpler than a real one would be for this process, but it illustrates the basic idea. Developing a flowchart is a good way to understand a process. You will need to meet with various stakeholders, ask questions, and take lots of notes. When you have a draft of the flowchart, you would meet with the stakeholders again, show them your flowchart, verify that it is correct or update it as needed.

The completed flowchart could then be used to visually communicate the process to various stakeholder groups. It would be suitable for programmers charged with writing the code, and for project sponsors concerned about the final product meeting all of their needs. It should be included in the project management plan and it could be used in training customer service representatives and help desk technicians.

Storyboards

I loved comic strips when I was a kid, especially the Sunday newspaper versions which were in color. Disney was my pre-teen favorites. As I grew older, I discovered Peanuts and Dilbert.

A storyboard is a sequential graphic display, much like a comic strip.[3] In a project management context, a storyboard might be used in the initiating process to "sell" the project to a potential sponsor. Later, in the planning process, and into the execution process, a storyboard could be used to share the "artist's conception" of the completed project with various stakeholders. In agile projects, a storyboard would be a communications tool shared by the product owner and the development team.

Storyboards are used to visualize future motion pictures and interactive media video games. Storyboards are frequently used to show what a future customer might see when they enter a shopping mall, an airport, a sports complex, or a similar structure. As we will see, storyboards can also be useful in visualizing the images of a web site under construction.

The required level of artistic quality depends upon the audience. Storyboards intended to be shared with the public or major stakeholders would probably benefit from the skills of a professional artist, but storyboards for use within the project team can be as simple as a few rough sketches scribbled on a whiteboard during a team meeting.

You do not have to be an artist to create a storyboard. If storyboards are a common requirement, you might want to consider purchasing a software product specifically designed to create storyboards. Several products are available, ranging in price from under $100 to over $1,000.

Scenario

Continuing with the Captain Hook website project, you decide to create a storyboard to ensure you and the sponsor agree on the project requirements. Again, we will focus on the checkout process. Your storybook will be the sequence of screen displays the customer will pass thru during the checkout process.

Results

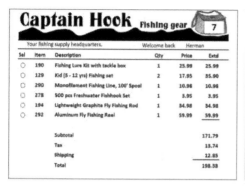

1. Original basket containing 7 items

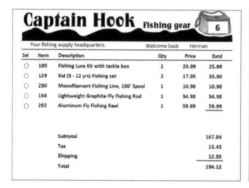

2. Customer has selected an item to be removed from his basket

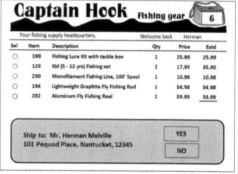

3. The item has been removed from the basket

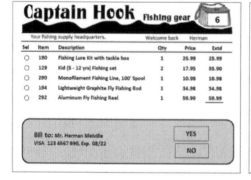

4. The ship-to address is verified

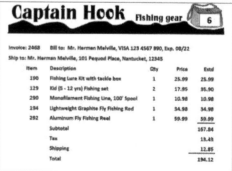

5. Bill to information is confirmed

6 Order is placed and printable invoice is produced

Statistical Process Control

Many quality tools use statistics to analyze data and, in fact, Statistical Process Control (SPC) is often considered the quantitative side of Total Quality Management (TQM). But where do we get the data in the first place?

In an ongoing process, we may set up some sort of device to take measurements automatically, but project management is not an ongoing process. We may need data on a particular topic only once during the project life cycle, so we are likely to favor simple, low cost solutions to the data-gathering process.

Checksheets

You cannot analyze data that does not exist, so the first step in data analysis is to get the data at the source in real time. A checksheet is perhaps the simplest data collection tool available; all you need is a pencil and a piece of paper, plus a little imagination. The checksheet itself is a blank table with column and row headings from your imagination. This hand-drawn example is perfectly useable.

Defects by shift, week of Feb 3	Mon	Tues	Wed	Thurs	Fri	Total
Day	//	///	####	///	///	16
Swing	///	//	///	//	####	15
Graveyard	/	####	///	///	//	14
Total	6	10	11	8	10	45

Scenario

Let's go back to the overheating motor we dealt with earlier in this topic. We began our investigation with a cause and effect diagram, and then, magically, we found that the root cause of the problem was that the legs on the case were too short. Okay, let's reveal the magic. Here's how to get from a problem to a solution.

Process

Our supplier has delivered 5 pallets of 240 motors each. We will take 20 motors from each pallet (n = 5 × 20 = 100) and visually inspect them for defects, then we will bench test them and see if they overheat. We record the results on a checksheet. The checksheet reveals that 3 of the 100 had visual defects but that none failed our bench test.

Test of 100 motors		
Pallet	Visual defect	Bench test
1	0	0
2	2	0
3	0	0
4	1	0
5	0	0
	3	0

We could build one of the prototypes and run it until it overheated, then take it apart and see what failed. That's called destructive testing. It might be fun, but probably a waste of time and money. Instead, let's run a prototype and take periodic temperature measurements of different components, turn it off before it dies, and then repeat the process, perhaps on another unit.

Below is a single run of our test. In practice, we would probably do this several times, hopefully at different starting ambient temperatures, and then average the results. But with just this first test, we can see that the motor has gone from 72 degrees to 110 degrees in 30 minutes. Also, and more importantly, we see that the temperature at the bottom grill has reached 101 degrees during the 30 minute test. Other components have gone up some, but have remained under 80 degrees. That's cool.

Checksheet: Temperature readings at various locations after start of test							
Area	0 Min	5 Min	10 Min	15 Min	20 Min	25 Min	30 Min
Side grill	72	72	72	72	73	73	74
Back grill	72	72	72	73	73	74	74
Bottom Grill	72	73	75	78	84	92	101
Battery	72	72	72	73	74	75	76
Motor	72	74	77	82	89	98	110
Ambient	72	72	72	73	73	73	73

Results

Remember that the checksheet is just the data-gathering tool in the process. The next step is to analyze the data. We used a simple line graph for that, just to get some closure on the checksheet discussion.

In the graph, note how the temperature of the bottom grill seems to follow the increase in temperature of the motor. It appears there is a very high correlation between the temperature of

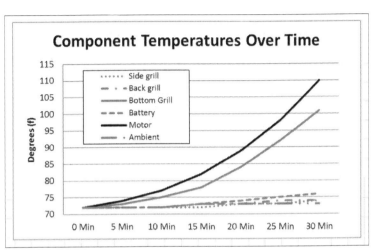

the motor and the temperature of the bottom grill.

We found that longer legs allowed hot air to exit the bottom grill more efficiently. Data analysis was the magic we used to find it.

Correlation

What does "a very high correlation between the temperature of the motor and the temperature of the bottom grill" mean? If we plan to write a change request proposing longer legs, which may be a very significant design change, we had better have more objective evidence than a couple lines on a graph.

Discussion

Correlation means that two sets of data, which we will call X and Y, appear to be related. A positive correlation coefficient means that as X increases, so does Y, and as X decreases, so does Y. A negative correlation coefficient means that as X increases, Y decreases; and as X decreases, Y increases.

Excel offers a very simple function that will give us the correlation between two arrays (sets of data). In this example spreadsheet, we listed the temperature readings for the motor (X) and the bottom grill (Y). The formula in cell B10 is =CORREL(A2:A8,B2:B8). A correlation of 1.0 means the data sets have a perfect positive correlation, while a correlation of 0 means there in no correlation; and a correlation of – 1.0 indicates a perfect negative correlation. The value of 0.9984 shows a very high positive correlation.

	A	B
1	X	Y
2	72	72
3	74	73
4	77	75
5	82	78
6	89	84
7	98	92
8	110	101
9		
10	Correl:	0.9984
11		

Correlation does not prove cause and effect. We cannot say that a change in X *caused* a change in Y any more than we can say that a change in Y *caused* a change in X. We could have switched X and Y in the function and the output would be the very same result of 0.9984.

What we have found is that the temperature of the bottom grill and the temperature of the motor are highly correlated, but does one cause the other, or does a third, currently unknown item, cause the motor and the bottom grill to overheat at about the same rate?

Scatter Charts

This chart was produced from the same data array we used for the Correlation function. We then added a least-squares linear trendline with equation and R^2 value. The trendline is the closest match to the data points, assuming the correlation is linear. The R^2 value indicates how well the trendline matches the data. The R^2 value can range from 0 (no correlation) to 1 (perfect correlation).

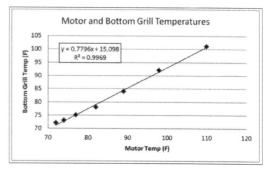

In our example, an R^2 value of 0.9969 is damned close to perfection!

Histograms

In the case of the overheating motor, we had only seven data points. In the real world, we may have thousands. Histograms help us understand large amounts of data by summarizing it into categories or bins.

Scenario

Your project is to design the new M120, which will eventually replace the venerable M100. One of the objectives for the M120 is a significant increase in reliability over the M100. Specifically, management would like to increase the mean time between failures (MTBF) by at least 50%. Over the years, more than 10,000 M100's have been returned for repair, or replacement parts have been ordered for field repair; some units have had multiple repairs. The company has data that includes the serial number, customer, hours in use before failure (each unit has a built-in clock), the failed component, and much more.

Let's learn more about the nature of the M100 failures. What is the MTBF for the M100? What components tended to fail the most often?

Process

You begin by downloading the M100 failure data into an Excel spreadsheet. The raw data fills 12 columns and 12,285 rows. You copy the hours and the name of the failed component into a new worksheet.[4] You now have two columns, one for hours before failure and one for the failed component, but you still have 12,285 rows to deal with. Yuk!

We need to summarize the data into a more manageable form.

Filler:

A histogram is one of the chart types built into Excel. It will automatically select the categories for you. Just select your data and then click Insert > Column or Bar Chart > More Column Charts > Histogram. I don't care for it as I like to have more control my categories. If specific categories are not that important to you, it's certainly quick and easy to use.

Results

For row 2 to row 12286, column A is the number of hours before the unit failed, and B is the cause of the failure. The mean time between failures for the old M100 product is 4638 hours. Of our 12286 failed units, the fastest failure was in 22 hours and the longest runner was 10,963 hours.

Hours	Failure					Bin	Count
5458	Control	Count	12285			0	2441
8550	Battery					1000	569
506	Battery	MTBF	4638			2000	798
375	Motor					3000	1044
9977	Motor	Target	6957			4000	1356
1033	Battery					5000	1584
2860	Motor	Min	22			6000	1763
4621	Battery					7000	1148
4986	Fan	Max	10963			8000	886
9532	Control					9000	477
2413	Fan					10000	219
3090	Battery						12285
4572	Battery						

The formula in cell E2 is =COUNT(A2:A12286). The formula in cell E4 is =AVERAGE(A2:A12286). The formula in cell E6 is E4*1.5. The target MTBF for the new M120 product is 6957 hours, which we decide to round up to 7000.

Of the 12,285 units reported, the shortest time before failure was 22 hours. The formula in cell E8 is =MIN(A2:A12286). The longest time was 10963 hours for the units that failed. Of course, if a unit has not failed, it is not included in this data. The formula in cell E10 is =MAX(A2:A12286).

Given the minimum and the maximum, we decide to create a histogram using bins of 1000, from 0 to 10,000. That will give us 11 data points, which is much easier to manage than 12,285.

We enter bin labels 0 thru 10,000 in cells G2:G12. We then enter formulas in cells H2:H12 that will count the number of values in each bin. Cell H4 is =COUNTIFS(A2:A12286,">="&G4,A2:A12286,"<"&G5). This formula will count the number of data points in the range A2:A12286 that are equal to or larger than cell G4 (3000) and less than cell G5 (4000).

The formula in H13 is =SUM(H2:H12). This sum, 12285, is the same as our count in cell E2 so we know that our COUNTIFS formulas in H2:H12 are counting everything once and nothing twice. Now we are ready to build our histogram. In Excel, we selected cells G2:H12 and then inserted a column chart, a vertical bar chart.

By default, Excel added gaps between the bars, which would be fine if we were comparing categorical data like motors and batteries, but we are not.

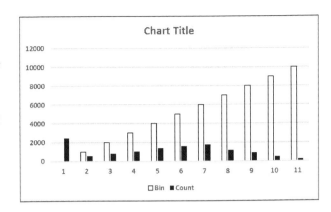

Excel also included our Bins as variables rather than labels. We edit the chart to remove Bins as a data series and use it instead as the labels for our horizontal axis.

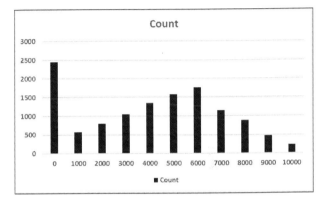

We are working with a continuous range of quantitative data that we have arbitrarily divided into bins of 1000; so we edit the chart and set the gap width to zero. That zero gap width is really the only difference between a histogram and a vertical bar chart, but it's an important distinction because it tells our audience that the underlying data are continuous and not discrete.

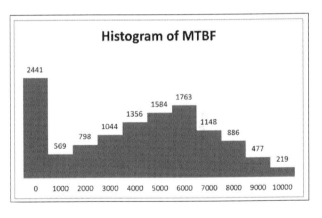

In the histogram we can easily see that the M100 suffers from early failures in the 0 to 1000 hour range, and then appears to have a normal distribution after that. Where should we start on our mission to improve the mean time between failures in our new M120 product? A good way to prioritize our efforts is a Pareto analysis.

Pareto Diagrams

A Pareto[5] diagram is a specific type of column and line chart. We will begin by creating a special table in Excel.

	A	B	C	D	E	F
1	**Hours**	**Failure**		**Failure**	**Count**	**Cum%**
2	5458	Control		Motor	5141	42%
3	8550	Battery		Battery	3122	67%
4	506	Battery		Fan	1792	82%
5	375	Motor		Control	956	90%
6	9977	Motor		Input	581	94%
7	1033	Battery		Output	463	98%
8	2860	Motor		Other	230	100%
9	4621	Battery			12285	
10	4986	Fan				

For our histogram, we used the COUNTIFS function to get the number of entries in each time bin. Note the plural "S" at the end of the function name. That allowed multiple criteria such as "bigger than this and smaller than that."

We can use COUNTIF (singular, no "s") if we only have a single criteria.

We listed all of the sources of failure in cells D2:D8. Cells E2:E8 contain our COUNTIF functions. Cell E2 is =COUNTIF(B2:B12286,D2) and it counts the number of times the label "Motor" (in cell D2) shows up in our data. Our total of 12285 in cell E9 confirms that we have included all of our data, and nothing more. The formula in cell E9 is =SUM(E2:E8).

We could have entered our categories (Motor, Battery, etc.) in any sequence, because the next step is to sort the table in descending order. Then we add a column for cumulative percent. The formula in cell F2 is E2/E9, formatted as a percent. We want the cumulative percent so each formula in the range E2:E8 is slightly different. For example, cell F3 is =SUM(E$2:E3)/E9 and cell F8 is =SUM(E$2:E8)/E9.

We could have entered the formula in cell F3, and then edited it to =SUM(E$2:E3)/E$9. The dollar signs change the row references from relative references to absolute references. That way we can copy the formula into cells F3:F8. In Excel, the function 4 (F4) key at the top of your keyboard is a quick way to change relative to absolute references.

Process

First, note that this column chart, or vertical bar chart, has gaps between the bars. That is because we are working with categorical data and not continuous data.

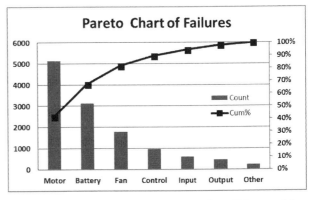

The bars are displayed in descending order of magnitude from left to right. That is because we sorted our table in descending order. We could have waited and edited the chart, but sorting the table is much easier, and makes the table easier to understand in the process.

The original column chart displayed the count bars as you see them, but the percent values, which ranged from 0 to 1, were all lost down at the horizontal axis. We edited the chart and added a second Y axis, which Excel placed on the right side of the chart. We then indicated that our "Cum%" data should be linked to the second Y axis and set the maximum value for that axis as 100%. Finally, we change the "chart type" for our cumulative percents from column to line with markers. This gives us a traditional Pareto diagram.

Results

Looking at our Pareto diagram, we see that motor failures are our biggest problem, representing over 40% of the problems, even though they only make up 14% of the categories (1/7 = 0.1429). Of the seven categories, we could solve 67% of our problems if we focused on the first two (motors and batteries) and we could solve 82% of our problems if we only focused on the top three out of the seven. That's the power of Pareto: prioritize the important few and deprioritize the trivial many, or in other words, let's get the biggest bang for our buck.

We dig a little deeper into the motors to see if we can find any opportunities for improvement.

Discussion

We begin with a new spreadsheet, focusing on motors.[6]

Cells A2:B12286 are the same as before. Cell E4 counts the number of motors in our sample, and cell E6 gives us the average number of hours before the motor failed.

	B	C	D	E	F	G	H	I
1	Failure		Motor			Bin	Count	Percent
2	Control					0	2297	0.4468
3	Battery					1000	496	0.0965
4	Battery		Count	5141		2000	927	0.1803
5	Motor					3000	503	0.0978
6	Motor		MTBF	1367		4000	388	0.0755
7	Battery					5000	280	0.0545
8	Motor					6000	198	0.0385
9	Battery					7000	52	0.0101
10	Fan					8000	0	0.0000
11	Control					9000	0	0.0000
12	Fan					10000	0	0.0000
13	Battery						5141	1.0000

The formula in E4 is =COUNTIF(B2:B12286,D1). Cell E6, the mean time between failures, MTBF, is =AVERAGEIF(B2:B12286,D1,A2:A12286). Note that we referenced cell D1 for our criteria rather than entering the label "Motor" directly in our Countif and Averageif functions. It is considered good practice to reference labels and values in other cells rather than "hiding" them inside formulas and functions.

About 45% (2297/5141 = .4468) of the motors failed in less than 1000 hours. The formula in cell I2 is =H2/H$13, and that formula was copied into cells I3:I12. Cell H13 is =SUM(H2:H12) and cell I13 is, of course, =SUM(I2:I12). The fact that cells E4 and H13 both report the same total motor failures value of 5141 tells us we probably don't have an error in our formulas.

The histogram for Motor tells us that much of the "less than 1000 hours" problem we had in the overall data set was caused by motors, and that motors have a much shorter life expectancy than the other components of the M100.

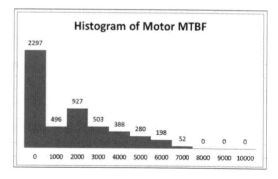

Procuring a more reliable motor should be the major objective of our efforts to improve the reliability of the new M120 product.

Discussion

It's late at night. You are driving home after a long day and you are tired. Your car drifts to the side of the road. Suddenly, Bang! Bang! Bang! as your right front wheel encounters the rumble strip along the side of the road. You quickly steer back to the center of your lane; now wide awake and back in control.

Scenario

The next day you are back at work on the erosion control project. Your team is placing bags of cement along the side of the creek, and things are not going well. The problem is that the bags do not fit together properly unless they are all the same size. You have developed a simple process that is supposed to fill each bag with exactly 40 pounds of cement, but some bags are under-filled and some over-filled and the odd sized bags don't line up as they should.

Control Charts

Control charts are like rumble strips on highways. A little wandering back and forth in your lane is natural, but if you go too far from the center line, you get a warning in time to take corrective action.

The objective of control charts is to give you feedback when assignable causes of variation are present. Assignable variations can be good or bad. If good, investigate, find the cause, and make it part of the process. If bad, investigate, find the cause, and prevent it from reoccurring.

Process

While there are several types of control charts, we will focus on two, the $\bar{X}$-chart (pronounced X bar chart) and the R chart (pronounced R chart).

Periodically, like every hour, we will take a small random sample (5 will do) of our cement-filled bags and weigh them. Next we determine the range (heaviest minus lightest) and the mean (total of all five, divided by five.)

We then post the range on our R chart. If it plots outside of control limits we will stop the process, quarantine our sample, determine the cause of the problem and fix it.

Otherwise we post the sample mean on the $\bar{X}$ chart. If it plots outside of our control limits we stop the process, quarantine the sample, determine the cause of the problem and fix it. Otherwise we put the sample bags back in line and continue the bag-filling operations.

Discussion

No special software is required to construct a control chart. All you need is paper (graph paper works best, but is not required) a pen or pencil, and a calculator to determine the sample average. You will also need a measuring instrument, such as a scale, ruler, micrometer, whatever, to measure the product attribute you are concerned with.

An important concept in total quality management, TQM, is "quality at the source." The idea is to empower the workers, the people actually making things, to be responsible for the quality of their output. To do this, they need tools and training to track the process and the output, and the authority to take corrective actions before the process gets so far out of control that the output becomes unacceptable. Worker empowerment is also a fundamental of agile project management.

Control charts are an excellent example of that. A quality control professional may create the chart, with upper and lower control limits based on standard deviations or factors from a table, but the person running the process is the one who collects the data, enters it in the chart, and decides, given some rules we'll discuss shortly, if the process should continue or if it should be shut down and corrective actions taken.

We empower the worker to take ownership of their process. We give them the tools needed to monitor the process; we give them training on how to use the tools; and we give them the authority to change the process, including halting production, if the process starts to get out of control. We even empower the worker to make or suggest changes to the process to improve the quality of the output. The benefits of worker empowerment far exceed the low cost of maintaining control charts.

Process

The first step in creating our control charts is to determine the mean and the range of the process when it is in control. We inspect the bag-filling machine and ensure everything is as expected. We then run it for a while, 30 bags should do, and weigh every bag. Let's say we get a mean of 40.1 pounds, which we will call $\bar{\bar{X}}$ (pronounced X bar bar) and a range of 2.6 pounds, $\bar{R}$, (pronounced R bar). Next we need some data from a "table of factors for control chart limits." These tables can be found in books on statistical process control or online. An example is included here.

From the table, for our intended samples of $n = 5$, we note that the "mean factor A_2" is 0.577, the "lower range factor D_3" is 0, and the "upper range factor D_4" is 2.115.

We use these factors to set the lower and upper control limits for our $\bar{X}$ chart and our R chart as follows:

n	A_2	D_3	D_4
2	1.880	0.000	3.267
3	1.023	0.000	2.575
4	0.729	0.000	2.282
5	0.577	0.000	2.115
6	0.483	0.000	2.004
7	0.419	0.076	1.924
8	0.373	0.136	1.834
9	0.337	0.184	1.816
10	0.308	0.223	1.777

$$\text{LCL}_{\bar{x}} = \bar{\bar{X}} - A_2(\bar{R}) = 40.1 - 0.577(2.6) = 40.1 - 1.5 = 38.6$$

$$\text{UCL}_{\bar{x}} = \bar{\bar{X}} + A_2(\bar{R}) = 40.1 + 0.577(2.6) = 40.1 + 1.5 = 41.6$$

$$\text{LCL}_R = D_3(\bar{R}) = 0.0(2.6) = 0 \text{ pounds}$$

$$\text{UCL}_R = D_4(\bar{R}) = 2.115(2.6) = 5.499 = 5.5 \text{ pounds}$$

After we construct the charts, we give them to the process operator along with instructions on how to complete them, tools for measurements (a scale), tools to compute the range and the sample mean (a calculator) and, most importantly, the responsibility and authority to control the process.

Periodically, like "on the hour," the operator selects five bags at random, weighs the samples, writes the weights in a table, and calculates the sample range and the sample mean. The sample range is the weight of the heaviest bag minus the weight of the lightest bag. The sample mean is the total weight of all 5 bags, divided by 5.

This is our table of samples. It is prepared by hand at the work site by the operator.

The data are not sent to some office to be entered into a spreadsheet by an administrative assistant.

The sample range and sample mean are calculated by the operator, the process owner.

Time	Bag 1	Bag 2	Bag 3	Bag 4	Bag 5	Range	Mean
8:00	38.8	39.0	39.2	41.0	40.7	2.2	39.7
8:57	38.4	39.2	40.5	38.9	41.0	2.6	39.6
10:09	40.5	38.0	39.2	39.4	38.9	2.5	39.2
11:07	39.1	40.0	41.6	39.5	40.0	2.5	40.0
12:04	39.1	41.4	41.8	38.9	40.5	2.9	40.3
13:02	41.9	41.0	39.2	41.0	41.1	2.7	40.8
14:07	39.0	40.2	40.5	39.3	38.9	1.6	39.6
15:06	38.7	41.2	38.2	40.2	40.1	3.0	39.7
16:03	40.3	39.4	38.5	38.3	41.4	3.1	39.6
17:01	42.0	41.1	39.3	40.1	40.8	2.7	40.7
17:59	41.0	39.1	39.3	38.1	41.0	2.9	39.7
18:59	41.6	39.8	41.3	41.2	41.0	1.8	41.0
20:01	40.3	38.9	39.6	41.7	40.3	2.8	40.2
20:59	42.0	38.6	41.0	38.1	39.1	3.9	39.8
21:56	42.0	38.8	39.1	40.3	39.4	3.2	39.9

Next, the process operator plots the sample range in the R chart and the sample mean in the $\overline{X}$ chart. If the sample range is above the upper control limit or below the lower control limit, the operator stops the process and investigates the problem. If the range is between the upper and lower control limits, the operator looks to $\overline{X}$ chart.

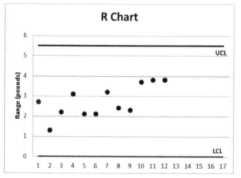
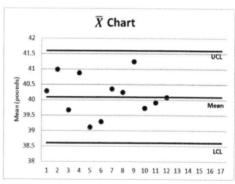

If a table of factors for control chart limits is not used, the upper and lower control limits are usually set to plus and minus three standard deviations from the mean. The empirical rule states that 68% of random sample means will fall within the first standard deviation, 95% within the first two standard deviations, and 99.7% will fall within the first three standard deviations of the process mean. If a sample average is outside the 3σ limits, there is less than 0.07 probability that the process is in control.

There are several things to look for in the $\bar{X}$ chart. Like the R Chart, if a sample mean plots above the upper control limit or below the lower control limit, the process is assumed to be out of control.

In addition, five consecutive plots in an upward or downward direction, two consecutive plots near a control limit, five consecutive plots above the mean, or below the mean, or very erratic behavior are all signs that the process should be watched carefully as it may be approaching an out of control state.

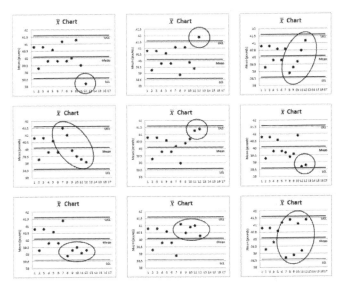

Check with your project management office for organizational guidelines on interpreting control chart plots.

Also, consider the impact of declaring a process to be out of control when it is not; known as a Type I error; or concluding that a process is in control when it is not; a Type II error.

Scenario

You are continuing your work on the erosion control project. Some portions of the creek have sharp turns and you decide to use 25 pound bags rather than 40 pound bags. Your process control charts worked well for the 40 pound bags, and you plan to continue using control charts for the 25 pound bags, however you decide to increase the sample size from 5 to 10 bags.

You reconfigure your bag filling system for 25 pound bags and run a test batch of 30 bags. The mean is 25.0 pounds and range is 2.5 pounds. From a table of factors for control chart limits, for samples of $n = 10$, you note

215

that the mean factor A_2 is 0.308, the lower range factor D_3 is 0.223, and the upper range factor D_4 is 1.777. What are the upper and lower control limits for an R chart and an $\bar{X}$ chart?

Scenario

You are instructing the bag-filling operators in the proper use of control charts. You tell the operators to weigh 10 bags at random every hour and record the weights in a table. At the end of the day, you return and show the operators how to calculate the sample range and the sample mean, and how to plot them on the control charts. You conclude by saying that in the future, the data is to be plotted every hour, so that corrective actions can be taken immediately if needed. Draw the control charts and plot the data. Is the process in control?

Sample	Bag 1	Bag 2	Bag 3	Bag 4	Bag 5	Bag 6	Bag 7	Bag 8	Bag 9	Bag 10	Range	Mean
1	24.7	25.1	25.5	24.2	24.1	25.1	24.8	25.0	24.0	25.0	1.5	24.8
2	24.2	24.5	26.5	25.2	24.5	25.6	25.3	24.1	25.2	24.3	2.4	24.9
3	24.5	25.1	26.0	27.5	24.3	25.2	25.6	25.4	25.2	25.2	3.2	25.4
4	24.3	25.4	24.6	24.5	24.2	24.3	26.0	25.2	24.2	22.0	4.0	24.5
5	24.8	25.3	24.7	23.5	25.8	25.8	24.9	25.8	24.1	24.2	2.3	24.9
6	24.0	24.1	24.4	24.2	24.9	24.3	25.8	24.6	24.3	25.0	1.8	24.6
7	24.3	24.7	23.8	24.2	22.5	25.7	24.0	24.0	25.5	24.1	3.2	24.3
8	23.9	24.3	24.1	22.8	25.2	24.8	21.4	25.6	25.7	24.0	4.3	24.2
9												
10												

Process

$$\text{LCL}_{\bar{X}} = \bar{\bar{X}} - A_2(\bar{R}) = 25.0 - 0.308(2.5) = 25.0 - 0.77 = 24.23$$

$$\text{UCL}_{\bar{X}} = \bar{\bar{X}} + A_2(\bar{R}) = 25.0 + 0.308(2.5) = 25.0 + 0.77 = 25.77$$

$$\text{LCL}_R = D_3(\bar{R}) = 0.223(2.5) = 0.5575 \text{ pounds}$$

$$\text{UCL}_R = D_4(\bar{R}) = 1.777(2.5) = 4.4425 \text{ pounds}$$

Working with the process operators, you calculate the sample ranges and the sample means, and record them in the table. You then ask the process operators to plot the data on the control charts.

Sample	Range	Mean
1	1.5	24.8
2	2.4	24.9
3	3.2	25.4
4	4.0	24.5
5	2.3	24.9
6	1.8	24.6
7	3.2	24.3
8	4.3	24.2

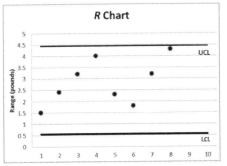

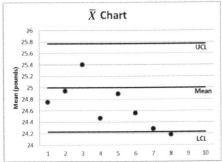

The process is not in control. The R chart is borderline but technically acceptable, but the $\bar{X}$ chart clearly indicates a problem because there are five consecutive samples below the mean and also because the sample mean for hour number eight is under the lower control limit.

You and the operators agree that the process will be fully inspected in the morning and that the control charts will be updated every hour.

You remind the operators that they are responsible for the quality of their output, and that they have full authority to stop the bag-filling process and make adjustments as needed. You make a mental note to drop by the bag-filling station tomorrow morning and have a look at the control charts.

Did I say a mental note? There would be nothing wrong with a notation in the issues log whenever a quality control chart indicates a process is out of control, even if the problem was corrected as soon as it was observed.

For example, the problem is a loose nut and bolt, and the solution has been simply to tighten it. If you notice this entry frequently in the issues log, you could look into a more permanent solution such a self-locking nuts.

Perhaps you decide to upgrade all of your equipment with self-locking nuts, requiring some expense and downtime, and therefore a change request. Having a detailed history of the problem in the issues log will make that change request a lot easier to justify.

<u>Footnotes</u>

(1) Prior to World War II, US factories were run by men mostly with engineering degrees. They did it the way they had been taught, the way it had always been done. Then came the war and the men went to fight for their country. A lot of women stepped up to run the factories, providing the equipment and munitions that eventually won the war. The federal government sent consultants to help the women run the factories efficiently. One of the consultants was Dr. W. Edwards Deming. He developed many innovations in management and quality. The women, receptive to anything that would help, and not having a bias for the old established methods, eagerly implemented Deming's suggestions.

At the end of the war, the men returned to the factories where they quickly replaced the innovations with the old, established methods; and the women went home to give birth to the baby boom.

Having learned the mistakes made at the end of the first World War, the US government sent consultants to help rebuild the Axis nations. Deming and others were sent to Japan where they would continue to develop management practices and later become known as the "quality gurus."

In the 1970's and 80's, US manufacturing executives visited japan to see how the Japanese were able to build the high quality, low cost products they had become known for. The answer the Japanese gave their guests was "We got it from you. Deming gave it to us."

Today, the highest award for quality in Japan is the Deming Prize.

(2) Flowcharts were first presented by Frank and Lillian Gilbreth in 1921. The Gilbreths, well-known for their pioneering work in time and motion studies, were the subject of the 1948 book and the 1950 movie *Cheaper by the Dozen.* In addition to their work, the Gilbreths found time to raise twelve children. A "therblig" (Gilbreth respelled) is one of 13 manual, visual, or mental elements into which an industrial manual operation may be analyzed in a time and motion study.

218

(3) A storyboard uses pictures to describe something that could have been described by words. A comic strip is a good example. According to Wikipedia, a similar phrase dates back to a 1911 newspaper editorial; and storyboards were used in advertising as early as 1913. The exact phrase "storyboard" was used in a 1918 newspaper advertisement for a "pictorial magazine," *The San Antonio Light.*

(4) When you have a large data set like this download, I recommend keeping it as is, and doing all your work on copies of it. I frequently rename the worksheet "Data" or "Original." I might change the font and widen some columns to make it easier to read, and I might add a comment about the source of the data and the date of the download. Also, I might add a background color that will remind me I am looking at the original and complete data set, and not to mess with it.

I can then make multiple copies of it, either by copy and paste of selected portions, or making a copy of the entire worksheet, renaming the copy, and removing the background color. Then if I make a mistake, delete something in error, or change my mind, I can always go back to the original data set.

(5) Vilfredo Pareto (1812 – 1882) was an Italian economist. He developed the "Pareto Principle," sometimes called the rule of 80/20. He noted that 80% of the land in Italy was owned by 20% of the population and he popularized the use of the term "elite" in social analysis. He focused on identifying "the important few from the trivial many," an important factor in total quality management; or in politics. He told the government at the time that all they needed to do to stay in power was to please the 20% social elite. The other 80% of the population did not matter.

(6) When I devote a spreadsheet to a particular topic, I like to rename it from "Sheet3" (or whatever) to "Motors" or some other short name that helps identify the spreadsheet. Short names will allow you to quickly find the spreadsheet you are looking for, and their names will appear in formulas that refer to them. You can move them so frequently used spreadsheets are at the front of your file and reference tables are at the back. You can also move similar worksheets are next to each other and you can change the color of their tabs so similar worksheets have similar colored tabs.

Earned Value Management

Earned value management (EVM) analysis is a methodology used to compare our current results (earned value) to our planned (baseline) scope, cost and schedule. It can tell us how we are doing compared to plan and help us predict how the project will finish compared to our planned finish.

We will cover planned value, earned value, and actual cost in this first topic. Following EVM topics will include schedule variance, cost variance, schedule performance index, cost performance index, forecasting, to-complete performance index, and performance reviews. Each EVM topic will build on prior EVM topics.

<u>Discussion</u>

Planned value is frequently referred to as "PV" in project management literature, but that could easily be confused with present value in financial management. I will do my best to avoid acronyms as much as I can, following the rule: Avoid Acronyms Whenever Possible, or AAWP.

Planned value is the dollar value of the amount of work we had planned to have accomplished by a given date. The best way to get this is bottom-up. We add the planned costs from the work breakdown structure for all of the activities that should have been completed as of today. If an activity is currently underway, we estimate the percent complete and apply that percent to the planned cost for the completed activity.

The planned value as of a particular point in time, sometimes called the performance measure baseline, is a combination of the cost, schedule, and scope baselines. It states, in monetary terms, what we expected to have accomplished, not what we expected to have spent. If we had planned to complete activities A and B at this point, then our planned value is the sum of the budgeted costs for activities A and B, even if, in fact, we have only completed activity A, or we have completed activities, A, B and C.

The planned value for the entire project is the same as the budget for the project, including contingency reserves but not management reserves.

Earned value is the value of the work we actually did complete as of a given point in time. If we have completed activities A, B and half of C, the earned value is the budgeted amount for activities A, B and half of C. The earned value is not the amount we have spent, but rather the amount budgeted for the work that we have completed, paid for or not.

Actual cost is the total of the costs incurred, for or not. If we have accomplished all of activities A and B, and half of activity C, then the actual costs would be the labor, materials, and overhead used to complete activities A, B and whatever we have incurred on activity C.

Scenario

Activity A has a total budgeted cost of $20,000. Activity B has a total budgeted cost of $45,000. Our schedule was to complete activity A on April 1 and activity B on April 30. We planned to begin activity C, which has a planned cost of $30,000 on May 1.

In the afternoon of April 30, we visit the site and learn that both activities A and B have been completed, and that the supervisor took the initiative to begin work on activity C, which she reports as being 50% complete. We also learn that the total costs for labor, materials, and overhead, were $22,500 for activity A and $41,350 for activity B. In addition, $12,500 has been spent so far on activity C.

What are the planned value, the earned value, and the actual cost for the project as of April 30?

Results

The planned value for April 30 is the budgeted costs for activities A and B is $20,000 + $45,000 = $65,000.

The earned value as of April 30 is $20,000 + $45,000 + $30,000/2 = $80,000.

The actual cost as of April 30 is $22,500 + $41,350 + $12,500 =$76,350.

In summary, we had planned to accomplish $65,000 worth of work by April 30, but, in fact, we actually accomplished $80,000 worth of work. We had planned to incur $65,000 in costs as of April 30, and we have actually incurred costs totaling $76,350. We are ahead of schedule but over budget.

Practice

Today is day 50 in your project to restore Veterans' Park. Five activities should be completed, or underway, by now. The data in the table are your most recent status update.

The critical path is not identified. Earned value analysis includes all of the relevant activities as of the specified date, not just the critical path activities. Activity F, which is not scheduled to begin until after day 50, and has not begun, is not considered in our analysis.

Activity	Start	Duration	Finish	Planned Cost	Actual Cost	Complete
A	1	24	25	$20,000	$22,000	100%
B	25	20	45	$40,000	$25,000	70%
C	25	40	65	$60,000	$20,000	30%
D	25	10	35	$30,000	$28,000	100%
E	35	36	71	$60,000	$45,000	80%
F	71	8	79	$10,000	$0	0%

What are the planned value, the earned value, and the actual cost for your project as of day 50?

The completed activities are easy; the incompletes are the problem. Take your time and think about where each activity should be on day 50.

Process

	A	B	C	D	E	F	G	H	I	J
1	Activity	Start	Duration	Finish	Planned Cost	Actual Cost	Percent Complete	Planned Value	Earned Value	Actual Cost
2	A	1	24	25	$20,000	$22,000	100%	$20,000	$20,000	$22,000
3	B	25	20	45	$40,000	$25,000	70%	$40,000	$28,000	$25,000
4	C	25	40	65	$60,000	$24,000	30%	$37,500	$18,000	$24,000
5	D	25	10	35	$30,000	$28,000	100%	$30,000	$30,000	$28,000
6	E	35	36	71	$60,000	$42,000	80%	$25,000	$48,000	$42,000
7								$152,500	$144,000	$141,000

Note the finish dates in cells D2:D6. Activities A, B and D should have been completed by day 50. Planned values as of day 50 are in cells H2:H6. For activities A, B and D, the planned value in column H is the planned cost in column E. This is true even for activity B, which is behind schedule and only 70% complete as of day 50 (it should have been fully completed by day 45).

Activity C was scheduled to begin on day 25 and conclude on day 65. On day 50, activity C should have been 25 days into its 40 day duration, or $25/40 = 0.625 = 62.5\%$ complete. When complete, activity C will have a planned value of $60,000 so on day 50 it has a planned value of $60,000 X $0.625 = $37,500$.

The same logic applies to activity E, which was scheduled to begin on day 35 and conclude on day 71. On day 50, activity E should have been 15 days into its 36 day duration, or $15/36 = 0.416667 = 41.67\%$ complete. When complete, activity E will have a planned value of $60,000 so on day 50 it has a planned value of $60,000 X $0.416667 = $25,000$.

The planned value on day 50 is the total of the planned value for each of the five planned as of day 50 activities: $152,500.

The earned value for completed activities is their respective planned value. For incomplete activities, it is their planned value times their percent complete. The total earned value for the project as of day 50 is $144,000.

223

The actual cost for the project, as of day 50, is the sum of the actual activity costs: $141,000.

Results

The bad news is that the project to restore Veterans' Park is behind schedule by about 5% (144,000 / 152,500 = 0.944).

The good news, is that we have spent about 2% less than planned to accomplish the work we did get done ($141,000 / $144,000 = 0.979)

Discussion

The math is the easy part. The challenges come before and after we crunch the numbers. What data do we include in our computations; and how do we place the results of our computations in a context suitable for stakeholders?

We are nearing the end of this book, so I'll take the risk of being a little philosophical. Project math, in my opinion, is unlike other forms of math because of the stakeholders.

Scientists present their findings to other scientists. Financial analysis present their findings to other financiers. But project managers must present their findings to a diverse group of stakeholders who, for the most part, are not actively involved in projects.

We cannot simply toss out a bunch of numbers. We need to be able to explain the significance of our numbers in the context of project success, organizational goals and objectives and most importantly, the unique concerns of each of our different stakeholder groups. We need to be able to express the meaning of terms like earned value and expected value (plus a lot more terms to follow shortly) into terms our stakeholder groups will understand and appreciate.

Schedule and Cost Variance

In the Project Duration topic, we used the statistical terms standard deviation and variance; the variance being the square of the standard deviation and the standard deviation being the square root of the variance. In most project management literature, however, the term variance is used to describe the difference between the baseline or the expected value and the actual value. That is how we will define variance in this topic. No more squares, sum of squares, or roots of squares.

<u>Discussion</u>

If we tell senior management "The project to restore Veterans' Park is behind schedule but under budget both for the schedule and for the amount of work we have accomplished." Fair questions to expect in return would be:

"How much behind schedule?"

"How much under budget?"

Schedule variance is the difference between the earned value and the planned value as of a given point in time. The formula is:

$$Schedule\ Variance = Earned\ value - Planned\ value$$

Schedule variance can be used for all scheduled activities or just for activities on the critical path. In either case, at the end of the project, the schedule variance should be zero because we will have earned all the value that we planned to earn. We will have accomplished everything on the scope baseline, even if we had to modify the baseline via the change control process, in order to do it.

Cost variance is the difference between the earned value and the actual cost as of a given point in time. The formula is:

$$Cost\ Variance = Earned\ value - Actual\ cost$$

Cost variance should be used for all scheduled activities, critical path or not. Unlike the schedule variance, at the end of the project there is no guarantee that the cost variance will be zero. The only limit to how much we can spend is our good judgement and the size of our piggy bank.

Scenario

The planned value is $152,500, the earned value is $144,000, and the actual cost is $141,000. What are the schedule variance and the cost variance?

Results

The schedule variance is $144,000 – $152,500 = –$8,500. The fact that we have a negative variance means we are behind schedule. We have accomplished less work than we had planned to accomplish in the specified amount of time.

The cost variance is $144,000 – $141,000 = $3,000. The positive variance means we are below budget for the amount of work we have accomplished. In both cases, negative values are bad and positive values are good.

Discussion

I am not aware of an established variance formula in project management literature to compare planned cash flow to actual cash flow. If this is an important measurement to your sponsoring organization, you should discuss how best to communicate this information during the project planning process. You could define a "cash flow variance" as planned cash flow minus actual cash flow.[1]

What do –$8,500 and $3,000 really mean? Should we be concerned? If it's a ten thousand dollar project, probably yes; but if it's a ten million dollar project, probably no. We need a reference to put these values into perspective.

The schedule performance index is the ratio of earned value to planned value. The formula is:

$$Schedule\ Performance\ Index = \frac{Earned\ value}{Planned\ value}$$

The cost performance index does the same for cost:

$$Cost\ Performance\ Index = \frac{Earned\ value}{Actual\ cost}$$

Scenario

The planned value is $152,500, the earned value is $144,000, and the Actual cost is $141,000. What are the schedule performance index, SPI, and the cost performance index, CPI?

Results

The schedule performance index is $144,000 / $152,500 = 0.9443. A value below 1.0 is bad; we are behind schedule. A value above 1.0 is good; we are ahead of schedule, an SPI of 1.0 means we are exactly on schedule.

Our schedule variance was –$8,500, but that didn't give us anything to compare it to. The schedule performance index of 0.9443 tells us that we have accomplished about 94% of the work we had expected to have accomplished by this time.

The cost performance index is $144,000 / $141,000 = 1.0213. Like the schedule performance index, a value of 1.0 means we are right on target. A CPI greater than 1.0 is good; we have spent less than we planned to accomplish the earned value. A cost performance index less than 1.0 is bad; it spent more than we planned to accomplish the earned value.

Practice

Your project has a planned value of $240,000, an earned value of $252,000 and actual costs of $262,000. What is the schedule variance, the cost variance, the schedule performance index, and the cost performance index?

Answers

The schedule variance is $252,000 – $240,000 = $12,000. You are ahead of schedule. You have accomplished $12,000 more work than you had planned to accomplish by this date.

The cost variance is $252,000 – $262,000 = –$10,000. You have incurred expenses totaling $10,000 more than you had planned to incur given the amount of work accomplished. You are over budget by $10,000.

The schedule performance index is $252,000 / $262,000 = 1.05. You have accomplished 5% more than you had planned to accomplish by this date. You are 5% ahead of schedule.

The cost performance index is $252,000 / $262,000 = 0.9618. You are not earning the value you planned to earn. For the expenses incurred, you have only accomplished 96% of what you planned to accomplish.

You could say you are over budget by about 1.00 – 0.96 = 4%, but actually the cost performance index says you are under-producing by about 4%. It's like you didn't spend too much for that six-pack of beer. You spent what you planned to spend, but you walked out of the store with only five bottles. That's a scope problem, not a cost problem.

Footnote:

(1) Generally accepted accounting principles, GAAP, has a standardized financial report called a "statement of cash flows." If you need to monitor and report planned and actual cash flow, and cash flow variance, you might want to have a look at the statement of cash flows format before you try to reinvent one on your own.

Filler

Cowrie sea shells were used as currency in 1200 BC and bronze and copper imitation cowries were produced in China at the end of the stone age. Round stamped coins appeared around 600 BC. Leather banknotes were developed in China, as the first use of paper currency. Today, electronic fund transfers are replacing the need for physical currency.

Forecasting Estimate at Completion

Forecasting is quite common in business. We forecast demand for our products, we forecast interest rates for investments, and we forecast the weather for the company picnic. Forecasting involves making predictions about the future based on historical data, but understanding there is some uncertainty regarding events between now and then.

Discussion

In project management literature, the term forecasting usually means estimating the final cost or the final schedule of an ongoing project. We will refer to it as an estimate until a change request has been approved and our estimate becomes the new budget at completion or schedule at completion.

We made a lot of assumptions at the start of the project. Now that we are into the project and have some actual work performance data under our belt, we can replace some of those assumptions with facts, and that may warrant a revision of our expected project finish date and total costs, which we will call a cost estimate at completion or a schedule estimate at completion.

We will look at four common methods for calculating a cost estimate at completion. All involve the actual cost of work completed. The difference is how we estimate the cost to complete the unfinished work.

- The first method is based on the budgeted rate.

- The second method is based on the cost performance index.

- The third method is a bottom-up review of work to be completed.

- In the fourth method, we will include both the cost performance index and the schedule performance index.

We will conclude with an estimate of the schedule at completion.

Scenario

You are well into your project to implement the new order fulfillment system. You have encountered some unexpected expenses and you are concerned that the project might not finish in budget. You need to determine a revised cost estimate at completion. You assume that problems of the past were unique and will not continue; all future work will be at the budgeted rate (cost per day). Your formula is:

Estimate at Completion
$$= Actual\ cost + (Budget\ at\ completion - Earned\ value)$$

The planned budget at completion is $850,000. The earned value is $480,000 and the planned value is $500,000. Actual costs are $527,472. Based on this data, what is your revised estimate at completion?

Results

Assuming the budget variances you have encountered will not continue, you use the budgeted rate method and form an estimate at completion of $527,472 + $850,000 – $480,000 = $897,472.

The planned value was $500,000. Why didn't we use that in our calculations? The reason is that it is not part of the formula. This was not a sneaky trick on my part; it is a reminder of a common problem in the real world, as opposed to math textbooks. We frequently have more data than we need. It is important to know what we need, but it is equally important to recognize what we do not need, and not be fooled into using it. My grandmother used to tell me to eat everything on my plate; but my math teacher never told me to use all the numbers available.

You cannot undo the past, but you believe the future will continue as originally planned. You estimate the total project will cost $897,472 rather than the $850,000. You request a meeting with the project sponsor and you draft a change request to increase the budget from $850,000 to a rounded $900,000.

230

Scenario

At the meeting, the project sponsor asks why you assume the prior budget variances will not continue. After some consideration, you agree that you may have made an invalid assumption. Although each of the budget variances you encountered were unique, you cannot identify an underlying cause that no longer exists. You agree to assume the budget variances will continue at the same rate, and therefore, you can use the cost performance index to form a revised cost estimate at completion.

Discussion

There may be an underlying cause to the budget variances. Even though each of the activities were unique, the same logic was probably used to estimate their cost. Your estimation technique is common to all of the variances. Since you used the same technique to estimate the remaining activities, you should expect the variances to continue at the same rate.

Process

The formula is:

$$Estimate\ at\ Completion = \frac{Budget\ at\ completion}{Cost\ performance\ index}$$

You recall that the cost performance index formula is:

$$Cost\ Performance\ Index = \frac{Earned\ value}{Actual\ cost}$$

Results

The earned value is $480,000 and the actual cost is $527,472, so the cost performance index is $480,000 / $527,472 = 0.91.

The budget at completion is $850,000 so the new estimate at completion is $850,000 / 0.91 = $933,938, which we could round to $934,000.

Scenario

Let's assume that no systematic errors were found in the original cost estimating process.

If, other than a few ongoing activities, the work already completed is different than the work to be completed, there may be little justification to assume the past cost performance will be indicative of future cost performance. It may be worth our time (and money) to take a fresh look at the work ahead of us. This is known as a bottom-up estimate. The formula is:

$$Estimate\ at\ Completion = (Actual\ cost) + (Sum\ of\ future\ costs)$$

As you can see, the formula is quite simple; the difficulty is in gathering all of the future costs. We may have done this when we originally planned the project, but, as the saying goes, we are older and wiser now.

We make a list of all current and future activities, and break each activity down to its lowest cost elements. (The table is just an example. For instance, direct materials should be further decomposed into the different materials, quantities, freight, tax, etc.). Working with activity experts and our most recent performance data, we review each cost element and revise as necessary. For an activity currently underway, work already completed goes into the actual cost bucket, and work to be completed goes in to the future costs bucket. When finished, we add all of the future costs together and that becomes our estimate to complete, our "sum of future costs" in the above formula.

Activity	Element	Original	Revised
D	Direct labor	7,000	9,550
	Direct materials	5,000	7,800
	Indirect costs	1,000	1,700
E	Direct labor	25,000	34,000
	Direct materials	45,000	47,500
	Indirect costs	5,000	8,500
F	Direct labor	70,000	75,000
	Direct materials	60,000	64,900
	Indirect costs	4,000	4,650
G	Direct labor	15,000	17,000
	Direct materials	12,000	13,500
	Indirect costs	4,000	5,240
H	Direct labor	3,000	4,650
	Direct materials	8,000	8,470
	Indirect costs	2,000	2,580
I	Direct labor	4,000	5,200
	Direct materials	70,000	78,500
	Indirect costs	2,000	2,500
J	Direct labor	2,000	3,540
	Direct materials	4,000	5,950
	Indirect costs	2,000	2,500
Totals:		350,000	403,230

Using the bottom-up method, our estimate at completion is actual costs plus the sum of future costs, $527,472 + $403,230 = $930,702 = $930,700. You can't knock the logic of the bottom-up method, but it takes a lot of time, from some very valuable people, and that costs money. Also, to cost justify a new bottom-up estimate, we need to have learned enough from the work performance data that the quality of our new estimate is a significant improvement compared to our original estimate.

Scenario

Before you can draft a new change request, your project sponsor asks if you are on schedule. She points out that cost is frequently a function of time; the longer a project takes, the more it will cost. After all, time is money.

Process

Your planned value was $500,000 but your earned value is only $480,000, giving you a schedule variance of –$20,000. Remember that a negative schedule variance means you are behind schedule.

You review the causes for the various delays and conclude there is no reason to assume they will not continue. With that assumption, you can use the schedule performance index to form a better cost estimate at completion. The formula is:

$$Cost\ estimate\ at\ completion = Actual\ cost + \frac{Budget\ at\ completion - Earned\ value}{Cost\ performance\ index \times Schedule\ performance\ index}$$

Remember that the schedule performance index is:

$$Schedule\ Performance\ Index = \frac{Earned\ value}{Planned\ value}$$

Your schedule performance index is $480,000 / $500,000 = 0.96. A schedule performance index less than 1 means you are behind schedule. An SPI greater than 1 means you are ahead of schedule.

Results

Remember that your actual cost to date were $527,472, the current budget at completion is $850,000, your earned value is $480,000, the cost performance index is 0.91, and you have just determined that your schedule performance index is 0.96.

Given all that, your new cost estimate at completion is $527,472 + ($850,000 - $480,000) / (0.91 X 0.96) = $527,472 + ($370,000 / 0.8736) = $527,472 + $423,535 = $950,807. We could round that up to $951,000.

Scenario

Now that you have a valid cost estimate at completion, the sponsor asks you for a revised schedule estimate at completion. The formula is:

$$Schedule\ Estimate\ at\ Completion = \frac{Planned\ schedule\ at\ completion}{Schedule\ performance\ index}$$

The project was originally scheduled to take 216 days. Your revised project duration is 216 / 0.96 = 225 days.

Discussion

Our original budget at completion was $850,000. Using work performance data, we demonstrated four different methods to estimate a revised budget at completion: $897,472, $933,938, $930,702, and $$951,006, and we discussed the pros and cons of each. Which method we hang our hat on will depend on organization policies and guidance from the sponsor or project management office.

We also discovered a method to use the schedule performance index to calculate a revised schedule at completion from 216 days to 225 days.

Practice

You are about half way into a project to build a solar powered barbeque.

The original budget at completion was $750,000 and the project duration was 110 days.

As of today, the planned value is $450,000, the earned value is $495,000, the actual cost is $440,000, and a bottom-up analysis indicates there is $229,500 worth of work still to be completed.

1. What is the current cost variance?

2. What is the current cost performance index?

3. What is the current schedule variance?

4. What is the current schedule performance index?

5. Using the budgeted rate method, what is the cost estimate at completion?

6. Using the cost performance index only method, what is the cost estimate at completion?

7. Using the bottom-up method, what is the cost estimate at completion?

8. Using the cost performance index and schedule performance index method, what is the current cost estimate at completion?

9. What is the current schedule at completion?

Results

1. The cost variance is $495,000 – $440,000 = $55,000.

2. The cost performance index is $495,000 / $440,000 = 1.125.

3. The schedule variance is $495,000 – $450,000 = $45,000.

4. The schedule performance index $495,000 / $450,000 = 1.100.

5. Using the budgeted rate method, the cost estimate at completion is $440,000 + $750,000 – $495,000 = $695,000.

6. Using the cost performance index only method, the cost estimate at completion is $750,000 / 1.125 = $666,667.

7. Using the bottom-up method, the cost estimate at completion is $440,000 + $229,500 = $669,500.

8. Using the cost performance index and schedule performance index method, the cost estimate at completion is $440,000 + ($750,000 – $440,000 / 1.125 X 1.100) = $646,061.

9. The schedule at completion is 110 / 1.100 = 100 days.

Management summary:

> The project to build a solar powered barbeque is under budget and ahead of schedule. We should finish about day 100, rather than day 110, and have a total cost between $646,000 and $695,000; most likely between $666,700 and $669,500.

Discussion

Note the rounding in the management summary. If you tell someone $666,666.67; they will expect accuracy to the penny. If you tell them $666,700 they will expect accuracy to the nearest hundred. Since we are estimating the future, let's not overstate our clairvoyant powers.

To-Complete Performance Index

We have seen how we can use planned value, earned value, actual cost, schedule variance, cost variance, the schedule performance index, and the cost performance index to forecast a cost estimate at completion.

The results may not be acceptable if our estimate at completion is over budget (or if real-world conditions have changed and we need to finish the project at a lower cost than originally planned).

We may need to take actions to change the trends and get back on track, or to meet new cost requirements. The to-complete performance index (TCPI) will tell us what level of cost performance we must achieve in the time remaining to overcome our deficit and finish the project on budget.

Scenario

Continuing with the scenario introduced in the Forecasting topic, we will assume our change request for the new order fulfillment system was not approved. Instead, our project sponsor has asked us what level of performance will it take to finish the project within the original budget.

Remember that the budget is $850,000, the planned value is $500,000, the earned value is $480,000 and the actual cost is $527,472. The cost performance index is $480,000/ $527,472 = 0.91, so we are over budget.

Process

There are actually two to-complete performance index formulas, one using the budget at completion and one using the estimate at completion. The budget at completion formula is:

$$TCPI = \frac{(Budget\ at\ completion) - (Earned\ value)}{(Budget\ at\ completion) - (Actual\ cost)}$$

Results

Our to-complete performance index is ($850,000 – $480,000) / ($850,000 – $527,472) = 1.1472, which we round to 1.15.

Discussion

Until now our cost performance index has been 0.91, and from now until the conclusion of the project, we need a cost performance index of at least 1.15 if we are to finish the project on budget. We got a value of 91 cents for every dollar we spent; to recover, we need to start getting $1.15 for every dollar we spend.[1] Can we do that? Here is where we put down the calculator, get off the computer, and put on our leadership hat.[2]

Scenario

After team meetings and discussions with subject experts, we conclude that it would be unrealistic to assume we could improve our cost performance from 0.91 to 1.15, and it would be unethical to tell our sponsor that we could.

We discuss the situation with our sponsor, and learn that she has included a managerial reserve of $50,000 in addition to our project budget of $850,000. What to-complete performance index would we need to meet if our sponsor would accept $900,000 ($850,000 + $50,000) as the new budget at completion? The estimate at completion version of the to-complete performance index formula is:

$$TCPI = \frac{(Budget\ at\ completion) - (Earned\ value)}{(Estimate\ at\ completion) - (Actual\ cost)}$$

We retain the original budget at completion in the numerator ($850,000) but we use our new estimate at completion ($900,000) in the denominator.

Results

The to-complete performance index for our estimate at completion is ($850,000 – $480,000) / ($900,000 – $527,472) = 0.9932.

If we can bring our future performance up to 0.99, about equal to our original plan of 1.00, our cost at completion will be $900,000, which is equal to our original budget at completion of $850,000 plus the management reserve of $50,000.

238

Practice

You are working in the Project Management Office of a large organization. You currently have five ongoing projects.

- Project A has a budget of $80,000, earned value of $45,000, and actual costs of $48,000.

- Project B has a budget of $36,000, earned value of $12,000, and actual costs of $11,538.

- Project C has a budget of $120,000, earned value of $85,000, and actual costs of $90,425.

Compute the cost performance index, the cost estimate at completion, and the to-complete performance index for projects A, B and C.

- Project D has requested a budget increase from $250,000 to $265,000. Their earned value is $100,000 and their actual costs are $108,696.

- Project E has also requested a budget increase, from $450,000 to $475,000. Their earned value is $250,000 and their actual costs are $275,000.

Compute the cost performance index and the to-complete performance index for the requested budget amounts for projects D and E.

Write a short summary of your findings for each project.

Remember that the to-complete performance index formula is different for the budget at completion and the estimate at completion.

I recommend using Excel for this, but the choice is yours.

Results

The formula in cell B5 is B3/B4. The formula in cell B6 is B2/B5. The formula in B7 is (B2-B3)/(B2-B4).

Project A will be over budget by $5,333 unless they immediately improve their cost performance index from 0.94 to 1.09 or higher.

Project B should complete the project under budget as long as they maintain their cost performance index, which is currently 1.04, above 0.98.

Project C will finish about $7,600 over budget, $127,659 – $120,000, unless they immediately improve their cost performance index from 0.94 to 1.18. The formula in cell B31 is (B26 – B28)/(B27 – B29).

Project D has requested a budget increase from $250,000 to $265,000. If the new budget is approved, project D will still need to improve their cost performance index from 0.92 to 0.96.

Project E has requested a budget increase to $475,000. If it is approved, they will need to improve their cost performance from 0.91 to 1.00 for the remainder of the project.

	A	B
1	Project A	
2	Budget at completion	$80,000
3	Earned value	$45,000
4	Actual cost	$48,000
5	Cost performance index	0.94
6	Estimate at completion	$85,333
7	TCPI based on BAC	1.09
8		
9	Project B	
10	Budget at completion	$36,000
11	Earned value	$12,000
12	Actual cost	$11,538
13	Cost performance index	1.04
14	Estimate at completion	$34,614
15	TCPI based on BAC	0.98
16		
17	Project C	
18	Budget at completion	$120,000
19	Earned value	$85,000
20	Actual cost	$90,425
21	Cost performance index	0.94
22	Estimate at completion	$127,659
23	TCPI based on BAC	1.18
24		
25	Project D	
26	Budget at completion	$250,000
27	Estimate at completion	$265,000
28	Earned value	$100,000
29	Actual cost	$108,696
30	Cost performance index	0.92
31	TCPI based on EAC	0.96
32		
33	Project E	
34	Budget at completion	$450,000
35	Estimate at completion	$475,000
36	Earned value	$250,000
37	Actual cost	$275,000
38	Cost performance index	0.91
39	TCPI based on EAC	1.00
40		

Variance at Completion

This topic is only three pages long, and the math is super easy; but in some ways it is the most important topic in this text.

Discussion

We began this text with the statement that a successful project could be defined as one that finished on time, in budget, and in scope. Variance at completion is how we know if we are in time, budget, and scope.

The formulas are:

Schedule variance = Earned value – Planned value

Schedule performance index = Earned value / Planned value

Cost variance = Earned value – Actual cost

Cost performance index = Earned value / Actual cost

Scope variance = Delivered scope – Planned scope

Scope performance index = Delivered scope / Planned scope

In time, in budget, and in scope means a zero variance at completion for each of our three measurables. We delivered exactly what we planned to deliver (scope) for the amount of money we planned to spend (budget) and on the planned schedule (time).

A positive schedule variance, or a schedule performance index greater than 1, is good. We are ahead of schedule or finished the project earlier than we planned. A negative schedule variance, or a schedule performance index less than 1, is bad. We are behind schedule or finished the project later than we had planned.

Similarly, a positive cost variance, or a cost performance index greater than 1, is good. We spent less than we planned. A negative cost variance, or a cost performance index less than 1, is bad. We spent more than we planned.

In theory, a positive scope variance is good, we accomplished everything we planned, plus a little more; and a negative scope variance is bad, we did not accomplish everything we planned.

Scope variance is rarely discussed in project management literature for two reasons. During the project, scope variance is the same as schedule variance. Both use the same input, earned value and planned value, and both provide the value of the difference between the scope (planned value) we had expected to have accomplished by this date, and the amount of scope (earned value) we actually did accomplished. The other reason is that, at the end of the project, positive scope variance is subjective and difficult to calculate. If we produced deliverables that were not in scope, that were not planned, how do we know their value? Maybe they have a negative value as they will interfere with some other activity the organization is planning or working on.

A positive scope variance is also bad, as it indicates unauthorized scope creep, a sign of ineffective project management. If we had planned to increase scope, we should have requested a change to the scope baseline, thereby eliminating any positive scope variance.

Like activities on the non-critical path, we should be aware of positive scope variances, but not as our number one priority. Continuing the analogy, like activities on the critical path, negative scope variances are a number one priority to us.

A last thought about scope. A schedule performance index of 0.90 implies that we are 1.00 − 0.90 = 0.10 = 10% behind schedule, but it actually says we have only delivered 90% of the scope we had planned to deliver by this date.

Given all that, we will confine our discussion of project variances to schedule and cost variances, and their respective performance indices.

There are two times in a project where we should calculate and use the variance at completion; during the project and at the conclusion of the project in a performance review. The math is identical, but the purposes are different.

During the project, we should estimate the variance at completion to identify potential problems while we still have time to take corrective actions.

At the completion of the project, we need to identify and document the reason for any non-zero variance in the organizations' lessons learned repository so that future project managers may benefit from our (painful?) discoveries. Additionally, end-of-project incentive bonuses may be tied to positive cost or schedule variances.

Scenario

Your budget at completion is $250,000 and the schedule at completion is 380 days. Our schedule estimate at completion is 392 days and our cost estimate at completion is $256,500. What are the cost and schedule variances at completion?

Results

The cost variance at completion is $250,000 – $256,500 = –$6500. This negative value is not good. We will finish the project $6500 over budget. To put this in perspective, we are $6500 / $250,000 = 2.6% over budget.

The schedule variance at completion is 380 – 392 = –12 days. Bad news. We will finish the project 12 days late, or 12 / 380 = 3.16% late.

Practice

Your project budget at completion is $900,000 and the schedule at completion is 420 days. Your cost estimate at completion $936,000 and your schedule estimate at completion is 462 days.

What are the cost and schedule variances at completion, both in units (dollars or days) and as a percent of planned? What will be the schedule performance index and the cost performance index at completion?

Results

Your estimated cost variance at completion is $900,000 – $936,000 = –$36,000 and your cost performance index is $900,000 / $936,000 = 0.9615

Your schedule variance is 420 – 462 = –42 days and your schedule performance index is 420 / 462 = 0.9091.

Both are bad news because the variances are negative and the performance indices are less than 1. At your current rate, you will finish the project 42 days late and $36,000 over budget. Bummer!

Footnotes

(1) To put this in academic terms; a student has "C" on the mid-term. To get a "B" in the course, they need to get an "A" on the final exam.

(2) I once wrote an article entitled "Are we managers or are we mathematicians?" The idea was that doing the math, and doing it correctly, is important, but using the results to understand the situation, and to develop viable courses of action to influence future outcomes is even more important.

The to-complete performance index is where we become proactive, where we, as managers say "I have seen the future, I don't like it, and I am going to change it."

Mathematicians can see the future; leaders change it.

Filler:

Augury was one of the earliest forecasting methods. It involved predicting the future based on the flight of birds. There is some logic to this. For example, birds migrating north or south could predict seasons, and birds seeking shelter predict a storm approaching. Perhaps birds flocking to ripening fruit or, less appetizing, carrion-eating birds circling a fresh kill.

244

Earned Schedule

Earned schedule, first introduced in 2003, is referred to as an extension of earned value management. We will briefly describe it here.

<u>Discussion</u>

Earned value management is an extremely popular project management technique, but, according to advocates for earned schedule, EVM has a couple of drawbacks. It uses the cost of an activity rather than the time the activity should have been completed. Also, a project that is completed late will have a misleading schedule variance of zero and a schedule performance index of 1.00. That's caused by changing the baseline to match the estimate at completion. Earned schedule does not do that.

Earned schedule uses time units rather than monetary units, and it more accurately reflects the performance of projects that finished late.

We will discuss two earned schedule formulas and how they compare to earned value management. Other earned schedule formulas involve trigonometry and are well beyond the scope of this text.

The earned schedule is the point in time when the earned value should have been completed. Assume a project began on January 1st. Today is May 1st and we have just completed the work that was scheduled to be completed on April 1st. The earned schedule is 3 months (January, February and March) but, as of May 1st, the actual time is 4 months.

The schedule variance is the earned schedule minus the actual time: $3 - 4 = -1$ We have a schedule variance of negative 1 month.

The schedule performance index is the earned schedule divided by the actual time: $3 / 4 = 0.75$.

As with earned value management, a negative variance is bad and a positive variance is good. Likewise, a schedule performance index less than 1 is bad and a schedule performance index greater than 1 is good. With EMV we would be comparing the planned value to the actual value as of May 1st. Either method would have told us we are behind schedule.

Stakeholder Communication

Stakeholders are people or organizations that are, or will be, or perceive they will be effected by our project or its deliverable. If we are building a new factory, stakeholders include the organization, the project sponsor, the project management office, the project team members, our suppliers, our employees, our customers, the community, and the local government. Even the competition has an interest in our project. What are we doing and how will affect them?

I had a very experienced project manager in my class a few years back. His response to almost every case study was the same observation: the problem was a lack of appropriate communications.

A proper discussion of project communication would include oral, written, visual, and synchronous vs. asynchronous communications; even social media; but none of these really belong in a math text. There is, however, one aspect of project communications that does belong here, and that is the number of communications channels we must deal with.

Discussion

A major responsibility for project managers is to engage with our stakeholders, and that involves communications, from us to them, from them to us, and between the various stakeholder groups. The more stakeholders we have, the more complicated this becomes, but it's not a linear relationship. Adding one more stakeholder does not add one more communication channel, it might add hundreds more.

Scenario

There are four people on a team: Amy, Bill, Carlos, and Dim. How many communication channels are there? With only 4 stakeholders, we can count the communication channels: A – B, A – C, A – D, B – C, B – D, and C – D. There are six communication channels, each capable of carrying communications in both directions.

Edith joins our team. Now how many communications channels are there?

We have A – B, A – C, A – D, A – E, B – C, B – D, B – E, C – D, C – E, and D – E.

That is a total of ten communications channels; we went from six to ten communications channels just by increasing our team from four to five people. And if Fred joins the team, we will go from ten to fifteen. We can't keep counting as our team grows; we need a formula.

The formula is:

$$Communications\ channels = \frac{Stakeholders(Stakeholders - 1)}{2}$$

Process

$$Communications\ channels = \frac{4(4 - 1)}{2} = \frac{4(3)}{2} = \frac{12}{2} = 6$$

$$Communications\ channels = \frac{5(5 - 1)}{2} = \frac{5(4)}{2} = \frac{20}{2} = 10$$

$$Communications\ channels = \frac{6(6 - 1)}{2} = \frac{6(5)}{2} = \frac{30}{2} = 15$$

Discussion

Do we really care if we have six or ten or 15 communications channels? Probably not, but then a project with only a few stakeholders is not very realistic. Suppose we have a project with 1 sponsor, 1 project manager, 1 project management office, 15 team members, 8 vendors, 25 concerned citizens, 1 county planning department, and 7 county supervisors. That's not a big project, but it has 59 stakeholders and 1711 communications channels.

Other than taking a test, you will probably never need to calculate the number of communications channels you have to deal with, so why bother? Well, the reason is to get you to think about the increased complexity in your communications as your list of stakeholders grows. It's like scope creep. Add a stakeholder here, add another there, and in no time at all, you have "communication channel creep."

Scenario

Continuing with the 59 stakeholder example, is there any way we could reduce the number of communications channels?

Process

Yes, we can consolidate the stakeholders into groups. We can specify that all communications with vendors will go through our purchasing department. All communications with county supervisors and other agencies will go through our legal department. All communications with concerned citizens will be via a web site. Most communications with project team members will be in a weekly team meeting or as posted on the project bulletin board.

Results

By consolidating stakeholders into groups with common interests, we can significantly reduce the complexity of project communications. If we could consolidate the 59 stakeholders into 20 groups, for example, we could reduce our communications channels from 1711 down to 190, a reduction of 1521 channels. A whopping 89% reduction!

Discussion

Agile methodologies developed some communication techniques that may be useful to waterfall or hybrid projects.

Agile uses small teams co-located to facilitate osmotic communications. They use "information radiators" to post notes, messages, and charts.

They have short, frequent meetings. A good example is the daily standup meeting which is usually limited to 15 minutes. It follows a fixed, 3-question format. And, yes, everyone stands up to keep the meeting short.

Inventory Profile Analysis

We have seen how aggregating stakeholders into groups reduces the number of communication channels and makes our communication job a lot easier. The same is true of inventory. Line workers, inventory planners, and sales people are concerned with stock keeping units, SKU's, but senior management prefers to aggregate SKU details into categories such as product families or groups. The problem is that a lot of very important information is lost in the aggregation process. Inventory Profile Analysis is an aggregation technique that overcomes the problems associated with typical inventory data aggregation.[1]

Discussion

Individual stock keeping units, SKU's, are aggregated into product families. For example, all tee shirt sizes and colors are aggregated into the tee shirt product family. Senior management then reviews the product family data, frequently in a process known as Sales and Operations Planning, S&OP.

The two key indicators for each product family included in S&OP worksheets are: inventory level, expressed as periodic demand, such as days on hand, weeks on hand, or months on hand; and fill rate, expressed as the percent of customer order lines filled from stock on hand.[2] We would expect that higher inventory levels would correlate strongly with higher fill rates, but that is not always the case. The problem is in the aggregation process, what I call the agony of aggregation.

Scenario

Senior management needs something other than "months on hand" to determine if they have the right inventory to meet the expected demand, but they do not want SKU level data. They want a summary of the SKU data at the product family level. But they also want to know if the inventory is in balance.

Inventory balance, not total quantity, is the key to Inventory Profile Analysis.

Using pyramid forecasting, we expect tee shirt demand next month to be 20 small, 50 medium, and 30 large, for a total of 100 tee shirts. Senior management has authorized one month of inventory on hand, so we want to start the month with 100 tee shirts.

Discussion

Breaking News: An excess of one item does not compensate for a shortage of another item, even in the same product family. For example having too many small tee shirts will do nothing to solve the problem of not having enough large tee shirts. We might have the total number of tee shirts on hand to meet the expected total demand at the product family level, but if the balance is not correct we will have lost sales, disappointed customers, and unsold inventory at the end of the period. The dreaded triple whammy.

Process

Working at the detail level, we know we will start the month with 50 small tee shirts, 60 medium tee shirts, and 10 large tee shirts, for a total of 120 tee shirts. Senior management is not happy that we are overstocked by 120 – 100 = 20 = 20%, but they let it go, for now.

At the end of the month, we report that we sold 80 tee shirts. Further, we have 20 tee shirts on backorder and we have 40 unsold tee shirts remaining in inventory. This is not what senior management expected.

Senior management is no longer complacent. "How in the Hell could you have a fill rate of only 80% when you began the month with 20% excess inventory, and you finish with 40 units in stock? And don't you talk SKU's to us because we are senior management and we work at the product family level. We don't want to get involved in the details, but we want some answers we can understand and work with."

Scenario

Your project is to redesign the organizations' S&OP worksheet to include inventory balance at the product family level, not SKU level, along with expected inventory and demand, also at the product family level.

Answer

The answer is going to be two values, not one, because excess quantities of one item will never compensate for shortages of another item. The two values, defined in Inventory Profile Analysis, are excess and shortage. There is no way they can be summarized into a single value. Inventory Profile Analysis also includes target, actual, and coverage.

Process

I am not aware of any inventory management software programs that includes Inventory Profile Analysis, but that's not a problem as Microsoft Excel is all we need, and everyone has it.

	A	B	C	D	E	F
1	Item	Target	Actual	Excess	Shortage	Coverage
2	Small	20	50	30	0	20
3	Medium	50	60	10	0	50
4	Large	30	10	0	20	10
5	Total	100	120	40	20	80
6	Percent	100%	120%	40%	20%	80%

Our desired inventory, our target, was 20 small, 50 medium, and 30 large. Our expected inventory is 50 small, 60 medium, and 10 large. We have excess quantities of small 50 – 20 = 30, and excess medium 60 – 50 = 10. Our total excess is 30 + 10 = 40 tee shirts. Compared to our target of 100 tee shirts, we have an excess of 40 / 100 = 0.40 = 40%.

We have a shortage of large tee shirts of 30 – 10 = 20 units. Our total shortage is 100 / 20 = 0.20 or 20%. Coverage is the compliment of shortage. If we have a 20% shortage, we have coverage of 80%.

Our excess inventory does nothing to reduce the shortage or increase the coverage. All it does is sit on the shelf consuming working capital.

If the forecast that gave us our target inventory is correct, our service level, our line item fill rate, will directly correlate with our coverage. In this example, with a coverage of 80%, we should expect a service level of 80%. The excess 40% will have no influence on the service level.

We clearly need to change the aggregated data we reports to senior management. In addition to expected demand and expected inventory, we need to include the expected shortage or coverage, and the expected excess. These values will also define our inventory balance.

There is no single short-term solution to shortage and excess inventory. Both are unique problems that require unique solutions. We are not asking management to deal with problems at the SKU level, but we are forcing them to recognize that inventory shortages and excess inventory are separate problems requiring separate and unique solutions.[3]

Inventory Profile Analysis defines a balanced inventory as 0% shortage and 0% excess. This can be displayed on an S&OP worksheet as 0/0, or as in our example, 20/40, meaning 20% shortage and 40% excess.

<u>Practice</u>

Your company manufacturers running shoes and one of your most popular product lines is Lady Jogger, which is offered in 5 sizes and 7 colors, for a total of 35 stock keeping units. Expected demand next month is 16,446 pair and your projected available inventory is 16,644 pair. Given the SKU level detail, what is your projected shortage and excess percents for next month? What is your projected line item fill rate?

	A	B	C	D	E	F	G
1	Target	6	6.5	7	7.5	8	Total
2	Peach	478	573	678	783	736	
3	Lime	422	527	586	734	654	
4	Lemon	397	480	559	710	623	
5	Cream	324	434	443	547	528	
6	Apricot	288	365	417	480	449	
7	Vanilla	251	328	371	424	384	
8	Coffee	211	255	305	375	327	16,446
9							
10	Actual	6	6.5	7	7.5	8	Total
11	Peach	424	488	576	699	665	
12	Lime	387	468	534	698	603	
13	Lemon	374	469	570	691	586	
14	Cream	308	424	491	617	498	
15	Apricot	267	393	438	524	524	
16	Vanilla	265	355	417	474	413	
17	Coffee	287	344	424	485	464	16,644
18							

Answer

The formula in cell G8 is =SUM(B2:F8) and it was copied into cells G17, G26, and G35.

The formula in cell B20 is =MAX(B2-B11,0) and it was copied into cells B20:F26.

The formula in cell B29 is =MAX(B11-B2,0) and it was copied into cells B29:F35.

The formula in cell H26 is =G26/G8 and the formula in cell H35 is =G35/G8.[4]

	A	B	C	D	E	F	G	H
1	Target	6	6.5	7	7.5	8	Total	
2	Peach	478	573	678	783	736		
3	Lime	422	527	586	734	654		
4	Lemon	397	480	559	710	623		
5	Cream	324	434	443	547	528		
6	Apricot	288	365	417	480	449		
7	Vanilla	251	328	371	424	384		
8	Coffee	211	255	305	375	327	16,446	
9								
10	Actual	6	6.5	7	7.5	8	Total	
11	Peach	424	488	576	699	665		
12	Lime	387	468	534	698	603		
13	Lemon	374	469	570	691	586		
14	Cream	308	424	491	617	498		
15	Apricot	267	393	438	524	524		
16	Vanilla	265	355	417	474	413		
17	Coffee	287	344	424	485	464	16,644	
18								
19	Shortage	6	6.5	7	7.5	8	Total	Shortage
20	Peach	54	85	102	84	71		
21	Lime	35	59	52	36	51		
22	Lemon	23	11	0	19	37		
23	Cream	16	10	0	0	30		
24	Apricot	21	0	0	0	0		
25	Vanilla	0	0	0	0	0		
26	Coffee	0	0	0	0	0	796	4.84%
27								
28	Excess	6	6.5	7	7.5	8	Total	Excess
29	Peach	0	0	0	0	0		
30	Lime	0	0	0	0	0		
31	Lemon	0	0	11	0	0		
32	Cream	0	0	48	70	0		
33	Apricot	0	28	21	44	75		
34	Vanilla	14	27	46	50	29		
35	Coffee	76	89	119	110	137	994	6.04%
36								

Our target was 16,446 but our actual is 16,644, so we are over 198 units, or 1.20%. This is where traditional inventory management often stops.

But, Inventory Profile Analysis tells us we actually have 6.04% excess inventory and, despite the excess total, we have shortages of 4.84%.

The shortage of 4.84% and the excess of 6.04% would be indicated as such in the S&OP worksheet, or, using the format shorthand of shortage/excess, it could be displayed as 4.84/6.04 if you prefer.

The coverage, as you recall, is the compliment of the shortage, 1.00 - 4.84 = 95.16. Given the very high correlation between coverage and fill rate, we expect our line fill rate to be about 95% next month.[5]

Footnotes

(1) When I was being interviewed for the position of materials manager at SOLA Optical, I was shown some graphs with inventory levels, measured in months-on-hand, and order fill rate, the percent of customers' orders filled from available inventory, both aggregated at the product family level. In some cases, absolutely deplorable fill rates, like 50% to 60%, were accompanied by stock levels of 2.5 to 3.0 months on hand. How could that be?

My answer was that I had no idea, but that I would like to investigate and find out why. My honest answer may be what got me the job. It took me some time, but I eventually discovered the answer.

I called my discovery Inventory Profile Analysis. In 2001 I published an article about Inventory Profile Analysis in the Production and Inventory Management Journal. The article won "best article of the year" for which I received a trophy and a check for $2000. I still have the trophy, but the $2000 is long gone.

(2) A line order is some quantity of a specific stock keeping unit.

(3) The official definition of a stock keeping unit, SKU, is an item at a location. So an excess of small tee shirts at the distribution center will not compensate for a shortage of small tee shirts at the retail store. That gets into Distribution Resource Planning, DRP, which is, although a fascinating topic, beyond the scope of this humble publication.

(4) Note that shortage and excess quantities are compared to the target total and not the actual total.

(5) This example is very typical of fashion retailing. Some colors or designs within a product group are more popular than originally planned, and others are less popular. Further, managing "fringe sizes" is more challenging than managing "core sizes." That's due to a principle called the Law of Large Numbers. Forecasting demand for large numbers, like core sizes, is usually more accurate; with less forecast error; than forecasting demand for relatively small numbers, like fringe sizes.

Index

Major topics are displayed in bold font
Excel function begin with an equal sign (=)

271

Made in the USA
Columbia, SC
09 August 2019